PIMPS, HOs,

PLAYA HATAS,

AND ALL THE REST OF

MY HOLLYWOOD FRIENDS

Also by John Leguizamo

THE WORKS OF JOHN LEGUIZAMO

SEXAHOLIX

FREAK

SPIC-O-RAMA

MAMBO MOUTH

AN ecco BOOK

HARPER

NEW YORK • LONDON • TORONTO • SYDNEY

PIMPS, HOS,

PLAYA HATAS,

AND ALL THE REST OF

MY HOLLYWOOD FRIENDS

MY LIFE

JOHN LEGUIZAMO

HARPER

A hardcover edition of this book was published in 2006 by Ecco, an imprint of HarperCollins Publishers.

PIMPS, HOS, PLAYA HATAS, AND ALL THE REST OF MY HOLLYWOOD FRIENDS. Copyright © 2006 by John Leguizamo. All rights reserved. Printed in the United States of America. No part of this book may be used or reproduced in any manner whatsoever without written permission except in the case of brief quotations embodied in critical articles and reviews. For information address HarperCollins Publishers, 10 East 53rd Street, New York, NY 10022.

HarperCollins books may be purchased for educational, business, or sales promotional use. For information please write: Special Markets Department, HarperCollins Publishers, 10 East 53rd Street, New York, NY 10022.

FIRST HARPER PAPERBACK PUBLISHED 2007.

Designed by Cassandra J. Pappas

Library of Congress Cataloging-in-Publication Data is available upon request.

ISBN: 978-0-06-052072-4 (pbk.)
ISBN-10: 0-06-052072-8 (pbk.)

07 08 09 10 11 ID/RRD 10 9 8 7 6 5 4 3 2 1

To all the actors, directors, writers, and producers, or anybody that was a part of trying to make some piece of art or some commercial crap disguised as something to say: here's to you. I respect you all because it's never easy . . . even when it's supposed to be, it's not.

They say never write your autobiography till you're about to die or too old to work. Well, I never listened to good advice so why should I start now? I think of this book less as an autobiography and more of a way of keeping score with the people who have wronged me. No, that would be negative . . . it's more of a personal inventory.

Oh, forget the half-lie. It's what happened as best as I can tell it without bitching or whining or gossiping, which is pretty hard for me to do. I've taken out some good slander insurance and have gotten the name of a killer lawyer (not killer like in cool, but as in cold-blooded hit man). So I'm kind of prepared . . . but probably not for the emotional fallout. That's much harder to deal with.

I've had to change some names because some people I know are very litigious and it's just a good idea to . . . Otherwise they'll feel like they own you or you owe them. It's just very messy. I should have written a fiction piece, but as I didn't, I've had to modify identifying features, so instead of a flat nose, I've said an aquiline nose, including physical descriptions and occupations of other individuals in order to preserve their anonymity. In some cases, composite characters have been created or timelines have been compressed in order to further preserve privacy and maintain narrative flow. The goal in all cases was to protect people's privacy without damaging the integrity of my life story.

So why did I write this? Maybe because I'm a recovering Catholic and I never really got the whole priest-confession thing right. Or maybe I'm just masochistic—that's just the artist in me, the one I try to empower over the commercial whore who mostly runs my inner and regular life.

For me, there's always been a fine line between acting and acting out. Like this one afternoon me, English, Xerox, and Fucks Funny are riding the 7 train, the elevated subway that runs from Manhattan way the hell out into Queens. I see that the door to the conductor's booth at the front of the car is open, and no one's inside. And I get this sudden idea for my first public performance. Call it guerrilla theater, except at the time I was a clueless youth and thought guerrilla theater was a show they put on in the monkey house at the Bronx Zoo.

I was fourteen. That's thirty in ghetto years, so you might say I was a late bloomer, but I'd had other things on my mind before then. Like girls. And dodging my old man's fists. And girls. And dodging my old man's fists. And girls.

English, Xerox, and Fucks Funny were my homies, my half-assed gang. We called ourselves the Sexaholix. We hadn't had any sex yet, except the kind you have by yourself in the bathroom with the door locked, but we already knew we were addicts. Fucks Funny's nickname was a takeoff on Bugs Bunny; we called him that because he had big rabbit ears and a bent dick. Xerox said everything twice, everything twice. He repeated everything everyone else said, too. English was a second language for English, like it was for the rest of us, and he still didn't really have the hang of it yet. Past tense always screwed him up.

"Yo man, I haded a quarter but I losteded it," he'd say.

And Xerox would say, "He losteded it. Losteded it. Word."

So we're heading home on the 7. The 7 train is like an artery pumping little brown, black, and yellow people into the city every morning, where they do all the work the white people don't want to do, and then squirting them back out to the vast urban sprawl of Queens at night, so the white people don't have to eat and sleep with them. Queens is the modern-day Ellis Island, where all the immigrants from all over the world are dumped when they come to this country. There are more ethnicities and nationalities crowded together in Queens than anywhere else on the planet, and there's always some new ethnic group piling on. Like lately they call the 7 the "Mariachi Line," because it's full of Mexicans. Before that it was the "Curry in a Hurry," because of all the Pakistanis and Indians riding back and forth to Jamaica, the New New Delhi. And before that it was the "Whiskey Train," because of all the Irish people from Sunnyside.

I see that empty conductor's booth and get this idea. English, who was kind of an Eeyore, always worrying, sees me heading for the booth and moans, "Yo yo, man, whatchoo doon? You gonna get us busteded."

"Word," Xerox nods. "Busteded."

But I didn't let them stop me. I was born to be on stage, baby. Even if the stage was a rickety subway car and my audience was sleepy janitors and maids.

In the booth I find the conductor's microphone. This is it. My moment to shine. "You'll be great, you'll be swell." All the clichés. I switch on the mic. Showtime.

And because I'm fourteen and don't know shit about theater, I just do all my impressions of cartoon characters from TV.

First, Foghorn Leghorn bursts out of the speakers in all the cars on the train. "BOY I SAY BOY C'MERE A MINUTE SON I WANNA TALK TO YA."

Then I do Snaggle Puss. "EXIT, STAGE LEFT."

Then Popeye. "ACK ACK ACK, TOUCH ME LOVE MUSKLE."

Oh I've got them now. Those maids and janitors are rolling in the aisles of every car. (Actually, they're just looking confused. Most of them don't speak English.)

"HEY THERE BOO BOO. I'M SMARTER THAN THE AV-ER-AGE BEAR."

Then I leave them with a song, like a little brown version of a Borscht Belt comedian. A Cuchifrito Belt comedian.

"AAAAAAH'M BRING-IN HOME A BAY-BEE BUM-BLE BEE . . ."

And for my finale, a transit cop grabs me by the nape of the neck and drags me out of the booth.

Busteded.

My first bad review.

I only spent a couple of hours behind bars, but that was enough. There were some scary, degenerate guys in there, and I was young, Latin, and friendly. I could see myself losing my virginity in a couple of ways I didn't want to lose it. I was saving myself for marriage.

This one huge, greasy gorilla had his eye on me. I couldn't quite tell which eye, because one of his eyes was higher than the other, like Quasimodo. But I could tell he liked me. You could see he'd spent a lot of time in prison, because he was built like a weightlifter, and he had tattoos all over his body. I mean his fingernails, his earlobes, his lips, and his gums were tattooed. When he grinned and licked those lips at me, I could see he had more gold teeth than Harlem.

"Mmmm, look at that tasty little motherfucker," he cooed. "I want that ass. Yum yum yum."

I knew I had to turn the situation around fast, or I'd be celebrating my fiftieth birthday as Lola the prison bitch. So for my second acting job of the day, I became the baddest, hardest punk alive.

"Who's gonna be my bitch?" I strutted. "I said *who's* gonna *be* my *bitch*? Cuz *somebody* gonna have to suck my dick. Oh yeah."

Now I got the laughs.

My father came down to the precinct to pick me up. But before he was going to pick me up, he was going to beat me up. Cuz that's the sort of dad he was.

He's swinging at me and I'm ducking behind this big Irish cop.

"I'm beating you because I love you," Pops explains.

"Yeah, and I can't wait to grow up and love you back," I say. "At least let me get the cuffs off."

Pops is reaching around that big Irishman's fat ass for me, and I'm ducking and weaving like Muhammad Ali.

"If you run away it's going to be worse," Pops warns.

"So you're saying if I stop running you gonna give me a discount on the ass beating?" I say.

"Discount on a ass beating?" Xerox repeats.

I hadn't noticed that he'd followed me to the station. We didn't call him Xerox for nothing. Word.

So my first public performance ended with me getting arrested and taking a beating. Not the most auspicious way to launch a career in show business.

But look at me now. I'm a star of stage, screen, and TV. I play myself to sold-out crowds everywhere from Broadway to the Mark

Taper Forum in L.A. I get to write, produce, direct, and star in my own films, and I always make sure I get at least one sex scene with a naked Latin honey. And rehearse it many, many times. (Don't tell my wife, 'kay? She thinks I use a stunt double.) My agent tells me I'm now the highest-paid Latin actor in the world. Then again, my agent's a liar who's been ripping me off for years. I'd fire him, but then I'd just have to pay somebody else to tell me how good I am.

Oh yeah, I'm bad. I'm happening. I'm the shit.

Funny thing, though. I still don't seem to know the difference between acting and acting out. I made it to Broadway and Hollywood the hard way. As a role model for aspiring actors I totally suck. I never quite figured out how to play the game of Hollywood the way you're supposed to. I've got a mouth. I've got a brain. I'm not just another idiot Hollywood movie star like . . . well, I won't name any names. (Yet. Keep reading. What, you think I'm gonna give it up on the first date? You calling me a ho?) I like to improvise and fool around and be creative in front of the camera, which has a way of pissing off other actors. I've been bitch-slapped and body-slammed and was once threatened by a certain very big, very macho movie star, who just happened to be in drag at the time. Talk about humiliating. I've made myself a persona non grata with Actor's Equity and the Emmy Awards people, and even the Democratic National Committee.

All because, hard as I tried at first, I just can't quite play along. I'll always be a comedian. In a way I'm not much different today from that kid who commandeered the stage of that 7 train. It's just that the stage has kept getting bigger and bigger.

Oh yeah, I've made more than my share of stupid mistakes. Taken roles I shouldn't have, and turned down ones that would've been great for my career. Hired and then had to fire some of the wrong people—my best friend, my brother, a psycho stalker bitch from hell. (My Moms still works for me. Yo lady, you next.) And I've suffered for my art, man. Spent one whole movie acting on my knees—and I'm not speaking metaphorically—and another in pumps and miniskirts, and still another bent over in a dwarf clown suit.

But I do it because I'm a driven man. I'm a perfectionist, a workaholic, an egomaniac, and a control freak. I've lost girlfriends, guy friends, and a wife, and I've pissed off my whole family. All for my art.

Yeah, I'm a horrible example of how to have a successful career.

But I made it anyway. Little by little, I figured out how to work the system, and make the system work for me. I've learned how to do things my way, follow my vision, and it's paid off.

I'm not just talking about the money—though the money is nice. Really, really nice. You grow up like I did, on the bottom rung of the ladder, making the kind of mad paper I do now is sweet. Nouveau is better than no riche at all, baby.

But it was never really about the money for me. Which is good, because my agent, my mom, the tax man, and my kids' dentist take it all away from me anyway. It's not about the fame either. It's all about what comes with the fame and fortune—power. The power to control my own destiny, the clout to shape my own career. Being in a position to create work for a lot of other Latin artists. Being able to do work that means something and says something, not just another stupid thrill-ride summer movie. Though I've made my share of those, too.

I know it isn't all my doing. I'm standing on the shoulders of a lot of Latin brothers and sisters who came before me—which is good, cuz I ain't that tall. I'm the brown Silver Surfer riding a cultural wave. In the twenty-first century, it's cool to be Latin. Now everyone wants to be Latin, the way everyone wanted to be black twenty years ago. Latin is the new black. Big ups to J-Lo. You my bitch, *mami*. I also owe mad props to some of the giant talents I've worked with, people like Brian De Palma and Spike Lee and Joseph Papp, who taught me so much.

I'm still working my ass off, though. Funny, I seem to be working harder now than ever. But that's all right. Like I said, I'm a workaholic—my Pops beat the work ethic into us as kids. And I'm doing work I find fulfilling and meaningful. How many people are lucky enough to say that? Especially if they're poor and Latin and from Queens?

Maybe it won't last forever. We all know how fleeting success and stardom can be. But while I got it, I'm-a flaunt it, yo. I'm gonna use it till I lose it.

And if I end up broke and busteded again, I can always go back to performing in the subway.

I got my first training as a comedian at home when I was a kid. It was a survival tactic. If I could make my Pops stop and laugh, it might give me that extra second I needed to run away from him.

My father was a strict autocrat-totalitarian-despot-dictator-disciplinarian. I blame it on his early life.

It's always been hard to get my dad to talk about his youth. Once you get my mom started, it's hard to get her to stop. Between the two of them, the stories come out like *Rashomon*, with all these conflicting points of view. But here's what I've pieced together:

My dad's father, a rich part Italian part Puerto Rican who lived in Colombia, left my dad's mother when my dad was a baby. My dad grew up in a big household with his mother, grandmother, aunt, uncles, and a cousin. Every Friday as a boy my dad went to meet with his father at the stock exchange, La Bolsa de Valores de Bogotá, and his father gave him money for his living expenses. My dad started saving this money from the time he was maybe thirteen.

After high school, he got a job at a big savings bank. He worked over-time and weekends and added every penny he made to the money his father gave him.

When he was eighteen or nineteen, he'd saved enough to pursue his dream. He was a big fan of European cinema, and had decided early on that he wanted to become a film director. So he gave his mother everything he'd earned, with the idea that she'd hold on to it and send him a monthly living allowance, while he went off to Italy to study film at the great film studio in Rome—Cinecittà. He always said it was the best time of his life. It's part of our family lore that he met Fellini at lunch in Cinecittà, in the studio cafeteria. I don't know what Fellini had for lunch. La dolce pizza or something.

My dad seemed to be on his way to becoming the Colombian Fellini when his mother and stepfather used his savings to pay for an operation for their son, who was born with encephalitis. The step-father promised to repay the money in a couple of months. He had a cooking-oil factory and was cooking up a big shipment that would turn a nice profit. Unfortunately, the factory burned down, and the stepfather had no insurance. After that, they stopped sending my dad the monthly allowance he lived on.

My dad had to quit Cinecittà. He left all his books and clothes with his landlord and moved to Spain, thinking he could find a job there and eventually return to Rome to complete his studies. But there was no work in Spain for foreign students, and my dad finally gave up. He stowed away on a boat to get home, was discovered and arrested. Maybe that's part of why he got so mad at me later when I got nabbed on the subway.

He was twenty-one when he got back to Bogotá. That's where he met my mom. She was an exotic beauty, with a mix of blood-lines that supposedly included Native American, Arabic, Spanish, Lebanese, and maybe some Jewish and African as well. Like his mom

My Moms and Pops in Bogotá, when they still got along.

and dad, hers had broken up—my Lebanese grandfather had left my grandmother—and my mom was forced to choose between them. She chose her mom. So my mom and dad had that in common.

She was such a looker she could have had any man in Bogotá, but she fell in love with my dad at first sight. He was handsome, distinguished, and had picked up a lot of European flair. He wore fine Italian shirts and silk ties, and sang her all the latest Italian and American pop tunes. Stuff like "Volare" and Dean Martin's "Inamorata" was huge in Bogotá. He took my mom to Italian restaurants, bought her Italian scarves and sweaters, wrote her love letters every day—he worked it, baby. My mom's girlfriends said she'd met her *Principe Azul*—her Prince Charming.

Everything was beautiful and romantic, straight out of a *telenovela* . . . until they got married. They were so young. He still had his dreams and wasn't really ready to settle down. And the worldly sophistication that made him so attractive to my mom also made her paranoid. All the ladies loved my dad, and he didn't mind their attention. At parties my mom would watch the women buzz around him and him flirting back. He was like a shark, smooth and sleek, swimming in a sea of tasty little fishies. Mmm mmm mmm.

So she freaked when he told her he was going to get a job in Colombian TV. There were only, like, four channels and they were all run by the government, but it was still really glamorous by local standards, and filled with beautiful women. She told him he had to choose—her or a TV career. She admits now that it was a terrible thing to do and probably ruined their marriage. She knows that this was when my dad's dream truly died, and that he probably never forgave her for it. But she was young and insecure and couldn't help herself.

So my dad shelved his plans to become a big director, and took a good job he probably hated, as a sales promotion manager for a big Swiss food company in Bogotá. He had an office and a whole department to run—a department, my mom soon found, that was full of beautiful young women. Oopsy. He got a company car and a membership in a swank country club and made mad pesos. He hired a live-in maid. They moved into a really nice apartment in the same small building where my dad's grandmother, aunt, and so on lived. In fact, pretty much all the apartments in the building were my dad's family. It's a Latin thing, yo. You know how the Godfather says to keep your friends close but your enemies closer? My peeps believe in that big-time. That's why we surround ourselves with family members.

Soon they had me. Later they gave me a little brother to torture, Sergio. I called him Serge and he called me Master. We shared the same bed until I went away to college. We drew a demilitarized zone down the middle to keep from killing each other.

We were living in the lap of luxury. At least from my mom's perspective. She'd grown up so poor that she and her brothers and sisters slept in dresser drawers because their folks couldn't afford cribs. But my dad still had other laps on his mind. He kept slipping off to party with his single friends, and inevitably my mom caught him cheating. When she threatened to leave and take me and Serge with her, my dad came up with a Hail Mary plan to save the marriage—he suggested they move out of Colombia, to remove him from temptation. At first they thought about going to France, but then decided the opportunities would be better in America. Why my mother believed his story that there would be no tempting wimmins in France or America is beyond me. I guess she was just young and naive.

We came to Queens when I was three and Serge was one and a half. New York City was tough for my parents. They were young, didn't speak a lot of English, didn't know anyone here. There weren't

Me and Sergio. I called him Serge and he called me Master.

many Colombians in Queens at the time. And even though they were all at least middle-class, educated, and had held good jobs back in Colombia, in Queens they were just more spics to add to all the other immigrants, so the only kind of jobs they could get were pretty low-level. My mom's first job was dressing dolls in a factory in Jamaica. My dad got a job as a maitre d' in an Italian restuarant. The boss liked him because he spoke Italian, and he thought Leguizamo was an Italian name. My dad despised that job. It was just so far beneath what he'd done before.

Serge and I saw very little of my dad when we were little, he was working so hard to make it. Both of my parents worked their butts off. The funny thing is that even though they came here to save their marriage, they spent their first few years here planning how to make a lot of money quick and go back to Colombia to live like big shots.

One scheme was appliances. They started buying and storing washers, driers, stoves, refrigerators—all stuff that wasn't so easy to get in Colombia. They were going to be the Latin Crazy Eddies. Eduardito Loco. When they'd built up enough stock, we moved back to Colombia, but it didn't work out the way they pictured it. All of those appliances, along with all our family belongings, were loaded off the boat into a couple of trucks. Then the trucks drove away with it all and we never saw any of it again. Yep, just like Crazy Eddie— everything must go! I have almost no family photos or other memorabilia. It was all stolen.

My parents decided to come back to the U.S. They left me and Serge with my dad's mom. Taking care of us for a year, until my folks could send for us, was her penance for having lost all of my dad's savings when he was in Italy.

My folks finally resigned themselves to living in Queens, becoming U.S. citizens, and forgetting their dream of ever going back to Colombia to live the high life. They dug in and worked their asses off to make it here. Reality had beaten their high hopes out of them. My dad still always had some scheme going, like his plan to become a big real estate magnate in Queens, but somehow they never quite worked out. And he still liked the wimmins, and they still liked him, which was a source of constant fighting with my mom.

*   *   *

My dad pinned a lot of his aspirations on me and Serge. It was like his own dreams had been crushed, so he was determined we were going to succeed where he'd failed. We were going to have class and manners and make something of ourselves, not like the rest of the no-future *pendejos* in the neighborhood. We were going to be cultured and successful if he had to kill us to make it happen. We never had so much homework that he couldn't give us more. We listened to Puccini and read Homer.

On top of being poor, he was still cheap. He always came up with

Me and my Pops, back when we still got along.

ways not to get us anything for Christmas. One year on Christmas Eve he told us that Santa wasn't giving out any presents because he was depressed and suicidal.

"He's up on the roof right now. He's gonna jump. You boys stay here, I'll go up and try to talk him out of it."

He went out the door, and a minute later we heard him outside yelling, "No, Santa, no! Don't jump! Think of the children! Aaayyy!"

Serge was scared and started bawling. But I was a little older and wiser.

"Santy didn't suicided," I told my dad.

"No? How you know that, Einstein?"

"Cuz there is no Santy Claus," I replied. "Come on, Pops. Ain't we been good this year? We want our toys."

You didn't talk to my dad that way.

"You want toys, you ungrateful ingrates?" he thundered. "I was so poor, thank God I was a boy or I wouldn't've had anything to play with. I hope you have greedy children like you someday. I curse you. *Sofrito cuchifrito que se joda un poquito.*" Which means, "I hope you get fucked—not too much, just enough."

And he did not spare the rod in teaching us discipline. He smacked us around for every infraction—when he could catch us. We came to respect that man's hand like the hand of God Himself— the wrathful, take-no-shit Old Testament God. He even beat us with the belt we made and gave him for Christmas. Cardboard stings! The ungrateful ingrate.

Serge and I would go outside to avoid getting beat on by our dad. And then we'd get beat up out on the street. Because we were always the new kids on the block. My dad kept moving us every year. From Jackson Heights to Elmhurst, Elmhurst to Astoria, Astoria to Jamaica. It was all part of my dad's grand plan, movin' on up every year, just like the Jeffersons. Only somehow we never seemed to get out of Queens. We started out in a tiny studio apartment with a Murphy bed, which looked like science fiction to my little Latin eyes. From there we kept movin' on up to slightly bigger and better apartments, until finally we had our own house, with a backyard and everything. Only my father, still scheming to get rich, rented out most of the rooms to strangers, so it was as though we were back in one room anyway.

It was a drag being the perpetual new kid on the block. And we were always the first Latins, too. We were like Latin pioneers, busting neighborhoods where no Latins had busted neighborhoods before. They were all Irish or exclusively Italian until we arrived. Yeah, I took a lot of beatings.

I became a comic because otherwise there was no fun at home.

The only time we had fun was when I would goof and get my father laughing, and that would break the tension.

Like one time after I hit puberty, I was in the bathroom playing with my *pinga*. Which I did a lot. What, you didn't? Liar. All guys jerk off. Even the pope does it. I taught Serge how to do it, too. Cuz that's what big brothers are for.

I was a dedicated little jerk-off. I shocked the monkey to death. I climbed Mount Baldy a thousand times. I caulked the entire bathroom.

So I'm in there one day, naked, standing at the sink, waxing the plantain, ready to launch, when the door, which I thought I had locked, bursts open, and my dad is there, looming and seething.

"WHAT THE HELL ARE YOU DOING?" he shouts.

"Hey Pops! I, uh, I'm, um . . . I'm changing the lightbulb!"

"WITH YOUR DICK?" he shouts. But I can see a bit of a grin forming.

"Well . . . I couldn't reach it with my hands?"

For a split second he teeters on the cusp of either busting my chops or bursting out laughing. Thank God he goes for the latter. Giving me time to grab my undies and slip down the hall past him, before he changes his mind.

I've been ad-libbing comedy ever since.

It wasn't that my mom and dad didn't like to party. They just didn't do it together, and they never did it in the house. My dad loved the ladies (he's remarried twice since my mom divorced him), and my Moms loved to party and hang out, as long as it wasn't at home. In fact, they were out often and partying hard. My brother and I were like latchkey kids.

But there was no fun at home. At home we had to address my dad as "sir." He was a typical overbearing Latin dad in that way. A Latin kid has to be very, very careful how he addresses his dad, because they all have this hair-trigger sense of when they're being disrespected. Especially back then. I guess it was because they got no respect out in the world, so they demanded extra at home.

Like my dad would be in another room and call for me: "John, you little shit!"

You're supposed to say, "Sir?" But sometimes I'd forget and go "What?" or "Yeah?" Not meaning any disrespect, it was just a reflex. But when a kid says "What?" or "Yeah," a Latin dad hears "Fuck you, Dad!"

And my dad would go off. He'd come storming into the room.

"WHAT DID YOU SAY TO ME?"

And poor little Serge would come walking in at just the wrong moment and say, "What?"

Pow. Serge is airborne. The youngest recruit in the Air Force. Flying without a plane.

My Moms and Pops spent a lot of time out of the house, because whenever they were home together they fought, constantly, like caged rats. Oh my God the fights Serge and I witnessed as kids. It was like HBO, except there wasn't a referee to keep them from fighting dirty. Or maybe it was more like Mexican wrestling. No rules, no holds barred, and use of furniture as weapons is okay.

I'd grab a spoon and pretend it was a microphone and I was the announcer.

"*Sábado, Sábado en Madison Square Garden! Lucha libre de la época! Leguizamo contra Leguizamo!*"

They fought about everything. Money—my dad wouldn't give my mom any. Toys, trips, cool clothes—we didn't have any of that, either. Women—the ones my dad was seeing on the side.

As I entered my teen years, I developed this mortal fear of death. For a while I woke up almost every night moaning and covered with sweat after some nightmare where a dark, shadowy figure climbed in from the fire escape to kill my folks or came up to my bed with a garbage bag to suffocate me, and I fought him off with whatever I could put my hands on. I'd lie there with my heart pounding in the dark and all the next day I'd brood over these morbid thoughts of death. Really, I was convinced I'd never live to see thirty.

Do all kids go through a period like that, obsessed with death and violence? Or just my Dad's?

After fifteen years of arguing my parents finally agreed on something. Divorce. It was a nasty-ass divorce—for everybody except my father. Because he walked away with everything—the house, the money, his leopard thong. And my Moms got . . . me and Serge. And she got to be a single mother, which is a polite way of saying broke, exhausted, and nobody'll date your ass.

My mom did a lot of complaining at Serge and me. She'd be standing in the kitchen making dinner. Which really wasn't that hard. After Pops left, she took a job, and she went back to college at night, so she was always too busy to cook. We ate Shake 'N Bake. Dry. Right out of the box. With no chicken. But she'd still complain.

"*Pedaso de mierda, inutil.* You need too much attention. That's why I have to be both mother and father to you. Why don't you just grow up and move out so I can party again?" And she'd prance around the stove, singing, "I love the night life, I love to boogie . . ."

Even after he and my mom split up, my dad still wanted to run my life and Serge's. He was always telling my mom she was doing a lousy job of raising us. He only lived a couple of blocks away, and he'd see me on the street after school, hanging with my friends. I had a lot of black friends, and I had grown my hair out into a kind of Latin afro—a spicfro—and he was convinced I was on my way to becoming a gangsta.

So he freaked when I got arrested on that 7 train. There was no way he was going to let his son grow up a no-good criminal. Of course, it

The high school spicfro convinced my Pops I was a gangsta.

never dawned on him that my getting popped had absofuckinglutely nothing to do with having black friends, it was all about me acting out because of *him*. Nope, he convinced my mom to send me back to Colombia, to get me away from the bad influence of my friends. They kept the plan a secret, like they were plotting D-Day or something. John's Departure Day. The idea was they were going to spring it on me the day after the school year ended. But a few days beforehand I caught my mom whispering on the phone. Something about plane tickets, school uniforms, my cousins in Bogotá.

When she hung up I was standing right behind her.

"Mom, are you sending me to Bogotá?"

She jumped.

"*Ay, Dios mio!* Why you sneak around like that? You scare me half to Brooklyn."

"Stop changing the subject, Ma. Are you and Dad sending me to Bogotá?"

I could see her trying to come up with some cover story, but then she started to cry. Latin moms are champions of crying. They cry when they're happy, they cry when they're sad, they cry just because it's been thirty minutes since the last time they cried.

"Ay, Johnito, your father is so worried for you. He thinks you are becoming a bum on the street."

My heart sank to my feet. Now I started crying too.

"Please don't send me away, Ma. I'll be good. I promise."

We hugged. We cried. But their minds were made up, the tickets bought, my bags packed. A few days later they put me on a plane.

I spent another year in Bogotá, living with relatives, going to a private school for American kids, where we wore uniforms and lined up to go pee, and the whole disciplinarian bit. My relatives were very strict with me—my dad had given them precise instructions. When I wasn't in school, I was home doing my homework. They were very sweet to me, but they kept me on a tight leash. I was miserable. I missed my friends, I missed my family, I even missed Queens. I got sick and lost a lot of weight, out of pure depression. I wrote my mom every week, begging her to let me come home. She saved those letters, and you can still see my tear stains.

Eventually they let me come back, and my dad's plan worked, sort of. I never reconnected with any of my old friends. My mom had moved to yet another part of Queens. So once again I had to make new friends, go to a new school, get beat up by new bullies.

So I blame my whole life on my parents. Especially my dad. Because being the son of an autocratic dictator dad like mine marks you for the rest of your life, man. Everything I've accomplished, and everything I've fucked up—I owe it all to you, Pops.

Look at all the books, plays, and movies that have been about the sons of overbearing fathers. *Amadeus* is about how Mozart spent his whole life trying to screw some praise and affection out of his father.

Death of a Salesman, one of my favorite plays, is about two sons struggling for their dad's love and respect. In *The Brothers Karamazov* you've got four sons who are so tormented about how to deal with their autocratic dad—how to earn his love, or at least get their hands on his money—that they end up murdering him. (Believe me, there were times.)

Shrinks say that when you're a little baby your relationship to your mother is so close it's like you, the baby, don't even realize she's a separate person. For nine months you shared her body, her blood, you ate what she ate, all that. And even after you're born, you're still attached to her by the umbilical cord, and then the breast, and all those other ways you're close to her like you'll never be close to another human being for the rest of your life.

Your father is the first person in the world you have a "social" relationship with. He's the first other, separate human being you're aware of in the world. He's your contact with the rest of the world, like your bridge to society.

So they say that how you related to your father as an infant and a kid can have a lot to do with how you relate to the rest of the world when you grow up.

If you were the son of a father like mine, a dad who was always running your life and bossing you around and punishing you at the smallest sign of independence or disobedience, you can go one of two ways as an adult. You can grow up to be weak, indecisive, reluctant to assert yourself, scared to make up your own mind or act out in any way. You're always flinching from the hand of that imaginary father figure who's like an angry giant in your head.

Or you go the opposite way and fight back against the giant— you're always asserting yourself, you're always acting out, you're always resisting authority and fucking up and clowning around. You're driven to create your own place in the world, and to succeed. You're driven to stand up for yourself and stand out as an independent individual who takes no shit from nobody no way.

The psychologist Alfred Adler said that if you go that route, you become "perfectionist, ambitious, egotistical and defiant." He also wrote: "Such children, in their everlasting greed for triumph, may at times even become the material from which, under favorable conditions, the great personages, the artists and poets develop."

Word!

Either way, you still always have that giant in your head, and your relationship with him will always have a lot to do with who you are, how you act, what you accomplish, and what kind of husband and friend and father you become. No matter how successful you are, no matter how much fame and fortune you pile up, you're still always trying to prove yourself to him.

Not that I'm comparing myself to Mozart. He died young. But still, when I look at my life and my career and my relationships . . .

s I was bouncing around between all those different parts of the ghetto, comedy became a survival tactic for me on the streets, too. I'd run into some bully and he'd go, "My pops can beat your pops."

And I'd say, "Oh yeah? When?"

"Oh, you funny. You ridonkeylous."

That was one of my nicknames in school. Ridonkeylous. Mr. Ridonkeylous. It beat Dickless.

I first started to write down my comedy ideas in high school because I wanted to be cool. This was at Murray Bergtraum High School in downtown Manhattan, right near One Police Plaza. I'd take the 7 in from Queens and transfer to the Lexington Avenue line every school day. It was a long ride and I had to work hard to resist taking over the mic and putting on a show.

At Bergtraum there was one table at lunch that was like our version of the Algonquin Round Table. You had to be funny, otherwise the other kids wouldn't let you partake. Only funny people got to sit.

Other kids would stand around and be entertained while you'd say crazy shit. It wasn't the coolest cool table. That was the table where all the gangstas and hoodlums sat. The kind of guys who called me Ridonkeylous. But still, it was a pretty cool table. There were girls hanging around and everything.

I didn't make it into this circle until late in sophomore year. The competition was fierce. Later I would audition at a lot of comedy clubs where it was easier to get a gig than it was to get a seat at that table. We had a lot of class clowns in the school. People knew who was funny and who wasn't, so to sit at that lunch table you had to be really funny. I'd start writing my jokes the day before, coming up with funny stuff of my own or stealing anything I heard that was good. That's how I started writing, working on my jokesmithing all the time. To be liked and to meet girls.

I was disruptive in high school. After my dad left, I was a handful for my mom. Not like I was a really bad or malicious kid. I just, well, lacked discipline. With my dad out of the house, I was like the news footage you always see of people running wild in the streets when some dictator dies.

My teachers were always bringing my mom in for conferences. Which was tough for her, because she had to take off from work.

"John is very bright," they'd tell her, "and completely undisciplined. If he would just shut up once in a while, he could be the best student in the school."

It wasn't just that I ran my mouth. I was always pulling some prank. Like we had this science teacher, Mrs. Sherman, who was so stiff and boring that I had to act out in her class just to stay awake. Once I got everyone in the class to sing "Jingle Bells" every time she turned to write something on the blackboard. It was a couple weeks before Christmas and I was in the holiday spirit. The first time we did it, she turned around and said, "Who did that?"

We all raised our hands.

"That'll be enough of that nonsense, you delinquents."

She turned to write on the board, and we all started to sing "Jingle Bells" again. This went on like a half dozen times, until she went running out the door to complain to the principal. I ran to the door behind her—and locked it. The whole class partied until the maintenance guy jimmied the door open and my classmates ratted me out.

I played hooky a lot too. Not just by myself—I'd organize half the kids in my class to cut school with me. We Latins don't like to do anything without a crowd.

One afternoon I orchestrated a walkout, and maybe twenty of us took the subway up to Times Square, which was still the Pit of All Sins in those days. It wasn't Disneyfied yet, it was more like this really twisted alternate-universe Disneyland for hookers, strippers, dope addicts, and assorted perverts of every disgusting type. It was like a little strip of Hell right in the middle of Manhattan, unbelievably scuzzy and depraved. Yeah baby.

We tried to get in to see this porn movie, *Yank My Doodle* or *Rambone* or whatever. Twenty high school kids all lined up at the box office window, with me in the lead, trying to talk our way in, when this huge pinky-white hand the size and heft of a frozen turkey falls on my shoulder.

It was like a scene from *Spanky & Our Gang*. This big Irish mook of a cop, really old-school, is like, "I'm runnin' ya in, Spanky." And me, Spanky, giving him attitude: "Ah, blow it out yer nose." Which of course got me nowhere but busteded. My second time behind bars.

And it still didn't learn me. I kept cutting school, and I kept giving cops lip. One afternoon me and a few pals ducked out of class and went down into the subway. I forget where we were heading—probably back up to Times Square, where *Rambone* was still playing. As we get to the turnstile a train is pulling in, and we all start scrambling for tokens, when out of nowhere this pair of transit cops appears.

"You boys goin' somewheres?"

One of my guys starts to panic. "We weren't gonna jump the turnstile, officer. Honest."

"So, you were gonna jump were ya?"

Their smug looks set me off.

"He said we *weren't* gonna jump," I said. "We got tokens. Look."

I pull my hand out of my pocket and all this stuff falls to the scummy subway floor—some change, some folded-up Kleenex (for use while viewing *Rambone*), a pack of matches, but no token.

"Uh-huh. Whyn't you boys in school?" one of them scowls.

"Whyn't you out bustin' some real criminals?" I fire back.

They both smile, real slow. And I go directly to jail. I do not pass the turnstile, I do not get to see *Rambone*.

I don't want to sound like I was a major juvenile delinquent or anything. Three busts was nothing where I came from. I knew guys who'd get busteded three times before breakfast. They had bail bondsmen on twenty-four-hour call. In high school. I guess I was showing off, trying to prove myself. I had never really been able to fight back against my dad, so I took it out on other authority figures. A behavior pattern I'd repeat often in my life.

Because I kept getting in trouble, my Moms tried to keep me on a tighter leash, but I made it hard for her. Serge and I were supposed to head straight home and do our homework. My mom would call from work at three every afternoon to make sure we were there.

"John, is that you?"

"No, Ma, it's a burglar. I was just about to take the phone when it rang."

"My son the clown. Are you doing your homework?"

"Yes, Ma."

"Is your brother helping you?"

"Jeez, Ma."

She'd hang up, and I'd go into the bedroom, where Serge would be dutifully studying. While I was becoming the class clown, he was on his way to class valedictorian. What a good, studious boy he was. As his older brother, I felt it was my duty to encourage him.

"Here," I'd say, dropping my books on top of his. "You like studying so much, do my homework too. I'm heading out."

"You can't make me!" he'd whine. "I'll tell Mom."

"Yeah? And I'll tell her you squeal like a monkey when you jerk off."

"You're the one who taught me!"

"And this is how you repay me?"

So he'd do my homework for me, and I'd go hang on the street a couple hours with friends before my mom got home from work.

Yeah, I was well on my way to becoming a major fuckup when my math teacher intervened. Mr. Zufa. Rhymes with "loofa." He was a white guy—very white, painfully white. He had a sort of British accent and a Tom Snyder laugh—"Haw haw haw haw." It almost made you sorry to be funny.

One day he says to me, "Mister Le-squeeze-mo, you have the attention span of a sperm." He was always finding new ways to mispronounce my name. "Why don't you rechannel your annoyingness? Instead of being a disruptive element, why don't you rechannel your attention deficit? Why don't you become a stand-up comedian, or an ack-tohr?"

I acted all punk and got up in his face. There were girls watching, you know.

"Fuck you. Don't tell me what I can and can't do. Just give me a referral to an acting school."

"This is going down on your permanent record, Mr. Le-grease-mo," he sighed.

Still, he got me thinking. Maybe I *should* look into this theater thing. There were lots of girls in acting classes, weren't there? And all the other guys would be into other guys. I'd have all the poonani I could eat. (Don't tell me you don't eat it, bro.)

So I went home and started looking up acting schools in the Yellow Pages. Because my Moms knew nothing about acting. Except once a month, when the rent was due.

"My mother died yesterday," she'd sob at the landlord.

"What? That's your fifth dead mother this year. Nobody has five mothers."

"We're Latino. It's an es-tended family."

I found an acting school in the Yellow Pages, Amanda Parsons' Showcase Theater. It cost $300 a semester. My mom didn't have that kind of money, so she asked my dad for it. Of course he said no.

"Acting lessons? What kind of a career is acting? A career for *maricones*, that's what. You let that boy become an actor, woman, and he'll spend the rest of his life sponging off you."

Now, I gotta say I've never really understood why my dad was so dead set, right from the start, against my becoming an actor. Mr. I Was Gonna Be The Latin Fellini. Was he worried that because his dreams had been crushed, mine would too? Was he jealous? Or was he just too damn cheap to fork over the three hundred clams? Honestly, I never figured it out.

But I wasn't going to let him stop me.

"Forget it, Ma," I said. "I'll get a job after school."

"A job? What kind of job can a boy like you get? When will you do your homework?"

"You let me worry about the homework," I said, making the jerk-off sign to Serge to keep him from saying anything.

So I got a job after school at a Kentucky Fried Chicken. I figured I'd already spent all that time choking the chicken, so frying them up was the logical next step. I worked there three afternoons a week, while Serge did my homework. What are little brothers for if you can't make them your slaves?

Two evenings a week I took the 7 train into Manhattan to acting class. Amanda Parsons was like a Vivien Leigh character, an old-school theater diva, a real Blanche Dubois. "I've always depended on the kindness of strangers. . . . Oh the light's too bright. Too harsh . . . " She was always on the brink of a nervous collapse, and her husband, who was a doctor, kept her supplied in pills. I'll never forget the first time I went to her place, a tiny apartment on Fifty-seventh street, not far from Carnegie Hall. I opened the door and she didn't have her wig on, and she was almost completely bald, with maybe three hairs on her head. She looked like Tweety Bird.

Mrs. Parsons had a real problem with my accent. It was too street, too homeboy.

"It has a Spanish, thuggish sound," she sniffed. "So primitive. Like a missing link."

And I'd be muttering things like, "Why you talking out the side a your face? I don't talkeded funny. Crazy-ass, smelly old *vieja*. You are *buggiando*. You know what time it is?"

But I listened to these pronunciation tapes she gave me, and I'd walk around the neighborhood all the time practicing how to get rid of my accent and develop more rounded, how-now-brown-cow vowels. I'd be spitting these tongue-twisters like "She sits on slitted sheets. She sits on slitted sheets. Red leather yellow leather red leather yellow leather . . . "

I didn't completely lose my accent, but I lost a lot of friends.

"Damn man, you talk funny. Wass wrong wichoo? You think you better than us cuz you overpronounciate your words?"

"How now, brown pal? Oh, how your brutish tones fall upon my ears."

"Keep talkin', motherfucker. My brutish foot gonna fall up you ass."

I should have been like James Gandolfini and kept the accent. Who knew talking ethnic would come into fashion later?

My mom and dad both came to see me do my first official performance at Mrs. Parsons' theater. It was a one-act play, and I had a big part, and I rocked it. My mom cried. The happy kind of crying.

"Who knew my son had such talent?"

My dad wasn't so impressed.

"I'm telling you, woman, nip this in the bud or he'll be living with you the rest of his life."

I didn't think I was going to learn much more from old Mrs. Parsons, so I switched acting schools. It was a real step up: I went to study under the illustrious Lee Strasberg. In the 1930s and 40s he worked with all the great American playwrights and directors, like Clifford Odets and Elia Kazan. Then he founded the Actors Studio and invented method acting. Marlon Brando, James Dean, Paul Newman, Marilyn Monroe, Jane Fonda, and Al Pacino all studied under him. He was a good actor in his own right, too—he played Hyman Roth in *The Godfather*. He was really old by the time I got there, but I figured he could still teach me a thing or two.

Boy, was I wrong.

One of Strasberg's most important innovations for actors was the "sense memory exercise." He figured that you don't remember key events just with your mind, but with all of your senses. Like when you remember the time your dog got run over by a car, you don't just see it in your mind, you feel it all over again. Actors can apply this on the stage. For a sad scene, you feel the sadness of when your dog died, and then you're not just acting sad or giving the impression of sadness, you're really feeling sad.

That's the theory anyway. I didn't get the hang of it right away. The first time I was called on to do a sense memory exercise in class, I was up there trying to feel like my dog died and Strasberg was going, "Come on, lose yourself in it. You barely have talent. You bore me. Get out of my class."

Those were the last words I ever heard him say. He died that night. I was like, "Oh my God, I must be a really bad actor. My acting is so bad it killed Lee Strasberg."

Okay, so maybe I wasn't a natural-born actor. But I was a workaholic. So I studied a lot and worked really hard until I was a natural. I got a job cleaning people's apartments to pay for it.

"You spent all those years getting an education to clean toilets?" my dad yelled when he heard.

Truth is I sucked as a Hazel. I'd be wandering around somebody's apartment memorizing my lines for the next day's class, and not a lot of cleaning got done. Once I was practicing my sword-fight moves with a broom and knocked a lamp off a table. I was standing there with the broken pieces in my hands when the woman whose apartment it was came in the door.

"Hi, John," she said, looking around. "Gee, the place looks . . . pretty much the way it did when I left this morning."

"You're welcome," I said, making past her for the door. "Oh, here." I handed her the pieces of the lamp. "It fell."

Exit, stage left.

Finally I found a teacher who loved my work. In fact, he loved it a bit too much.

"John darling, you have sooo much talent," he said. "But you need to experience more. Other lifestyles. Things that will open your worldview. That'll be five hundred dollars."

"Um, I don't have that kind of cash," I said.

"Oh? Well, then you can pay me . . . some other way." He smiled.

"No thanks," I said. "Trying to cut back."

Ah, you suck one dick and they call you a fag.

He died a year later.

I'm not saying I'm Carrie, but something was definitely going on. Word got around, and acting teachers stopped taking my calls.

My first real acting job was with a children's theater. Not because I wanted to do good for the kids or anything. It just was the only work I could get. I guess it was early affirmative action and they let a Latino in. Lowered their standards.

But I didn't care. I needed attention, even if it was kids. And the kids didn't care either. Kids can be so forgiving.

The repertoire was ghetto classics—like street versions of classic children's tales. There was one other comic in the company, and he and I became very competitive. Pretty soon we were just trying to outdo each other in voices. I'd say all my lines like Curly, throwing in a "Whoy sointly!" and a "Whoy Oy oughta!" and a "Woo woo woo woo woo."

He'd come back as Jerry Lewis. "Whoa Dean! Hey lady!"

And I'd go into Lou Costello. "Hey Abbott! Oh, I'm a baaaad boy."

The kids loved it. There's no accounting for children's tastes. But I didn't care about that. I can live for months on one good compliment.

It was time to have it out with my father about acting. He was still trying to convince my mother that it was all just a passing fancy. I told him I'd decided it was my life's calling. You'd think I'd said I was going to become a child-molesting serial killer.

"Don't waste our lives," he thundered. "We're immigrants. We gave you everything. We didn't come here for you to be an actor. You're deliberately wasting all our lives."

He shook his finger in my face.

"If you insist on becoming an actor," he warned, "you're dead to me."

So I became an actor. Partly to defy him, and partly to disobey him. That fine line between acting and acting out.

"Screw you, Pops," I said. "I'm not only going to be an actor, I'm gonna be a great one. I'm gonna get rich and famous doing it. And I'm gonna take care of Moms and Serge, cuz you sure ain't gonna do it."

Okay, I didn't say it to him. I said it to myself. If I'd said it to him he might have made good on his threat. I'd be dead to him all right. And to everyone else.

My nightmares would finally come true.

CHAPTER 4

When I got into NYU I started working to pay my own way by doing the comedy club circuit. It didn't pay very well. There were a lot of nights where you'd barely make your cab fare home. I became a vegan, not for religious or philosophical reasons but because I couldn't afford meat. Luckily I was used to it from my Shake 'N Bake days.

I joined a really amazing improv group called The First Amendment. Robin Williams had just quit, and Bruce Willis had stopped coming too. The company was on the way down, so they took me in. What did they have to lose?

My acting teacher at the time was an Italian mook named Joe. He was pretty critical.

"John, you need to be more worldly. You need content in your work. You need to be interesting to people when you're up there. You gotta get the girls talking about you. Like, 'What is he going to do next? What's he up to?'"

So I slept with all the girls in the company. And then I couldn't show up anymore, it was just too uncomfortable. They'd all be talking about me. Comparing notes. Making jokes about my dick and all.

It was then that I hooked up with Cathy, a fellow actor and co-median. She was a tall white girl—tall tall, like six foot two. Model wannabe. The Lexus of women. If you can climb her you can have her. When you've been with that girl, you know you've really been somewhere.

We became partners, doing comedy routines, and we became an item, living together. We made an odd couple. When we walked down the street we looked like Boris and Natasha. I was the Puerto Rican–Colombian homeboy from Queens; she was a total shiksa who came from money in the rich folks' suburb of Riverdale, up the Hudson from Manhattan. In fact, we lived together in her parents' house. And they didn't mind. They were really great to me. This Latin kid living in their house, schtupping their nice white daughter, and they were okay with that.

Our bedroom was right next to their bedroom, so we had to have Anne Frank sex. Hush-hush sex. Which was hard for me, because I'm Latin and very vocal. I like to make sure it sounds good. And after all those years of self-pleasuring I was enjoying it too much actually being with a real live woman.

So I'd be on top of her, slamming away, and I'd start to shout.

"Oh yeah, baby! *Ay, Dios mio!* Who's your man? Whoa, yeah! Two balls in the corner pocket!"

And she'd go, "SSSHHH!" And slap her hand over my mouth.

And I'd be like, "Mmmff mfff frmmma mmmf! Hummffa! Hummff! Wooo HOOO!"

Next day we'd get real funny looks from her parents.

"Um, we were working on a routine," she'd tell them.

Still, it was amazing that they were so open-minded. Later, they let us use an apartment they had in Riverdale, where we lived rent-free.

I was always expecting a big culture clash. Like when my family would come over. My family was all Latin-size people like me. Her family was gigantic. Her Wall Street stockbroker father was six-five, her brother was six-seven, the mom was five-ten. The sister was five-eight or five-nine—she was the only one that was normal-sized. It was like I was living in the Land of the Giants. My feet dangled when I sat in their chairs. It was so emasculating. Even their cats were big. I swear to God, they had the most enormous cats. They were like dogs. And of course I bring the typical Latin animal into their lives—a parrot. Cathy fell in love with that bird. She took custody of it when we broke up. (I got another parrot years later. His name's Homey. Parrots are a lifetime emotional investment. They can live like seventy-five years. Homey's gonna do my eulogy. Then he'll move in with one of my kids, like a cranky old grandparrot.)

I'd only been around people that white once before, when my parents enrolled me in the Fresh Air Fund so they could get rid of me for a couple weeks one summer. The Fresh Air Fund takes poor inner-city kids and sends them to a rich white family in the country for two weeks. So that just when you're getting comfortable with three meals a day, lead-free paint chips, and ketchup isn't a vegetable, they snatch it away. If you didn't know how poor you were before, now your ass really knows.

They put me on a Greyhound and I rode it all the way to Vermont, and when I got out, my perfect, white J. Crew family was waiting for me. The father looked like William F. Buckley Jr., and he was drunk twenty-four/seven.

"Oh look Marge," he said, patting me on the head. "We got our-selves a little Mexican. Would you like a drink, Jorge?" He pronounced it *You're-gay*. He had martini-olive breath.

"Yo, I ain't Mexican," I scowled.

"We do so love Cancún," Marge smiled. She patted my head, too. She looked like Mrs. Howell from *Gilligan's Island*.

"I said I ain't Mexican," I growled.

The dad haw-hawed. "Calm down there, *pequeño hombre*. You're going to like it here. We're going to buy you anything your little heart has ever desired."

When I heard that I decided okay, I'm Mexican. *Pues, orale, vato.* Can I get you a margarita?

Besides, it was such a relief to find out that white people could be just as fucked up as my people.

Cathy was great to me. She took care of me. I was living in poverty—I made $5,000 a year, if that. I had nothing. Her parents paid for everything, which was fantastic, because I didn't care about money. I just wanted to do what I wanted to do. I just wanted to be a funny man. I wanted to be a great comedian and comic actor.

It wasn't like I went with Cathy just to have somebody pay my bills so I could be an artist. I wasn't a ho. I really loved her. But it did work out nicely.

We worked the performance-art circles that were big in the 80s. Lots of lesbians. The cast outnumbers the audience, and someone very unattractive is always naked, with pubic hair sprouting from the unlikeliest of places.

It was with Cathy that I first learned a very important lesson: Never work with the person you sleep with.

Cathy and I had crazy fights, and it was all because we were a comedy team. Her dad wanted her to be a comedian and thought she was hilarious. We performed at the Comic Strip one night, and she didn't get certain laughs. On the drive home he started saying, "You guys are doing so great. I'm so proud of you . . . But John, you're getting a lot of the laughs, huh? Maybe it's not written really fairly."

I kicked her foot and gave her a what-the-fuck look.

"Maybe you guys should share the jokes more," he was saying. "It seems like John has all the punchlines."

That was the first drop of poison in our relationship, right there. From that moment on she started to hate me, thinking that I had bamboozled her somehow. We were writing our material together, and she was funny, but still. I had been doing it longer. Maybe I was a bit more polished than she was.

We kept doing the circuit, and started to meet some successful comics. We opened for Rodney Dangerfield in his club and he hit on Cathy, right in front of my face.

"You're a hot girl, you're beautiful, baby, what are you doing with him?"

I'm muttering, "Come here, you popeyed fuck, I'll give you a little respect. I got your respect right here."

Ray Romano was performing back then, and Mario Cantone. When we played the Comic Strip we'd open for Chris Rock, who would blow up the place. Just blow it up. This was after Cathy and I would do our thing and get a few laughs, but not exactly set the place on fire. We were funny, but it was not typical stand-up comedy. It was more like acting sketches and telling stories, not just joketelling, so it was strange and different for audiences. And then Chris Rock would go on and slowly, slowly wind the crowd up until they exploded with laughter. They'd be roaring.

Our routines were very physical. In one sketch I played a Japanese guy who was on the phone trying to get a report on my stocks from my broker. Cathy played the broker, and as the conversation progressed it became like phone-sex, but using stock terms. In another sketch we were a couple and she busted me for sleeping around. That turned into a very physical, slapping, beating-on-each-other routine.

Late in our relationship, when she really had caught me sleeping around, that sketch had a way of turning a little too violent. She'd really throw herself into it. Her whole six-foot Amazon self. She'd crack me so hard my head would go *boi-yoi-yoing* like one of those bobble dolls, and I'd see little Amanda Parsons tweety-birds circling before my eyes.

"Ow, baby. You gotta to try not to hit me that hard."

"Sorry," she'd say. But acting suspiciously unrepentant. "I was trying to make it look real."

Well, there does have to be some impact for it to look right. And sometimes you can't totally control the force of the blow. So sometimes when I hit her back I'd go too far and swell up her face.

The odd thing is, we got crazy laughs for that piece. That became our best-liked piece, because of the violence. Audiences loved it. "Oh shit, they're fucking beating each other!" People do like to see other couples beat on each other. It's a vicarious thrill.

One time, though, it looked a little too real. Some guys in the audience thought I was really beating on her. They ganged up on me after the performance and were actually ready to beat me up.

"You can't treat a lady like that, man."

"That was no lady, that was my— Ow."

Yep, still clowning around. Still getting my ass beat. But at least it was proof I was believable delivering my lines.

*　*　*

From all that performing, I got the balls to go be in a real play. And I did it in style: Joseph Papp's Public Theater, one of the most prestigious theaters in the country, where people like Meryl Streep and Kevin Kline performed.

I did two plays there, wham bam. The first was *La Puta Vida*, by Reinaldo Povod. Povod was a friend and protégé of the great Nuyorican poet and playwright Miguel Piñero, who wrote the play *Short Eyes*, which was also made into a film. I'm not the biggest fan of *Short Eyes*. It's about a child molester's tough time in prison, which is exactly what I think he should be having. But I'm a huge fan of Piñero as a Nuyorican poet. He broke a lot of ground for Latins by bringing the language of the street into his art. He was the first Puerto Rican playwright on Broadway, and it was a smash hit. And the movie version of *Short Eyes* was the screen debut of my friend Luis Guzmán, so it can't be all bad.

I must have done all right in *La Puta Vida*, because right away they asked me to be in another play, and it was huge. They asked me to play Puck in *A Midsummer Night's Dream*. The original Puck dropped out of the production and they were in a bind, but whatever. I was gonna do Shakespeare, baby. I was legit.

Sort of. The rest of the cast was awesome: Elizabeth McGovern, Fisher Stevens, F. Murray Abraham, Joe Morton, Lorraine Toussaint. I was the only pissant on the team. My name was so far down at the bottom of the program I was getting orders for printing. But I was still legit, right?

Now, I had not really done Shakespeare before, and I am not exactly a Shakespearean actor. The language was like a foreign tongue to me. I'm good with languages and accents and all that, because I grew up in Queens. I was used to Spanglish, Yiddish, Irish, takeout Chinese, deli-man Korean, Jamaican patois, whatever. But nobody in the neighborhood spoke Elizabethan pentameter. Nobody went into the bodega and said, "Prithee, I shall haveth yon pack o' Bubblicious or 'swounds shalt thou feeleth the kiss of my ponyard." Before I studied under Lee Strasberg, I tried a Shakespeare monologue when I auditioned to get into acting classes at Juilliard. It came out so ghetto they rejected me.

The night for the critics to come review the show was approaching, and the director was so nervous about my performance that he asked the great Joe Papp himself to tutor me in Shakespeare. Papp was a very interesting character, very patriarchal. Bossy would be the polite word for him. He was really more of an impresario than a director, and I'm not sure how much good his talking to me did.

Also, there was the problem that I was still a green idiot and didn't really get what he was trying to tell me.

At first he said to me, "If you have loved wisely but not too well, if you have felt the unkindest cut of all, if you have held the mirror up to nature and asked what's in a name, you are thinking Shakespeare. If you have considered yourself of this happy breed of men, or of this sceptered isle—when you have demanded your pound of flesh or called down a plague on both your houses, you are thinking Shakespeare. If you suspect we are pigeon-livered or believe the play's the thing, you are thinking Shakespeare. If you believe music is the food of love and that you should first kill all the lawyers, you are thinking Shakespeare."

And I was like, "Huh?"

I mean, I got some of it. I didn't know what the hell severed aisles or pigeon livers or quarter-pounders of flesh had to do with theater, and I hadn't been around lawyers enough yet to want to kill them all. But I had certainly loved not too well, and I did believe this play was the thing—the thing that was either gonna make my career or end it quick.

I must have looked pretty confused, cuz he tried again.

"Look, Shakespeare's not like conversation, John. It's heightened reality. Don't make it so casual. You're not ordering fries at McDonald's. Give it passion. Passion! Feel it deeply. Don't be afraid to over-act. Don't be afraid to be too big. Just be."

That's when the lightbulb went off. The trick to Shakespeare was overacting? Hell, I could do that. I practically specialized in it. Over-acting "R" Me. I thanked him, and he looked kind of dubious.

And that was the last time I saw him. He died soon after meeting me. Another great man of the theater killed by my bad acting.

Even with Papp's help, Shakespeare was not my thing. I was more street, colloquial, improv. Shakespeare was almost the opposite of what I do. It's all verbal, and I was so physical. Shakespeare is so set, it's so precise, you can't mess with it. In the theater, Shakespeare is like a religion. If you change one syllable, you're blaspheming.

We'd be in rehearsal, and I'd have a line like, "This is the woman, but not this the man."

Only it'd come out, "This is the woman, but that ain't the guy, yo."

The whole cast would gasp. The great F. Murray Abraham would cover his ears and run from the stage.

I'd be like, "What? What I say?"

The director would rub his face. "John, please say the line the way the Bard wrote it."

And I'd go, "Bart? His name was Bart Shakespeare?"

Okay, so Shakespeare did not come naturally to me. It was a whole different language, almost a whole different art form from what I knew. It's like if you're a jazz musician, classical music is not your thing, and vice versa. You may dabble, but you're not going to excel.

But I was a driven young man. I was compelled to excel. I hated screwing up in front of the cast, all these more seasoned ak-tohrs and ak-tohresses. I was determined to nail this thing. I'd show them. I was gonna be the best damn Puck I could be. The puckiest Puck the world had ever puckin' seen.

So I became a Method Puck. I was in character all the time. I wouldn't just be Puck on stage, I'd be Puck everywhere. I wouldn't just act Puck, I'd live Puck. A prankster. A trickster. A pain in the ass.

I started pulling practical jokes on the rest of the cast. One day I went to a novelty store and bought it out of itching powder. Which I put in everyone's costume—Fisher's drawers, Elizabeth's bra. Then I stood back and waited for the fun.

Suddenly I hear Fisher screaming, "Aaaaah! What the fuck is that?" This is backstage, during the performance. He's hopping up and down like he's got ants in his pants. Only this was worse. Itching powder doesn't just itch, it actually hurts. Because it's not a powder, it's sharp little nettles that prick your flesh. If I'd known that, maybe I would've thought twice. Maybe.

There was so much uproar backstage that it kind of upstaged what was going on in front of the audience. Where the great F. Murray Abraham was performing. And the great F. Murray Abraham takes himself and his craft v-e-r-y seriously. He carries his *Amadeus* Oscar with him everywhere, in the dressing room, even brings it onstage and hides it behind scenery. I'm not kidding. He grew up in Texas with a lot of Mexicans, but he thinks he's British. He has a very toffy accent—old Mrs. Parsons would've given him straight A's.

So the great F. Murray Abraham comes offstage after I've just ruined his big scene, and he's very upset. He's clutching his Oscar and drops down on his knees in front of me.

"Please be quiet, I beseech you," he implored in the plummy, red-leather-yellow-leather tones of a great Shakespearean ack-tohr. "Please allow me to have my moe-ment on stage." He was actually wringing his hands around the Oscar. "I don't rob you of your moe-ment. Please reciprocate the undeservéd respect I have shown thee."

I was mortified.

"Oh man, I'm sorry. Get up."

The great F. Murray Abraham.
I drove him puckin' crazy.

I was reported to Equity and fined a couple of hundred dollars.

After that I was even more nervous and torqued-up than before. Now I really had to redeem myself and show them I could pull this off. I worked myself up into such a state that there was no way I wasn't going to screw up on stage.

So the critics came to review us, and fuck me if I didn't forget my lines. Just went completely blank out of sheer nerves and panic. Standing in the spotlight like a deer in the headlights. Wracking my brains, but the lines were not there, and I had no idea of how to get out of it. You can't improv your way out in Shakespeare.

Joe Morton, who was playing Oberon, had to feed me my lines.

"Here comes my messenger," he said. "How now, mad spirit!"

I blinked into the lights and made fish lips, but no words came out.

Joe tried to prompt me.

" . . . And what of thy mistress?"

"Oh yeah!" I said. "Right! My mistress! . . . Uh, what about her?"

"Thine mistress with a monster is in love . . . "

"No shit! I mean, verily she ist. Milord and whatnot. We've gottest beef. I wilst pimp-slappeth and bitch-slappeth himeth. I've gotteth thine back . . . "

Oh, it was fucking awful. I was just babbling anything that came to mind. I could hear actresses fainting backstage. When I finally crawled off, totally humiliated, no one would meet my eye.

I was torn up by the critics. I was called "feckless" in the *New York Times*. I had to look it up—I had no idea what it meant. Even though I'd gotten a 1,600 on my SATs. If you count all four times I took them. The only reason I didn't kill myself after I read those reviews was because we have two rivers in Manhattan and I couldn't decide which one to jump into.

A Midsummer Night's Dream enjoyed a continuous run of one successive night. My father came to see it, but left before the second act.

"Dad, why didn't you stay?" I asked him afterward.

"I couldn't wait. It said on the program 'Second Act: a year later.'"

Despite the fiasco, Fisher Stevens and I became friends. He would soon suffer through *Super Mario Bros.* with me, and much later he produced and had a small part in *Piñero*, which my partner Kathy De-Marco and I coproduced with him. I really liked Joe Morton as well.

Looking back, I'd have to say I was a better Puck offstage than on. I admit it, I went into overdrive. That part played right into two of my worst and most conflicting instincts: the need to prove myself on the one hand, and the urge to act out and clown around on the other. Kind of a self-destructive combo, and boy did I self-destruct.

Joe Morton feeding me my lines in *A Midsummer Night's Dream*.

In many ways that Method Puck has been dogging me ever since. I have a long record of getting on actors' and directors' nerves. Still trying to prove myself, but still always feeling this itch to resist authority, to screw around, to ad-lib and act out.

My Achilles' heel.

By the way, two or three people from those plays died soon afterward. I'm serious. F. Murray Abraham should've been relieved that all I did was give him an itch.

My first step into movie acting was a baby step: a short NYU student film. The director, Daniel Taplitz (who later went on to a successful career in TV and film), saw me in an acting class and recruited me. I was flattered. Feed my ego and I'll follow you anywhere. Still, even at the dawn of my movie career, I was giving the director a hard time.

"So what's this movie called?" I asked Daniel.

"*The Cow*," he said.

"*The Cow*? Are you buggin'? Who's gonna want to see a movie about a cow? Who's the star, Elsie?"

"Well, it's not really about a cow . . ." he explained.

"I ain't appearin' in no barnyard tales, yo," I insisted. "Change the title."

What balls. But he did it. When it came out it was called *Five Out of Six*. Not a real grabber of a title, maybe, but at least it didn't sound like it was about Old Mac-Donald.

Five Out of Six won a Spielberg Focus Award, and despite being a short student film, got me some notice. Bonnie Timmermann, then a TV casting director, saw it and called me in for an audition.

Now, you have to understand what it was like to be a Latin actor auditioning in the 1980s. Basically, they didn't want to hear from Latin guys. They didn't know yet that we were going to be a trend. They only wanted to see Latin guys audition for two kinds of roles: gangsters or janitors.

But it was work, and we all went out for it. You'd see the same guys at every audition: me, Benicio del Toro, Benjamin Bratt, Luis Guz-

Practicing my serious, broody Latin lover look.

mán, and lots of other Latin brothers who never made it. All these Latin guys coming together, and everybody trying to be ghetto. People who weren't ghetto trying to be ghetto—bandannas, leather jackets, chains, the whole bit, strutting around. Guys who'd trained in Shakespeare going, "Yo, waddup homes? Dag." "Yeah, G. Word up."

Or if we were trying out for a janitor role, we'd all be in our coveralls, shucking and jiving like Latin Stepin Fetchits.

"How joo doon, sir? Nice day today, *hombre* sir."

One of the regulars wasn't even Latin. He was an Italian guy, Victor Colicchio, who was trying to pass for Latin. He did a pretty good impersonation—until he opened his mouth.

"Eh, fuggedaboudit! You're a mook. Gedoudda here."

He had a great scam going, when you think about it. You could play both sides, be gangstering your whole career. Mafia gangster, Puerto Rican gangster, same difference. Just go from gangster to gangster. (Ironically, Victor later wrote one of my very favorite movies I've been in, *Summer of Sam*.)

Of course what we all wanted was to make it in movies. We traded tips about how to make it, like any of us knew at the time. One bit of wisdom we all accepted as gospel was, "If you're ever in a movie poster, don't smile with your mouth open." Cuz if you did, some wise guy down in the subway would always draw a dick going into your mouth. To this day, you'll never see my teeth in a movie poster.

Auditioning for Bonnie Timmermann was special. Bonnie Timmermann single-handedly lowered the unemployment rate for Latin actors in the 80s, because Bonnie Timmermann was the casting director for *Miami Vice*. The premiere spixploitation TV series of the 80s, *Miami Vice* hired more Latin actors than had ever appeared on TV before. They needed us to play a different villain in every episode. And everybody was doing it. We knew we were denigrating our race, but we were making paper at the same time.

So I went up to Bonnie's office in midtown Manhattan, at Fifty-fourth Street and Park Avenue. Swanky place, big brass doors that shone like gold. And I was sick as a dog. I had a terrible fever and my voice was really hoarse. Which turned out to be a blessing. They gave me a few pages from a script to read, and with my low, raspy voice I sounded really thuggish—perfect for a *Miami Vice* bad guy.

And there was another thing. I hated TV. Maybe some of my dad's European art-cinema snobbery had rubbed off on me, cuz I thought TV was beneath me. I may have been nineteen and broke, but I was cocky. I was a theater actor, and to me TV was the lowest you could go. I thought acting on stage and in film was real acting, TV was just hack work. I always remembered something my Gramps said to me when I was young.

"TV? *Ay, fo!* When I was a kid we didn't have TV. We had a window."

So even though this audition was a big opportunity for me, the kind of break most starving young actors would kill for, I went in there with an attitude. I thought I was the flava, yo. And ironically, that worked in my favor too. Between my bad attitude and my fever and my raspy voice, I came off older than I was, like one badass thug. Which was just what they were looking for.

When I was through, Bonnie said, "You were really good. We loved you in *Five Out of Six.*"

And then I went away and waited to hear from her. Much as I looked down on TV, I knew this had been a big audition. Getting work on *Miami Vice* would get my face out there, and help me land an agent to get me more work. At that point, no agent would represent me. Taplitz's girlfriend Robin was a big wheel at Don Buchwald & Associates, Howard Stern's agency. She wanted to represent me, but she said, "You gotta get a gig first." I said, "How am I gonna get a gig first if you don't represent me?" Catch-22.

I got the part—Ivan Calderone Jr., a Colombian cocaine mafia prince coming to Miami to avenge his father's death. It was the two-episode season opener. And Miguel Piñero played my father.

They flew me to Miami. God's waiting room. Put me up in one of those crazy Miami Beach hotels. I'd go down to eat and there'd be all these old folks at the other tables, waiting for the early-bird specials and looking like they were about to die. And the menu had all this crazy shit on it—lion, alligator, ostrich. For a nineteen-year-old from Queens it was like "What the fuck? Did they raid the zoo?"

And then I discovered why TV sucks. Everything is so rushed. Everything's shot in two takes, tops. I ended up doing scenes for three episodes, and we shot them all in a couple days. And I had a lot of scenes. The pace was insane. The dialogue hurt my mouth to say, it was so awful. And they dressed me up to look like some Third World country's flag—a gold satin shirt, blue pants—like a parody of bad, flashy Latin taste. Flashy Latin taste is loud. Fake flashy Latin taste is deafening. I felt so stupid in those outfits. I looked like one of Ricky Ricardo's backup singers—colorized.

Oh God it was a terrible part, too. This Calderone fuck was such a melodramatic bad guy I could've played him as Snidely Whiplash. In one scene I had my sister tied to the steering wheel of a car, and the door rigged with a bomb. So when Tubbs, who's in love with her, goes to let her out—KA-BOOM!

And I sneer, in this really oily Latin accent, "You killed my father. Now you're gonna have to pay." Followed by an evil Snidely laugh.

It was so bad that I never felt like I was getting it right. I'd say to John Nicolella, the director, "That wasn't very good. Can I take another one?"

And he'd say, "No, no, that was perfect, that was great."

"Are you sure? It doesn't sound right. I feel kind of stiff."

"No, no, you looked terrific, you were amazing."

I'd be like, "All right, sure . . ."

My sense of what was good work was derailed. I'd say to myself, "That was great? Could I have possibly been that amazing, even though I thought I sucked? I must be a genius! Even when I suck, I'm amazing!"

We rushed through everything. I was in and out, there and gone. Meanwhile I would be panicking in my hotel room, working on my lines, trying to be just right for this part. I still didn't give a damn about *Miami Vice*. It was all about me. I'd be reading the script like, "My line, my line, bullshit bullshit bullshit, my line, my line, bullshit bullshit . . ."

The whole process violated my perfectionist urges. I knew I wasn't giving my best and it depressed the hell out of me. My control-freak side was totally frustrated too. I had zero control. I was just a cog in this well-oiled TV-making machine. Just a body and a voice to be ordered around. Stand on this mark. Deliver your lines. Now go sit over there until we call you.

Later, when I watched the show on TV, I found out I'd been right all along. I did suck. It was terrible. I was in such agony watching myself. I kept moaning, "God, I'm so fucking horrible." It taught me a very important career lesson: always ask for more takes. And never, never listen to anybody else about my acting, just trust myself. Trust my own eye, my own ear.

Of course, early in your career it's always pretty horrifying to see yourself up there on the screen. Everything is so annoying and magnified—the way you tawk, the way you look, the way you act. Everything you hate about yourself is put out there for everyone to see. It's hard to find anything good in it. Eventually you get used to it, but at first it's a rude awakening.

The fast pace and the lousy dialogue and the ugly costumes didn't do anything to improve my attitude on the set. I had a chance to meet

Don Johnson, but I was such an arrogant little prick and in such a foul mood that I pretty much blew him off. I was sitting in one of the tents on location, and he came over to sit next to me. He was trying to be friendly, and when he saw how nervous and miserable I was he offered me some advice.

"Hey, don't sweat it," he said to me. "TV is all about personality and charm. After that, you better have a big willy or big boobs."

It was good advice, but I didn't listen. I got up and walked away. Partly because I didn't have either a big willy or big boobs. But mostly because I was a rude, pretentious punk. I wasn't just young and cocky, I was young and a total dick.

"I don't have to listen to him," I said to myself. "I'm an ack-tohr in the theatuh."

Luckily, I don't think Don Johnson remembers me doing that. I've seen him at a lot of premieres and such over the years and he's always been really friendly. I still feel bad about it, though. I know that someday some young actor punk is going to do that to me. I'll go over to talk to him and he'll move away, because I represent every- thing he hates. That'll be my payback, dissed in my sunset years by a cocky young dickhead on the set of the Latin-flavored sitcom I'll be starring in, *Santos & Son*.

I just barely met Michael Mann, the show's producer. He'd get in the van with us sometimes as we drove to different locations around Miami, but he was always busy, always on the phone. He hardly noticed I was alive. Man, I was so impressed with him at the time. Michael Fucking Mann. He seemed like such a huge, unapproach- able figure. Now, I've drunk a lot of beers with him. He's just another guy in the business. Just another one of us hos.

Which is definitely how I felt when they handed me the big pay- check for my work. I was a real Jekyll and Hyde about that. On the one hand, my eyes popped out of my head like a cartoon character's when I saw the amount. Like a big cartoon horn in my head went *AH-OOO-GA!* I'd been skimming the bottom of the economic pool, somewhere down so low that the poverty line looked up to me. Panhandlers gave *me* spare change. So this one check was a king's ransom to me. The king, queen, all the princesses and the whole castle. I ran, skipping and laughing merrily, all the way to the bank. But there was still that other side of me, who had trained with some of the great acting teachers of the time. Like my dad, they had passed their standards along to me, and playing stereotyped scumbags in TV cop shows did not meet their criteria. Somewhere, I felt, the great F. Murray Abraham was watching *Miami Vice* and smirking.

Still, as bad as I felt about my part in it, *Miami Vice* was really important to my career. Because it was shot on film, it got me into the Screen Actors Guild (SAG). And it got me Robin as my agent. I went with her to a bar across the street from Don Buchwald's midtown Manhattan offices to celebrate and drank five martinis. I felt so cool drinking martinis, like a real grownup. Didn't feel a thing through the first four, and then *bong.* They had to carry me home.

Robin was a sweet, beautiful lady. Tragically, she would die of an aneurysm a few years later. And John Nicolella died of cancer after directing me in *Miami Vice.* Okay, it was a long time after—he died in 1998—but still. Steve James, the lead actor in one of my early films, *Street Hunter,* died not much later of pancreatic cancer.

I'm like a curse, man. I'm the Monkey's Paw. No wonder I had all those teenage death dreams. You shouldn't even be reading this. It could be hazardous to your health. You should sell this book, take the money, and buy cigarettes. It'd be better for you.

After Robin passed away I got a new agent, a classic New York–agent type, Morty Bartz.

"You were piss-poor on *Vice,*" he told me. "It's gonna be an uphill battle. But if anybody can get you your dreams, I might be the one. Look at it this way—I won't be making 10 percent of your salary, you'll be making 90 percent of mine. That's how good I am."

* * *

M iami Vice didn't improve my deteriorating relationship with Cathy. I was on a major TV show, I had my SAG card—my career was pulling way ahead of hers. And she was jealous. That's how actors are. We're superficial fucks. Even if you love someone, if they're an actor they're your competition. It really puts a strain on the relationship. You wonder why all those movie stars keep getting married and divorced, married and divorced, married and divorced? That's one way you can tell I'm not a typical Hollywood movie star— as of this writing, I've been with the same woman for ten whole years. That's like ten centuries in Hollywood-relationship years.

But then, Teeny, my wife, isn't an actress. I finally learned my lesson, even though it took a long time. Because I was acting all the time, and around actors all the time, and the only girls I knew to hook up with were actors. Eventually you come to realize that actors are not human beings. They may be great in bed, and crazy fun to hang out with, but then things always turn sour. Young actors and actresses are too selfish, too self-involved, too into themselves and their careers to really care about anyone else. I'm saying that about myself, too. My mantra in those days was, "Nothing will distract me from what I want. Nothing. Nothing will take me away from my work. My work is everything."

It can make you kind of hard to live with.

Like Cathy would go, "John? Oh my God, something weird's happening to me. I've lost the feeling in the whole left side of my body. I think I'm having a stroke."

And I'd be looking at myself in the mirror, trying out different expressions for my publicity photos. Serious, broody Latin lover. Wild, goofy comic genius.

"JOHN?"

"Hm? One second honey." Wonder if I should have my teeth whitened again.

"JOHN, I THINK I'M DYING OVER HERE."

"Be right there, sweets." Maybe I should be parting my hair the other way . . .

So Cathy and I struggled to keep it together, both on stage and off, and meanwhile the movie roles were coming in for me. At first they were tiny. I was an extra in a film called *Mixed Blood*, about drug wars in Alphabet City on Manhattan's Lower East Side.

It was the first and last time I was an extra. Extras are treated like shit. Especially by the first AD—the top assistant director. On most film shoots, the first AD is a Nazi, cuz they have to be. The director's busy being all arty and shit, but it's the first AD's job to make sure things actually get done, and done on schedule.

So we extras would be off to one side goofing around, wolfing down all the free food we could stuff in our faces, and the first AD would come by and say, "Do I have to open a can of Shut the Fuck Up?"

And I'd be like, "Hey man, if you gonna treat me like an animal, then give me a bunch of bananas and a big red bucket so I can shit in it and throw it at you."

First ADs have their own lingo, and some of it's pretty funny. Like they'll say, "All right everybody, quiet on the set. Lock it up. Nobody moves, nobody gets hurt. We're going for the mother-and-daughter shot." Which means shooting the same scene again, but with tighter focus. Or for a two-shot (two people in the frame) they'll say, "Okie and Dokie, my two favorite guinea pigs. Don't try this at home.

Rolling. Speed. Action." And the next-to-last shot of the day is "the martini."

People always tell young actors, "Don't be an extra, because they'll always think of you as an extra after that." Extras are the slaves of the film industry. If you're an extra, you're nothing. You're just extra. And the whole industry colludes to keep the extras down. It's a plantation mentality. It's like they're worried that if they give the extras the slightest bit of recognition, they'll get uppity. Maybe form an extras' union. Rise up and demand their rights. Hey, it could happen. Extras have a lot of time on their hands.

* * *

Then came my first real part in a big commercial film: *Casualties of War*, Brian De Palma's Vietnam War movie, with Sean Penn, Michael J. Fox, John C. Reilly, Ving Rhames. It was Michael J. Fox's first dramatic movie role. And his last.

I played Private Diaz, the token spic in Sergeant Meserve's squad. Sean Penn's Sergeant Meserve had been in-country too long and had lost his humanity. He goaded his men to do some brutal, ugly things. Diaz resisted weakly, but soon joined in. Only Private Eriksson (Fox) resisted. I came into things in midstream and didn't have a lot of lines, but I did a lot of mugging and face-acting in the background.

We spent four months in Phuket, Thailand. They don't call it Fuckit for nothing. It was crazy. Crazy crazy crazy. All us young guys, set loose in Thailand. Boys will be boys. I was twenty-four, a red-blooded Latin male. We did some wild partying. Just the drinking alone was incredible. I was drinking a bottle of whiskey a day, eating caffeine pills, staying up all night, getting fucked up. And then there was this mad brothel we all went to. The girls were behind a glass wall, and they were all dressed like they were going to a prom. Really young, beautiful girls, not like what you'd think of as hookers. And they all had numbers on their dresses. You just picked the number of the girl you liked, and you'd go back with her to this sort of bathroom-bedroom where she'd shower you, bathe and scrub you, and then you'd get busy with her.

I fell in love with one of those Thai girls. She was hot, and we had a great time together. I got a Thai-English dictionary and learned a few phrases:

"*Pud thai nic noi.*" I speak a little Thai.

"*Kup cun cap.*" Thank you.

"*Mai ben rai.*" Never mind.

"*Doh.*" Dick.

I was tighter with the black crew than the white crew on the shoot. Sometimes you just feel closer to the people you grew up with, and I had a lot more in common with the brothers. And forget the big movie stars—I mostly just saw them on the set. And there was so much racism in Thailand. The white crew got a little spoiled by it, I think, and they started saying all kinds of racist shit about the Thais, making a lot of comments about the waiters and such.

I grew up in a racist world, at the bottom of the ladder, so I'm hypersensitive to it. I don't take it well. One night at a public dinner one of the white actors was saying some really ugly things about the Thai people and I jumped in. We had a big yelling match and were ready to throw down.

"Shut the fuck up with your racist bullshit," I was yelling. Kind of ruined the evening for everybody. I felt like a killjoy, but I just couldn't take it anymore.

I won't say who the actor was. He never did much with his career. Some people deserve their anonymity.

De Palma was cool to work with. He's got a great, quirky sense of humor. He's got his eccentric side. He always wears the same outfit when he's shooting his films. A safari vest, gray pants, and a kind of safari hat. He wore the same clothes when we made *Carlito's Way* a few years later. Some directors are superstitious that way.

Acting in *Casualties* was a lot more satisfying for me than doing *Miami Vice*. Because there's so much money on the line, everything and everyone in movies is much more meticulous. It takes years to get a commercial film ready, so that by the time they start shooting they've polished and polished the script. A TV show they write in a week. And in film, you get time to work on a scene, do plenty of rehearsals and multiple takes.

Sean Penn was real aloof through the whole shoot. Didn't party with the rest of us, wouldn't even say hello. He gets totally absorbed in his role. He's a method actor's method actor.

He was like a god to me, so I kept saying hello to him. I'd say hello like three times a day and he'd ignore me every time.

"Hey Sean, how's it hanging?"

Nothing.

"Yo Sean, waddup, B?"

Silence.

". . . Hello?"

Nada.

"Wow," I thought. "That's how a real actor behaves. I must not have what it takes. I need people to like me too much. I wonder if I'll ever get to be as obnoxious as him?"

There was one scene I didn't like doing over and over. The one where Penn, playing the rogue sergeant, slaps me around for not wanting to help gang-rape the Vietnamese girl he's kidnapped. Because Sean Penn doesn't believe in staged combat. He's too method for that shit. When Sean Penn slaps you, he really wallops you. It was no joke. By the thirteenth take my face was beginning to swell up so badly I couldn't even say my lines clearly.

"Look, Mithter De Palma, thir," I mumbled. "I like realithm. I

Sean Penn prepares to give me a thmack in *Casualties of War.*

know realithm ith important. But if we have to do one more take, I'm gonna thtart flipping out."

I don't know, but I think Brian was getting off on it.

"Just one more take." He smiled. "You're doing great. It's so believable. No really. Just a few more angles and we'll have it."

I could swear he smirked at one of his assistants.

So we did another take, and Penn really laid into me. I was seeing stars.

"That'th it," I said. "Which way to my union reprethentative? Even for Thean Penn, man, I have to thet limith. I don't even let my girlfriend thlap me that hard."

I mean, come on. I didn't want to be typecast as the guy who likes to be bitch-slapped.

I was away from Cathy for four months shooting *Casualties* and messing around with the Thai girls, and when I came back she knew I'd been up to something. Women know. They always know. So she began to grill me.

"C'mon now, tell me. Just be honest. I promise you everything will be fine. I just gotta know."

And I go, "No honey, nothing ever happened."

She insists, "No, really. Just be honest. Look, I'm not gonna be upset. I just need to know the truth."

So I decided to fess up. "Okay, I was seeing this girl—"

She blew up. "I knew it! You fucking asshole! You piece of shit!" And she went off, breaking everything in the house.

Isn't that always the way? People always say, "I just wanna know the truth. I'm not gonna be upset." And then you tell the truth and they go apeshit.

I learned my lesson. Never be honest.

Casualties of War was my first big "Hollywood movie," but I didn't go for all that Hollywood shit. Still don't. Still a New York boy. I didn't go to the premiere. I don't hardly ever go to the Academy Awards. Like Sean Penn, man. We're too method for that. I didn't care for any of it. It just seemed superfluous.

See, I didn't want to be a movie star, I wanted to be an ak-tohr. There's a big difference. Most movie stars aren't very good. They're usually not talented. They're people who have a look the public likes, or they're clever enough businesswise to manipulate the system, or they're all drive and ambition. But they're not real actors.

Do I sound bitter? I don't think I am. Just realistic.

Then again, New York isn't the New York it used to be, either. There was a time when New York was the Mecca for all the best actors in America. They all came here to be the best and work with the best. That's changed now, for a lot of reasons. For one thing, there's not a whole lot of real acting roles on Broadway anymore. It's all revivals of like *Showboat* or whatever. Or worse. You go to the theater in New York City now, you're gonna see something like *Puppetry of the Penis*. And let me tell you, those penises'll be some of the best actors in town. Not the biggest dickheads in show business, but some of the most talented.

Meanwhile, the finances of making movies in New York became crazy expensive. It all but shut the city down as a place to make movies, and drove all the actors out to Hollywood, or Toronto. Toronto stands in for New York in so many movies now the two cities should just swap names. Or merge. Newronto.

When I got to produce and direct *Undefeated* we shot everything on location right here in New York Fucking City. Madison Square Garden, the streets of Queens, a gay bar in Chelsea. Homeboy keeps it real, yo.

Not that I have anything against Toronto. It's a cool city. Hip, but clean. And everybody's so polite. That's one way you know you're not in New York City. You bump into someone on the sidewalk in Canada, it's like a contest to see which one of you can apologize fastest.

"Oh I'm sorry, eh."

"No no, excuse me. My bad, eh."

"Rubbish, my good man. My fault entirely, eh."

It can go on for an hour. No wonder hockey's the national sport. They need to get out all that pent-up aggression somewhere.

It's why the entire nation of Canada got into such an uproar when Triumph the Insult Dog said nasty things about French Canadians on Conan O'Brien's show. Members of the Canadian Parliament getting up to denounce a rubber dog puppet as a racist. It looked pretty silly to us Americans, but after spending some time in Canada, I understood it better. You just don't do things like that in Canada.

Anyway, movies aren't really about acting anymore. They're thrill rides. They aren't about drama anymore; it's all action movies and big, goofy comedies. So it isn't really necessary to have great actors anymore. They just need guys who've been to the gym. And actresses who look good naked.

Not that I have anything against actresses who look good naked. Word.

Still, that's why whenever I get the chance I focus on making the kind of movies they used to make in the 1970s, dramas with strong stories and real acting. *King of the Jungle, Empire, Undefeated, Cronicas.* They're character-driven, not formula movies. Unfortunately there's no money in them, but it's the most exciting thing to do.

That's how I keep explaining it to my wife, my agent, and my kids' dentist, anyway.

My family and friends had funny reactions when they saw me on the screen in my first big Hollywood movie. When my father, Mr. Tough Love, saw *Casualties of War,* he said, "I have two things to say. That was good. And it wasn't so good."

I was like, "*Coño!* What are you, a Zen master?" I was expecting "You're in a Hollywood movie!" Instead I get Yoda. "Good your performance was, and not so good."

But that's my dad. I think down deep inside he was proud of me, but he wasn't going to show it. Maybe he really was angry that I was making it where he'd failed. Hard as I worked to prove myself to him, he worked just as hard not to let me see him be impressed. *Leguizamo contra Leguizamo, lucha libre de la época!*

Moms was different. She was like, "Oh, that was great—you were the best of them all!"

"Okay, Ma. Let's not go crazy."

Serge was excited for me too. Well, he and my mom had gone to every show I'd ever done. My cousin, the whole family went to everything I did. So did Cathy's parents. They went to everything. Her sister and brothers too.

As for my friends from back in the neighborhood, my old posse from Queens . . . well, I don't know, really. I had moved away from so many people, my life had changed so much, and I didn't see any of them anymore. I was a fish out of water. All the friends I had, really, were other actors, or comedians from when Cathy and I were doing the clubs. I don't know if you could really call them friends. It was too competitive a world.

In '89, I went off to do a small part in *Revenge*, a romantic thriller starring Kevin Costner, Anthony Quinn (who's dead now, but I had nothing to do with that one), and Madeleine Stowe.

Kevin was indisputably the star of the picture and I was just a pissant, but we still got into some macho competition stuff. Like there were all these groupies sniffing around the set, and I guess Kevin thought that as the star he'd automatically get the choicest cuts. But I was the one who walked off with the hottest hottie, this black sex-bomb named Infinity.

Infinity claimed to be an actress. Or as she put it, a "blacktress." She and I were drinking tons of tequila together one night, and between the booze and the fact that I was looking at her through my dick-prism, she just got hotter and hotter as the night went on. We ate a crazy Mexican specialty, *chapulines*. Fried grasshoppers. They're crunchy and taste like fried chicken skin. No kidding, they're delicious.

So Infinity and I go to her room, and we groove it. I believe I hit it five times that night. I could do that back then. Now once is enough.

Teeny and I get our freak on, and then if she wants more I'm like, "Honey, I owe you one. The vibrator's in the drawer. I'll hold your hand."

But I was young, and Infinity and I rocked all night. Then it was time to make my escape. Because we didn't really know each other, and that one-night stand shit always gets awkward the next morning. It was five a.m. and I had to report to the set in twenty minutes. I tried to slip my arm from under her head, but my watch got caught on her weave and she woke up.

"Na-ah," she snaps, all blackalicious and righteous. "Don't you try to leave me. Nobody leaves me. You can't just have sex and leave me."

I looked at my dick and thought, "No wonder they call you a prick."

"You can't just take my black love and break my black heart," Infinity is going on, really warming up now. "Cuz if you do, then I'm-a take my black foot and shove it up your yellow ass."

I was throwing on my clothes and trying to placate her at the same time.

"Hey, we're not even going out together," I'm saying. "Just chill. I gotta get to work. If the phone doesn't ring—it's me."

I ran to the set. Everybody could see I was still drunk and hadn't slept and feeling sick and in no shape for acting.

Tony Scott was the director. I liked him, but his coaching wasn't helping this time.

"Think rock and roll, John," he's egging me on in his British accent. "Think hot pussy." It sounded so weird with that British accent. Hot pussy.

"No more," I moan.

"Come on, John," he urges me. "Is that all you've got? Is that the best you can do?"

And that's when I showed him what more I had. I threw up all over him. Grasshopper thoraxes, legs, wings. I was like some strange Biblical piñata. A one-man plague of locusts.

Well, at least I didn't kill him.

Kevin loved watching me humiliate myself that way. Later that day he found a way to drive home which one of us was the star and which was the pissant with grasshopper vomit on his shirt.

"I want to teach you something, son," he said to me on the set. "I'm gonna teach you about lighting: get out of my light. Now if you can just manage that we might have a good movie here."

I'll never forget that. Never block a star's light. Got it. Cocksucker.

✳   ✳   ✳

Next I did *Die Hard 2*. Everybody thought that was going to be a big movie, and I thought it was going to be another good career move for me. Boy, was I disappointed.

When I did an audition video for it in New York I rocked it hard and they gave me the part of the lead terrorist. But I guess they couldn't see on video how short I am, because when I got to the set in L.A. all the other terrorists were like six-two, pumped out of their minds, and I was just this scrawny little guy, a vegan among all these enormous meat-eaters, who was supposed to be Terrorist #1.

One of them, Tony Ganios, was like six-five and built like a weight lifter. He was very friendly for his size. When they were lining us all up to have a look at us together he came over and threw his huge arm around my shoulders. He had arms bigger than my legs.

"Hey, little man. Aren't you from Queens? Me too. Hey, I got tickets to the Lakers. You wanna go?"

And I'm pleading with him out of the corner of my mouth, like Lenny in *Of Mice and Men*.

Die Hard 2. Tony Gainos stands in the back so I don't look so small.

"Yo, get away from me. Stand back. Don't talk to me."

I figured if he was way behind me and I stood on my tiptoes it would have like a tromp l'oeil effect and I wouldn't look so tiny.

It didn't work. They took one look at me lined up with all those giant carnivores and instantly demoted me from Terrorist #1 to Terrorist #7. From the lead bad guy with a lot of lines to just one of his henchmen. And then, as we're shooting, my part keeps getting smaller and smaller. Originally I was going to be in the whole movie, with this really dramatic death scene at the end. Now they decide to kill me off halfway through. Even worse, I'm wearing a black ski mask. Nobody's even going to recognize me dying.

So I was depressed and bored through the whole shoot. An actor on per diem with nothing to do is a dangerous creature. We were out on location, and there were all these tough local towny girls hanging around who said they liked bad boys. So I tried to be bad. I played tons of poker. Smoked a bunch of Lucky Strikes, nonfilter. Drank too much. I was trying to kill myself. See, when women say they like tough guys, outlaws, bad boys, that's when men smoke too much, drink too much, and drive motorcycles without helmets. But women don't say that because they really dig us. They're just trying to kill us.

There weren't even all that many women to be had, because we were running all around the place chasing snow. They needed snow, and the snow kept melting everywhere we went, because it was an unseasonably warm winter that year. We started out in Denver, where there was no snow, so we went to Seattle. No snow there, either. So we ran off to Alpine, Michigan. There had been tons of snow there when they scouted the location, but by the time we arrived it had melted there, too. They ended up having to use a lot of fake snow, all soap and foam.

Eventually I got cut down to one single line of dialogue: "No complications. Operation is green light." Wotta line. And even that wound up being dubbed by someone else. See, a lot of the dialogue actors speak when you're shooting a scene is rerecorded in the studio later, so you can hear it clearly. But when the initial shooting was done and I came home to New York, the part was so small that they didn't want to pay to fly me back to L.A. to record the line. So they just had somebody out there do it, which was really cheap, like Kmart dubbing.

Later, when my folks went to see it, my Moms tried to be supportive.

"At least you were subliminal."

And my Pops, as always, was like, "You know the kind of movie I'd like to see you in? A snuff picture."

Thanks, Dad. I love you too.

* * *

I got my first lead in a sweet little movie *Hangin' with the Homeboys*. I didn't actually want the lead, who was an innocent, romantic, kind of corny guy. I wanted the funny part, the showboat part where I could use my comedy chops. Joe Vasquez, who wrote and directed it (his first feature film), didn't really want me in the movie at first. Well, it wasn't that, but he'd promised a part to his best friend. But the studio wanted me. I'm not saying I was a better actor than Joe's friend. But I was. We had a big audition showdown, and I beat the other guy out. Still, I didn't get the part I wanted. Later in my career, I'd earn the cred and the clout to pick my roles. It's all about clout, baby.

Doug E. Doug was in this movie, and he was funny, man. Chris Rock was originally supposed to be in it too, but it didn't work out for some reason. That was all right for him. He got *Saturday Night Live* like the week after.

Homeboys was so different from the other crap I was doing and auditioning for at the time. It wasn't Latin gangsta stereotypes. They were real characters, like the guys I'd grown up with. Joe Vasquez had grown up the same way, in the Bronx, so he knew. It was like a ghetto buddy picture, a guys-on-the-road movie from the Bronx to Manhattan. *Homeboys* plays a lot with relations between blacks and Latins—with what it was like to be Puerto Rican and at the bottom of the social pecking order, lower even than blacks. The black guys are constantly putting the Puerto Rican guys down.

But despite ragging on each other, these guys are all best buddies. That's how it was when I was growing up. Black people have always been so cool to me. I wanted to be black when I was young. I was a spigger. Like a wigger, only spic. Those were the days when everybody wanted to be black. Wiggers, spiggers—in Chinatown there were even chiggers. All my girlfriends and friends in high school were black. They accepted me so freely. There wasn't any of the prejudice and racist shit I got from white kids—it was the opposite really, a huge embrace.

The script also dealt with what I call "toxic shame." Latin people can be so ashamed of their heritage they try to pass for something else. One of the Puerto Rican characters, Fernando, makes everybody call him Vinny and pretends to be Italian. Like the opposite of Victor Colicchio. When the guys get popped for fare-hopping in the subway, a white cop grills Fernando.

"Why your friends call you Vinny?" the cop asks.

"It's a nickname, that's all," Fernando mumbles.

"From Fernando to Vinny? I mean, why isn't it something like Fer-man or Fer-ball or something?"

"He thinks he's Italian," Doug E. Doug explains.

The cop is pissed. "So you think you're Italian, eh? Lemme tell you something. I'm Italian, okay? . . . No matter what you do, no matter what you say, you will never be Italian. Scum like you could never be in the same company as me."

Homeboys wasn't a big career move for me. Probably like 1 percent of the people who saw *Casualties of War* saw *Homeboys*. But it was a lot closer to my heart. Race, ethnicity, toxic shame were all issues I was thinking and writing about myself at the time. And it all came out in my first solo stage show, *Mambo Mouth*.

started writing *Mambo Mouth* the day Cathy and I first broke up. We got back together again briefly, and then broke up again for good, and lost touch with each other after that. I hear she got married, has a couple of kids, and became a Scientologist. I don't know if she's still acting. I know she made at least a couple small movies in the mid-90s. One was called *Cracking Up*, and the other was *Men Lie*. Both seem to have been about a Lower East Side performance dude with self-destructive tendencies and an inability to express true love. Hmm . . .

I had really wanted to do a one-man show for some time. Lily Tomlin, Eric Bogosian, and Whoopi Goldberg's solo shows were huge influences. I loved Lily for her theatrics, and Whoopi for her poetic simplicity, the economy of what she did, and Bogosian just because he was so angry and satirical and ballsy. Now I've done four shows—*Mambo Mouth, Spic-*

O-Rama, Freak, and *Sexaholix*—and I love the format. It's the most personal and intimate kind of performance you can do. The audience is right there, and you're putting out your thoughts, your feelings, your life. You're playing yourself on stage. Cool, right? Kinda terrifying too, and another good way to piss off friends and family, but still cool.

I was sick of always playing and seeing two-dimensional Latin stereotypes. I felt it was time to portray Latin characters that were three-dimensional, more than just the drug dealer, the guy with the gun, and the conga-player. *Mambo Mouth* was my funny-angry portrait of *real* Latin life. We were like this invisible race in America—like our aspirations, our experiences, our contributions to America didn't count. Nobody was documenting us. I mean, have you ever noticed how there were no Latins aboard the *Enterprise* on the original *Star Trek*? They had everything else—white people, black people, Chinese people, green and purple people—but no spics. I always took this as a sign that they weren't planning on having us around in the future.

I felt a longing to create some kind of legacy, a memory about surviving, about people who made it against the odds. If you're a minority in this country and you want to see your people accurately documented, it's a do-it-yourself project. So I decided to do it myself.

At the same time, though, I didn't want to fall into the trap some minority writers do, of trying to counter the ridiculous negative stereotypes with ridiculously positive stereotypes. You know, where every character is noble, every character is heroic, and they're all victims. I didn't want to do the Latin *Roots*. Not to knock *Roots*, it was hugely important in its time, it's just not what I thought I could contribute. I wanted to create real Latin people, a gallery of characters, good and bad, strong and weak, warts and all. Of course, they had to be "real" within a comic context, so they had to be kind of broad. But they weren't stereotypes. They were prototypes. Prototypes are the foundation of comic theater.

At first there were ten characters, but eventually it got whittled down to seven. I know that the impulse to do a lot of characters and voices goes back to growing up in Queens. All those different ethnicities crammed together like different ingredients in one big, multiculti *sopa*. You had the nice Jewish couple around the corner who were always complaining about how loud we were, and the Indian guy at the deli, the cranky old Chinese man in the Chino-Latino takeout, the big Irish oafs, the Italian meatheads, the Jamaicans. As kids we used to imitate them all—and make fun of each other, because a lot of us had ridiculous accents, too. It was a way of relieving some of the tension of being a mongrel pack of immigrant kids in the city.

I also used to make fun of my parents all the time, with their thick Colombian accents. That was my one way of having a little power over them, making fun of their accents. It was their one weakness. They couldn't pronounce shit correctly, and still can't. To this day they annoy me when they try to get uppity on me and say "pluh-THOR-a" instead of "PLETH-ora" and "keen-say-dential" for "quintessential." Or make "Sean Penn" sound like "champagne." Or "flee flaw" for "flip flops."

When you're a teenager, your parents are always humiliating you anyway, but mine went the extra mile, man. My folks would embarrass the shit out of me with their accents and their Old Country ways. They weren't as hip as everybody else's parents. Besides being crazy workaholics they were always trying to be so proper and were determined to get us moving up the social ladder. My friends would come over and we had to be very quiet. We could barely sit on the living-room furniture—it was that Latin thing where the living-room furniture is for show, it really isn't for sitting on. The living room was roped off, like at Lincoln's log cabin. Like we were expecting the pope for tea. And you never ate at the dining room table, you might mess it up. You ate over the kitchen sink. My father didn't want us to watch TV. He said we were using it up. If he came home and it was warm we'd get a beating. That sort of thing.

All of that somehow went into the characters I came up with for *Mambo Mouth*. I was performing them one character at a time at all the performance art spaces in downtown Manhattan—PS 122, a place called Home (where Camryn Manheim was stage manager), Dixon Place, Gusto House in Alphabet City. That's why I moved to Alphabet City, because I was there all the time performing, and it was a really creative, fecund, fertile place back then, the late 80s and early 90s. The coolest white people I ever met were hanging out there then. I was always so impressed by how cool they were. There were several generations of hip white folks layered on top of one another then. The last of the old Beats, like Allen Ginsberg, and the Warhol survivors like Taylor Mead. Punk rockers from the CBGB era, like Richard Hell. And the then-current generation of young performance artists, painters, DJs, all that. You'd see Eric Bogosian at the bodega, Steve Buscemi buying a coffee, Iggy Pop at the health food store, Quentin Crisp tottering down the street.

And there were still a lot of Latin families in the neighborhood, crowded into the tenements and projects. Puerto Ricans, Dominicans. A Santeria botanica on almost every block. Oxtail soup, plantains, and *cafe con leche* at little lunch counters. Salsa on every car stereo. Everybody mixing together, everybody cool. It was a really nice atmosphere, a good vibe. A lot of that would be gone by the end of the 90s as the neighborhood was cleaned up and gentrified.

The great acting coach Wynn Handman, director of the American Place Theatre, helped me pull the show together. I went to study with him because I knew he'd taught Bogosian. Wynn hooked me up with Peter Askin, who was studying to be a director then. Peter would go on to direct *Mambo Mouth*, *Spic-O-Rama*, and *Sexaholix* for me.

I started out the show with a character called Agamemnon (remember, my dad beat Homer into me), a cable-access show host who's the stereotype of the Latin Lothario, real greasy. I guess he was inspired by my dad's womanizing, that whole supermacho thing Latin men of my dad's generation were into. That, plus Spanish television talk shows and the phone-in cable-access shows that were all the rage in the late 80s.

Agamemnon mambos his way into the spotlight and declares, "*Hola, hola,* people, and welcome to *Naked Personalities,* the most dangerous show on public access TV. Where we take an uncensored look at your most favorite celebrity—me! That's right. And for the few of you who don't know me," he winks, "my name is Agamemnon Jesus Roberto Rafael Rodrigo Papo Pablo Pacheco Pachuco del Valle del Rio Monte del Coño de su Madre . . ." He pauses, swigs from a wine cooler, then continues. ". . . Lopez Sanchez Rodriguez Martinez Morales Mendoza y Mendoza.

"But you can call me Handsome."

Agamemnon answers letters and calls from viewers and gives them lousy, supermisogynist sex advice (". . . if you have a woman in your life, you gotta be suffering from estrogen poisoning"). By the end of the sketch you've come to see that under the tipo suave macho exterior he's a loser and lonely as hell.

"I don't get involved with my women," he brags. "I'm a short-term guy. I don't fall in love, and I certainly won't marry you. The only thing you can count on me for is satisfaction, gratification, ecstasy, passion, decadence, debauchery—and maybe kissing."

Loco Louie is a sex-starved fourteen-year-old who loses his cherry at Nilda's Bodega & Bordello. He is based on me and my crazy pals when I was a kid. Losing your virginity is such a big deal in the ghetto. You don't have computers, you don't get big vacations to Italy. The only thing you have is losing your virginity and bragging about girls. It's a different aspect of the supermachismo, the adolescent version.

When *Mambo Mouth* appeared on HBO, Loco Louie was, as far as I know, the first person to do the cabbage-patch dance on TV. "Go Loco! Go Loco! Go Loco!" It was big right then in Latin and black dance clubs. I brought it to HBO, and then everybody was doing it— football players when they made a touchdown, celebrities, everybody. Imitating me.

"Oh, big cultural contribution," you say.

Fuck you, I reply.

Pepe is an illegal alien who's been caught by the INS and is in jail waiting to be deported. He's maybe the angriest and definitely the most political character. I'd spent that time in L.A. and met a lot of Mexican brothers there, and they were all very political. I was so inspired by their political plight. Because after the Indians, the Spanish were the first ones here. We got here long before the Anglos. All of the Mexican people I know have some Indian in them, so they've got this sense of ownership, like they've been here since the beginning of time, you know. They never emigrated here, they've been here. You're the newcomer, White Man. And there was so much turmoil and controversy back then about the U.S. blocking its borders to keep the Latin people out, and the INS making all these raids and busts, and that's what Pepe represents:

"*Orale*, you Americans act like you own this place, but we were here first. That's right, the Spaniards were here first. Ponce de Leon, Cortés, Vasquez, Cabeza de Vaca. If it's not true, then how come your country has all our names? Florida, California, Nevada, Arizona, Las Vegas, Los Angeles, San Bernardino, San Antonio, Santa Fe, Nueva York!

"Tell you what I'm gonna do. I'll let you stay if you let me go."

Probably everybody's favorite character was Manny the Fanny, the transvestite hooker. That was the first time I did drag, in the skintight miniskirt, the heels, flipping my straight-hair wig. I looked hot, I don't mind saying. I'd do me.

Latin drag queens are hilarious. At first I was really stiff and stupid and boring, just like a typical comedian goofing on drag queens. But after a couple months of working on it I was like, yo, damn, I'm getting good at this shit. Girls gave me a lot of good tips. Showed me how to walk and stuff. I interviewed a drag queen over by Manhattan's meatpacking district, which was notorious for all the tranny hookers working the area. If you met a girl there and she seemed too beautiful and too easy to be real, she was. A lonely conventioneer from out of town who didn't know the score in that neighborhood was in for a big surprise. I can see the guy back in Omaha: "Man, the girls in New York are real different from what we got here. They're all gorgeous, they'll suck you off at the drop of a hat—and they have dicks!" While I was interviewing this one named Sassy, I saw another one get beat up in a car and stomped on the street. I decided then and there not to test out my routine in public.

Sassy's story didn't really work for me, but her behavior was really helpful. She was such a girl. In the wrong situation you could think she was female. After meeting her I knew I had to aim a little higher with Manny, make her really think she's a woman. Manny may be a tranny, she might not have a pussy, but she's got a heart of gold. And it melts when she sees that her friend Rosanna's been beaten up by her boyfriend again:

"*Ay*, listen to me. *Ay, fo! Mira, neña*, I know exactly what you are going through, because I have been there myself. I was a *pendeja* too. A regular little Miss Masoquista. Just like those poor sick bitches you see across the street. . . . Always hooked up with abusive pricks, that was *moi*. Because I thought getting slapped around and kicked up-side my head was better than nothing, as long as there was somebody in my bed when I woke up in the morning. Because somewhere in this warped mind of mine, I just convinced myself that it was love. And from then on I was lost *en el mundo* de 'cheap thrills *y* expensive regrets,' *tu sabes?*"

Manny the Fanny explains to Rosanna how she got back at the boyfriend who mistreated her: she Krazy Glued his dick to his thigh. Women in the audience loved that.

The Crossover King was usually the funniest segment of the night, and the one that pissed people off the most. Well, they say it ain't comedy unless you make somebody mad. He's a Latin guy with such a bad case of toxic shame he's not even trying to pass for white anymore—he's trying to pass for Japanese. The Japanese were taking over the world right then, and he wanted to be on the winning side. I played him really broadly, a full-tilt Japanese stereotype—squinty eyes, big teeth (easy for me), bowing all the time, and shouting *"Hai!"*

He gives a slide lecture on how to pass.

"Now, what exactly is a crossing over, you ask? That's a good question. Crossing over is the art of passing for someone that you are not in order to get something that you have not. The reason for this is there is no room in the corporate upscale world for flamboyant, fun-loving spicy people. So get used to it. I did."

As the sketch progresses, his Japanese shtick slips further and further, and his Latin self escapes. He's like Dr. Strangelove when he couldn't stop heil-Hitlering. Only this guy can't stop doing the mambo.

"Excuse me! This never happened to me before. I had a little Latino relapse."

That bit punched a lot of people's buttons. Latin people walked out sometimes. They thought I was self-hating. They missed the whole point that I was making fun of this guy. They thought I was actually advocating that Latins should learn to act Japanese.

Oh well. You can fool some of the people all of the time. Without even trying to.

I did all the characters in costume, which was a first for that kind of show. Bogosian didn't do costumes, Lily Tomlin didn't do costumes, Whoopi Goldberg used maybe a prop here and there. I wanted to distinguish my act from all the others.

I didn't have a real theater when I first performed *Mambo Mouth*. My first performances were in the hallway of the American Place Theatre. They had a regular play going in the main space, with a set and everything, so they set me up doing an early show in the hall-way. They built me a platform stage, and we had like seventy folding chairs for the audience, and my program was just a sheet of paper folded over. When I got done they'd whisk the chairs away and get things squared away for the "real" show that was going on inside the theater.

But it caught on anyway. Audiences really got into it. They cheered me on. They stomped their feet. There was no other Latin person doing what I was doing, so there was an amazing vibe, really elec-tric. It was clear that people were hungry to see a different kind of Latin character than the cartoon cutout villains on *Miami Vice*. And I got mad crazy reviews. Critics kept saying I was like a younger Eric Bogosian, which was such an honor. Then the *New York Times* reviewer Stephen Holden said I was "like Eddie Murphy at his best." Dag! I had a full-body hard-on for like a week after that.

In fact, the *Times* couldn't stop writing about the show. They interviewed me about it, they even let me write about it myself. I gave them a long piece about what it meant to be a Latin actor and writer at the start of the 1990s. And it rocked, if I do say so myself. Which I do. Any chance I get.

Here, I'll give you a few excerpts. I began with:

"I am an Hispanic and an artist. They are both of profound importance to me. But until now, very few people have asked my opinion about what they mean. I was certainly both before 'Mambo Mouth,' and its existence does not suddenly make me a Latin oracle. Yet all of a sudden my opinion seems to matter. . . . In the Age of Marketing, John Leguizamo has achieved shelf life. For how long may even be up to me. What a concept . . . "

I explained how when I was growing up the only Latins I ever saw on TV were Desi Arnaz in *Lucy* reruns and Speedy Gonzalez in Saturday-morning cartoons. "Spanish people in most American films and on television are on the outside: they add spice to the story, but they are never what it is about. Today, as an actor, I could make a living in the Spicorama of television and film playing the drug pusher/terrorist/immigrant/gigolo. In fact, I *have* played to type." (Cultural historians of the future, please note the early use of the term Spicorama.) "I understood that because of the way I looked, there was a certain piece of the pie I would be given—the crust."

Ha! Good line, John.

Thank you, John.

I am your biggest fan, John.

Back at ya, John.

Anyway, I went on to say that things were changing. There were more and more Latins in the country, and we weren't going to keep playing to the stereotypes—we were gonna start telling our own stories our own way. We weren't going to totally assimilate, the way some previous immigrant cultures had done. We weren't going to quietly melt in the pot. Instead, I predicted, we were going to "co-assimilate." And one day the country would "come to understand and respect" us.

Which brought me back to *Mambo Mouth* and more free self-promotion. Never been one to pass up an opportunity to advertise myself, yo.

Seriously, looking back now from like fifteen years later, I think that my prediction has been coming true. As Latins have become the largest minority in this country, we're having increasing impact everywhere. We're not just blending into the soup, we're changing it as much as it changes us. Latin music, Latin actors, Latin literature, Latin style, Latin culture are everywhere now, and influential. As Latins are becoming more American, America is becoming more Latin. It's a beautiful thing. And I like to think I had some small part in helping it along. I hope so.

All the press and publicity started to bring in a lot of celebrities and giant stage talents to see what this Leg-goozy-whosit guy was up to. Sam Shepard came, and Olympia Dukakis, and George Plimpton, John Getty Jr., John Malkovich, Arthur Miller, Al Pacino, Raul Julia. In the hallway, sitting in the fold-up seats. It was incredible.

Sometimes I'd meet them after the show—but sometimes, if I thought my performance had sucked that night, I'd be too embarrassed. Like the night John F. Kennedy Jr. was in the audience, and I didn't get half as many laughs as usual. I just felt off. So I snuck out after the show. Just ducked out, and nobody knew Leguizamo Had Left the Building. I was told later that he waited around for twenty minutes to meet me. I did that again later when Tim Burton and Gloria Estefan came to see my next one-man show,

Spic-O-Rama, and I felt I had given a bad performance. I just ran out the door.

Eventually I became more seasoned, learned how to deal better with different audience reactions. I mean, I did *Mambo Mouth* for a year, my first long engagement. You learn that it's not always you—sometimes it's the audience. Like matinee audiences don't laugh as much as evening audiences. It's early, they're usually an older and family crowd, they're just not as lively as an evening crowd. At evening performances people have had a few drinks, they've been at work all day, they want to laugh. There are times when an audience isn't quiet because you're sucking, it's just that they're into it and paying attention and digging it quietly.

And sometimes it really is you fucking up.

Mambo Mouth got to be too big a phenomenon for the hallway, so they moved me into the main stage. And a few months later we moved from the American Place Theatre to the Orpheum in the East Village, where it had a long, very successful run. It won an Obie, became my first HBO special—which won me a Cable ACE Award—and came out on video.

Mambo Mouth also got me new management. I moved to ICM, where the Bregmans, Martin and his son Michael, took over my management. I thought the Bregmans were the shit. Martin managed stars like Al Pacino, Barbra Streisand, and Faye Dunaway, and he was a producer on a bunch of Pacino's films—*Serpico, Dog Day Afternoon, Carlito's Way, Scarface.* Michael would become a friend and supporter of mine, helping me produce *Spic-O-Rama*, my TV show *House of Buggin'*, and other things. Years later, my relationship with them would end in such a completely bizarre and nightmarish way that I still can't bring myself to write about it. Maybe my next book.

I had loyalty issues with my old agent, Morty. He was such an old-school guy, like a character out of *Broadway Danny Rose*, but I felt I owed him. When he first took me on, he said to me, "Kid, to live long in showbiz, you have to have the hide of a rhinoceros, the memory of an elephant, the persistence of a beaver, and the native friendliness of a mongrel pup." I was like huh? "You need the heart of a lion and the stomach of an ostrich. And it helps to have the humor of a crow. But all these combined are not enough, unless when it comes to matters of principle, you also have the stubbornness of a mule."

I didn't know what the fuck he was talking about, until he sent me out on my first audition—to be the clown with a traveling petting zoo at kids' birthday parties.

Now that I was making it, I couldn't just ditch the guy. I'd pay him 10 percent of my earnings to hear him say things like "You're doing great, kid. I mean you could be doing better but you're doing just great. I'm gonna make you big, kid."

Crime doesn't pay, unless you're an agent.

So when I went with the Bregmans, I made them bring him along to comanage me, and they split the commissions—each got 5 percent of my earnings. The Bregmans hated being around him. They felt so humiliated to be associated with this piker. The Bregmans thought they were class, pure silk, and Morty was a sow's ear. But I got a kick out of torturing them both.

While I was doing *Mambo Mouth* I met my new best friend, Derek Zola. He was a lawyer, but I liked him anyway. I'd been working too hard to do much hanging out, and Derek was a party animal. He came from money and good schooling, a nice Jewish kid. And I could beat him at basketball. Very important for my friendships. So we were instantly tight.

Derek got me into the Manhattan nightlife. We double-dated a lot. We'd pick up all these neurotic, messed-up, fucked-up New York chicks. My type. We were like a cleanup team. Complete bottom-feeders. We'd play all sorts of nasty, degrading sex games with these women, and they were the type of women who liked it. Oh man, we'd play Block the Box, the Altar Boy, the High Dive, the Boomerang, the Furball. If you don't know what those are—good. Everything but Dirty Sanchez, cuz I feel that's Latin defamation.

Derek and I used to compete over whose people were the most oppressed, Jews or Latins. He was a Jew, but a wayward one—a wandering Jew. I was a recovering Catholic. I had trouble being a Catholic because God is perfect and we're not. I sin all the time, and *He* never does anything wrong. And no matter what *He* does, we have to like Him anyway. Or be hurled into Hell forever and ever amen. I always felt rejected by the church. Now I realize it was because I just wasn't cute enough for the priests.

"Jewish people are more oppressed," he'd argue. "We were almost exterminated."

I'd be like, "Are you crazy? Do you know that over twenty-four million Aztecs, Mayans, and Incans were genocided during the conquest?"

"Yeah, but that's history," Derek would say. "A lot of people still hate the Jews. There's still a lot of anti-Semitism."

And I'd slam-dunk him with "Yeah, but we Latins hate *ourselves*."

From *Mambo Mouth* I got tons of offers to do TV. They offered me a place on *In Living Color*, but I didn't want it. I thought I was too hot for that. And NBC wanted to develop a series around me, like they ended up doing for another comedian, Ray Romano. Instead of *Everybody Loves Raymond*, it could have been *Everybody Loves Leguizamo*. Or *Everybody Loves the Latino*. But I didn't go for that either. I still thought TV was beneath me. Probably not a wise career move—Ray became the highest-paid actor on TV—but you have to be true to yourself, even if it means you make a fucked-up choice now and again. And again. I took the meetings, they kept trying to talk me into doing TV, and I said, "Nuh-uh. I'm an actor. I may be funny, but I want to be a great actor."

So I went and did *Super Mario Bros.* instead.

D on't hold *Super Mario Bros.* against me. I
mean, when you decide to do a movie, you
don't go into it saying, "Oh man, I'm so
excited to be making this movie. It's really
gonna suck!" You go into it thinking, "I'm gonna rock this
thing," and only then you find out it's gonna suck. And then
you'll say or do anything to try to get out of it. You're in your
trailer, they're waiting for you on the set, a production assistant is banging on the door, and you're like, "Tell them I'm
sick. Tell them I have brain cancer." Anything, just get me out
of this movie.

At first I was totally up for it. Computer games were huge, and
a movie based on one of the most popular ones seemed like such
a natural. It would jump my career to the next level. And I'd be getting to act with Bob Hoskins, Dennis Hopper, and Fisher Stevens.

But oh, I had a horrible time making that movie. What a nightmare. It almost killed me.

One of the few upsides was that I started to hang out with the lead actress, Samantha Mathis. Oy vey, another shiksa, blond, button nose, real pretty girl. *Coño me Jodi.* Maybe you saw her in *Broken Arrow* or *American Psycho* or *Rules of Attraction.* (You saw her in *Super Mario Bros.*? Dag, that makes two of us.) She was going out with Nicolas Cage at the time, and I stole her from him by accident. Then River Phoenix stole her away from me. That girl was like a heist movie. She liked to get stolen.

Man, I was into her. I bought her these earrings, very serious, *very* bling. But before I could give them to her my dog ate them. I'm serious. That dog would suck up anything I left lying around. I called him Hoover.

"Goddamn it, man, those things were expensive. Cough them up." I shook him around some, but he wouldn't give.

So I bought some Ex-Lax and mixed it into his food. Then I spent a whole day taking him for walks. We must've walked a marathon, with him stopping every hundred yards.

Eventually I got those earrings back. I like to think she's still wearing them to this day.

Meeting Samantha was just about the only good thing about making *Super Mario Bros.* I hated the movie, I hated what I was doing in it, I hated the whole situation. *Mario Bros.* was another movie set where I drank a lot out of pure depression. Drank too much, smoked weed, ate 'shrooms (it was the first time I had sex on 'shrooms— oh man, I'm coming colors!), partied with the rest of the crew, all of us whining and commiserating about this miserable experience. It's always that way. The worse the movie, the better the partying.

The directors were this British couple, Annabel Jankel and Rocky Morton, who had previously directed *Max Headroom* and the Dennis Quaid remake of *D.O.A.* Why is it that I was always working with British directors? Must have been payback for all those great talents I was killing off.

Annabel and Rocky had gotten me the part, for which I was grateful—at first. They were really charming and had terribly polite British accents, but you could hear the steel fists inside their velvet gloves.

In the first place, they were confused about what kind of movie we were making. They wanted to make an adult movie, and the studio wanted it to be a children's movie. In the end, I think the studio was right, but I was torn about it, too. I didn't want to make a children's movie, but I know that was the prime audience. It's eight-year-olds who played the Super Mario Bros. game, and that's where the movie needed to be aimed. But Annabel and Rocky kept trying to insert grown-up material. They shot scenes with strippers and with other sexually explicit content, which all got edited out in the end anyway.

They were confused about what they wanted from me, too. I was trying to ad-lib a lot, to get something good out of my awful part as Luigi. One day they would encourage me to do that; they would be like, "John, try to be funny. Please, be as funny as you can." And then the next morning they would complain, "John, what are you, a clown?"

And like any married couple, they argued between themselves all the time. In a very suave and polite way, but it got to be hell for us as actors.

Annabel would say something like "I'm not feeling these costumes at all, darling. There's something about them so, I don't know . . ." She'd wrinkle her nose with distaste. ". . . So Oompa Loompa."

And Rocky would instantly reply, "I think they're smashing, my pet. Besides, Oompa Loompas were little people."

"Dear, not in front of John," she'd say. "No, the costumes absolutely are an offense. They must go."

"Nothing offensive about them at all, my pigeon," Rocky would say. "No, the costumes stay."

"They go."

"Stay."

"Go."

"Stay."

And they'd spend a half-hour going back and forth like that. It drove me to drink. It was like being directed by Chip & Dale. That's why a ship only has one captain.

"A two-headed monster doesn't last long," Bob Hoskins grumbled to me one day.

At least I think that's what he said. Because even though he was doing his best Brooklyn accent on-camera, the rest of the time he spoke in his normal Cockney. Cockney is a foreign language to me. It isn't even English.

After a while, Annabel and Rocky turned a lot of the crew against them. One day, Rocky's looking at all the extras on the set and he's not happy.

"Bloody geezer! Me Jerry Springer's coals 'n' coke!"

"These costumes are too pristine," he says. "They look horrible. I can't believe it."

And he grabs a coffee and pours it all over one of the extras. The extra's in a rubber mask, but it's not sealed at the neck, so hot coffee pours through and burns him. The guy's screaming, and Rocky shrugs, "Oh well, he's just an extra."

The crew was aghast. They made T-shirts with all the kinds of dismissive comments the directors made. People wore them on the set.

Evidently Rocky and Annabel weren't having such a good time either. To the best of my knowledge, they've never made another commercial feature film.

Bob Hoskins, on the other hand, was great to work with. Thank God I had him around to drink with.

"John, so sorry about these Brits," he said to me one day. "Not all English people are like them. He's a cunt and she's a cow. Care for a mild sensation?"

I followed him to his trailer and stood in the doorway, wondering what the hell a mild sensation was. He filled two shot glasses with scotch and handed one to me.

"Well then," he toasted, lifting his, "past the heath and out yer Khyber."

"Could you repeat that in English?" I said.

He sighed. "Past your teeth and out your Khyber Pass. Your ass. Gor, you're a right berk, aren't ya?"

"Um, if you say so," I shrugged.

He was always doing that, talking that Cockney rhyming slang. After a while I figured out that a mild sensation meant "libation." I never did figure out what a berk is, but I decided I was insulted.

Bob and I had a lot of mild sensations on that set. Those Brits can drink—especially the Cockneys. We'd have a shot together at lunch.

And after lunch. And before lunch. And later in the afternoon. And he's babbling his Cockney gibberish at me, and I'm getting totally fucked up.

But Bob is a stud. We'd do all that drinking, then it'd be time to shoot a scene and he'd say, "Come on, John, let's hurry up before I forget what it is I do for a living. I'm not getting any younger. Grab your cobblers, me old china, time to scarper."

And I'm like, "Uh, right. Let's scarper."

And I follow him out of the trailer, weaving and bumping into things. We had a big stunt to shoot. Never let an actor do his own stunts. Especially if he's been having mild sensations all day.

So I'm driving the Mario Bros. van. I'm trying to be cool and studly like Bob, but I'm wasted. Bob is standing by the sliding door looking very virile. "Come on, Luigi!" he says. "Koopa's getting away!" And I step on the gas, hard. The van shoots forward. Then I step on the brake, hard. The van practically tips over. Bob grabs the door frame to keep from pitching out of the thing. And as he does, the sliding door slams shut on his hand. And breaks his finger.

Ooo, was he pissed.

"Shit shit shit! Fucking wanker!"

"Oh my God, I'm sorry."

He goes into a kind of Cockney Tourettes.

"Cunt fuck piss dick cunt! Bloody geezer! Me Jerry Springer's coals 'n' coke!"

I'm not sure what that means, but I'm begging him for forgiveness anyway. "I'm so sorry, man. This movie already sucks, and now I go and break your hand!"

"It's not your fault, china," he winces. "Fucking shit cunt piss bollocksy bloody hell."

At least I didn't kill him.

If you ever watch that movie—not that I'm advocating that—in the last scene you'll see one of his hands is weirdly stiff. It's a cast. They painted it pink to look like a hand.

That shoot seemed to take forever. It was in Wilmington, North Carolina. Nice enough place to visit, I guess, but unless you're a real down-with-the-rich, pro-life Republican cracker, you wouldn't want to spend five months there. But at least there was Samantha. And Bob. And Bob's scotch.

Oh man that movie sucks. And I suck in it. But I don't just blame myself. Every director should try acting, just as every judge should spend some weeks in jail, to find out what he's handing out to others.

I got terrible reviews. One was so bad I got the critic's number and called him up.

"I'm in the smallest room in my house," I hissed into the phone. "I got your review in front of me. Soon it's gonna be behind me."

Ask any actors what they think about critics. It's like asking a lamppost what he thinks about dogs.

Then again, I have eight-year-olds all the time tell me, "I love Luigi!" At least it found some audience.

One place everyone thought *Super Mario Bros.* would have a built-in audience was Japan. The game was created there. Young people in Japan are so into computer games, computer anything, that it seemed a natural. The studio flew me, Bob Hoskins, and Dennis Hopper to Tokyo for the premiere. We pulled up in front of the theater in our limo, and damn if there weren't hundreds of people milling around outside, and TV camera crews and photographers and everything.

I was ecstatic.

"Look guys, we're a hit in Japan!"

Dennis and Bob were more professional and blasé.

"One for the road, Dennis?" Bob said, reaching for the minibar, which we'd already significantly depleted of its stock.

"Don't mind if I do, Bob."

So we had one more mild sensation, and then stepped out, steeling ourselves for the mad crush of fans.

But no one rushed us. No autograph hounds, no flashbulbs blinding us, no microphones stuck in our faces. In fact, the crowd shooed us to one side.

"Maybe they don't recognize us," Bob mused. "Maybe all Westerners look alike to them."

"We shoulda worn our Luigi and Mario costumes," I grumbled.

Dennis asked one of our escort-interpreters what was going on. Turned out the crowd wasn't there for us at all, but for some famous Japanese theater troupe that was performing next door.

Bummer.

Actually, there was one other audience for that movie. A famous porn starlet at the time got in touch with me.

"I loved *Super Mario Bros.* so much I'll give you a blow job for your birthday," she purred.

Yo, I'm down wid dat. I met up with her in L.A. We went out on a date, but it didn't really work out. For one thing, it's intimidating being with a porn star. There's just too much traffic, too much mileage. You can't help thinking about all the guys she's done all those things with before you. All those porn studs. You can't help wondering how you, you know, measure up.

Also, she was hot, but not as hot in person as in her movies. And for her part, I think she was trying not to be a porn star with me. She wanted to be just a regular chick. Like she wanted to be respected. So she wasn't the wild sex-fiend you'd expect. I never did get that blow job.

* * *

A couple other movies I did around that time were *Out for Justice*, a typical Steven Seagal flick, and *Regarding Henry*. I was really beginning to feel how acting in movies is a completely different experience from acting on stage in front of an audience. With *Homeboys* I really began to enjoy making movies. Acting for the camera is like acting in your own bathroom. It's kind of real but not real at the same time. It's very strange. On stage, the audience feeds you; it's a totally different energy.

Doing a show like *Mambo Mouth* gave me this incredible sense of accomplishment. It was so empowering to know that I could take something that was just an idea in my head and successfully turn it into action. It's so confidence-building and rewarding. You feel like you can do anything, like you can control your destiny.

When you're in a movie, even a great movie, it's not quite so personally rewarding. Theater is the actor's medium, film the director's, and TV the producer's. When the actor is on stage, it's all yours, and you can do whatever you want. It's your butt up there every night— the producers aren't watching, the director's moved on to his next show, and you're free to play. That's why they call it a play. By the same token, it's your ass on the line, too—nobody's going to save you from a botched scene by yelling "Cut!"

I like the intimacy of movies, but the director's in control. He's going to guide you toward a certain performance he wants. Fellini was infamous for treating his actors like puppets, moving them around precisely the way he wanted. That's why American actors had trouble working with him. If Fellini told an Italian actor to walk to the door, the Italian actor would walk to the door, then knock off for lunch. If he told an American actor to walk to the door, the American actor would ask, "What's my motivation?" Fellini would be like,

"Your motivation is to walk to the door." "But why?" "Because I told you so." That doesn't cut it with American actors. Homey don't play that. We're method-trained. We want to know why we're doing something. Most actors are savvy enough to go with their instincts, even if that opposes the director's ideas. But when you're done acting, the director's still going to edit it, shape it the way he wants, maybe cut you out of it, whatever. You don't have anything to say about your performance at the end of the day.

Television is a personality-driven medium, because the material's usually not that well written. And the producers in TV are more powerful than either the actors or the director. In TV, they do all the work a director usually does in movies or theater. They shape it. That's why they're called show-runners.

The only thing significant for me about *Out for Justice* is that I met Steven Seagal for the first time auditioning for it. He gave me the part, and he was really cool at the auditions. He was fun and nice. The next time I worked with him, though, a few years later, he was a total ass.

I don't even like to think about *Regarding Henry*. It's a complete embarrassment to me. I only did it to work with the great director Mike Nichols. This man was a god to me. He'd pretty much invented American improv comedy as half of the team Nichols & [Elaine] May in the 50s and 60s. He'd directed Whoopi's show on Broadway. And he'd produced or directed so many incredible movies—*Who's Afraid of Virginia Woolf?*, *The Graduate*, *Carnal Knowledge*, *Catch-22*, *Silkwood* . . . He's a giant.

But *Regarding Henry* . . . I am proud to say I'm the only man in the history of the cinema to successfully shoot Harrison Ford. And boy, did I get hate mail for it. People wrote things like "He just wanted a pack of cigarettes, you bastard!"

That was my one scene in *Regarding Henry*—I'm the nameless

gunman who shoots Harrison Ford and starts the whole plot rolling. It was such a horrible Latin stereotype that I was completely mortified to be playing it, and still am to this day. I did it only because I wanted to work with Mike Nichols.

Nichols didn't force me to do it. It was just the way the part was written. I knew what it entailed and I took the job anyway. And there wasn't much you could do to soften the character up any. It was hardly even a two-dimensional character to begin with—not much room for improvement. All I could do was be as real as possible and move on to the next project.

Well, things come to you for a reason, and you learn from your experiences, the good and the bad. There's a story they tell about Frank Capra in the 1930s. There was a script he wanted to direct, and none of the studios liked it. He ended up doing it for Columbia, which was like the bottom-of-the-barrel, B-movie studio. They gave him Clark Gable to star in it, because some studio executive was mad at Gable and thought it would teach him a lesson. The movie was *It Happened One Night*, and it turned out to be a huge smash hit and swept the Oscars in 1934. It was the first real romantic comedy in American film.

The thing is, Capra hadn't directed anything for a while before making that movie. He was creatively blocked, and the studios couldn't get him to make any of the movies they wanted him to. Then he met an American Indian, a wise older man, who told him, "Get your ego out of the way. It's not about you. You were given a gift, and you have to use it. Just do. And that's all there is to it."

Sometimes that's the way you gotta be to stay creative: Get your ego out of the way and just do. Don't sit around wondering, "Am I good enough for this? Is this good enough for me?" Especially when you've had some success, and the stakes get higher, and now you're afraid of failing. Your ego and your vanity make you afraid to take chances, and then you just create the same shit you've always created because it's safe and you know people like it. But you can't live like that, and you sure can't be creative like that. You've gotta take risks all the time, and you gotta be able to fail sometimes.

Regarding Henry taught me a lot about what I was and wasn't willing to do to be successful. I've failed other times since, taking chances, taking risks, and it's like they say: you learn more from your failures than your successes.

At least Mike Nichols turned out to be cool. Well, pretty cool. He had his own private cappuccino machine on the set, and he wouldn't let anyone else touch it. He was drinking his cappuccino all the time. And complaining about it all the time to the crew.

"This coffee tastes like piss water," he'd yell. "It's undrinkable." He'd pour it out and say, "Go make me another, and get it right."

After a while of this, the crew got their revenge. They pissed in his precious cappuccino machine. And he liked it!

"Now that's a cup of coffee!"

That was another important lesson for me. Never fuck with the crew. Cuz they will fuck with your happiness.

I started writing *Spic-O-Rama* while I was still doing *Mambo Mouth*. I never expected to do another one-man show after *Mambo Mouth*. I really thought that would be the first and last. I was surprised when *Spic-O-Rama* started coming to me.

Spic-O-Rama is my favorite of my one-man shows so far. It wrote itself so easily. I started workshopping little pieces of it at the Garage in downtown Manhattan. I was cockier than I had been working on *Mambo Mouth*. Now I had a little celebrity behind me, so I could force people to watch half-baked material. Which turned out to be really productive—for me, if not for the audience. The fear of sucking in public goads you to work hard and fix things really quickly.

Spic-O-Rama was a big leap forward on a lot of levels: the characters, the poetry, the structure, the meaning. *Mambo Mouth* had been a collection of sketches with unrelated characters. In *Spic-O-Rama* all the characters and monologues were related, and each sketch moved the story along. No one had ever done that with monologues before. I mean, it ain't *Rashomon*—the characters don't present conflicting views of reality—but each one gives his or her own perspective and commentary on the central story.

Even though I wanted it to have that more narrative structure, I knew I wanted to stick with the one-man monologue form. I think it's the oldest and most organic form of storytelling. There's a book from the 1970s called *Comedy High & Low*, by Rutgers professor Maurice Charney. He theorized that the origins of speech probably didn't come from prehistoric man trying to communicate important information—like "Look out for that lion!"—but from telling jokes, poking fun, some guy trying to lighten up the mood in the cave.

I've always thought that. Speech began with the comic monologue; I'm convinced of it. A guy coming back from the hunt and acting it out around the fire. A prehistoric smartass. And he's making fun of the other guy who tripped and speared himself as they were stalking the mastodon. Now that poor mook has to explain to his wife why everyone else is eating mastodon steaks and they're eating veggies. This prehistoric comic is making this whole long Lenny Bruce skit out of it, and everyone else around the fire is laughing and laughing. It took their minds off all the predators eyeing them and licking their chops at the edge of the clearing. It's ancient and ingrained. I watch my kids. When my daughter, Boogie, could barely talk, already she was making fun of me, imitating me, repeating everything I said. That's how it starts.

Spic-O-Rama also turned into a much more personal work than *Mambo Mouth*. It's my first attempt to write about myself and my family. *Spic-O-Rama* was my family in disguise—and with me taking a lot of liberties. It was inspired by Eugene O'Neill's masterpiece *Long Day's Journey into Night*, my favorite play in the world. It's his fictionalized autobiographical drama about his own dysfunctional family dealing with all their demons—one son hates his father, the other's an alcoholic, the mother's on drugs, and the father is tormented by all that.

I used that play as my model for how to deal with some of my own family's darkest secrets. Only, of course, I wanted to make it funny. I wanted it to have its serious or touching moments, but within a comic framework.

Another difference: O'Neill would not let his play be performed during his lifetime. He didn't want to have to deal with the fallout. I was going to perform mine myself. And I knew I could be nuked with a lethal dose of fallout from it.

I had no idea at the time, but *Spic-O-Rama* was the first of what became my "family trilogy," followed by *Freak* and *Sexaholix*. It says a lot more about life and family and love and hate than I was able to say with *Mambo Mouth*. The family is where everything begins, for all of us. So much great stage literature is about family: *Oedipus Rex*, *The Odyssey*, *Hamlet*, *Othello*, *Death of a Salesman*, you name it. Our families make us all who we are, even when they're not as intense and crazy as mine. We all have some wretched inner child who's been damaged or traumatized, and it drives all our lives. No one gets off easy.

I can see it now, someday Boogie will do her own one-woman show about what a horrible father I was. The way I see it, my parents damaged me, but I forgive them—it made me what I am today. So I'm-a damage my kids too.

Nah, just kidding. I don't need my kids to be that successful. Especially if they're just going to talk trash about me up on stage like that. Ungrateful ingrates.

The idea for *Spic-O-Rama* started with this guy I saw on the street one day while I was doing *Mambo Mouth*. What a character. A young Latin guy in army fatigues, obviously a Desert Storm vet, just hanging on the corner with his boombox. He looked like a character out of a Latin version of *Waiting for Godot*. I started wondering what he did for a living, what his life was like. He reminded me of all the guys I grew up with who'd gone into the service.

When I was twelve or thirteen, there was this older guy in my neighborhood, Chouchi. Chouchi was a marine vet. He wore his fatigues all the time, that floppy hat. And he was insane. Like all the guys I looked up to then, he was in a bunch of gangs, and I thought he was so cool. He had so much life experience compared to me and my boring friends.

Chouchi was the first guy I got drunk with. I was thirteen and we did that thing where you steal a little bit of every kind of liquor in your parents' house—everything on my mother's minibar, vodka, whiskey, rum—and mixed it all together in one ridiculous drink, a trashcan. We got completely fucked up and started fighting. Of course he knocked me down and started beating on me, but I was laughing through it. The next day I was black-and-blue—and sicker than I'd ever been in my life. My first hangover, at age thirteen. Too bad that was another lesson I didn't learn so well.

I put Chouchi and that guy on the street together into the character Krazy Willie. He's the oldest brother in *Spic-O-Rama*'s dysfunctional family. He's twenty-nine, back from Desert Storm, and he's doing nothing with his life. Drinking beer, hanging with his burnout friends Chewy and Boulevard. And he's about to get married to his sexy little eleventh-grade girlfriend, Yvonne. And of course they're fighting all the time, even on their wedding day, because he's an adult and a loser and she's a high-school tramp, and he still chases girls and can't afford to take her anywhere, so she's always busting his balls. He complains to Chewy, "Why can't she just lower her standards? I did."

As the show began to fall into place for me, their wedding, the start of what you just know is going to be a train wreck of a marriage, became the centerpiece of the story, with all the other monologues building up to and commenting on it somehow.

Then there's the youngest brother, Miguel—"Miggy." He's a smart and nerdy nine-year-old, cool and smart-ass funny, but also a dork and an egghead. He's one of the brainy kids. His best friend is a fat egghead like him, Ivan. Miggy does the Cabbage Patch and cheers Ivan on: "Go chubby! Go chubby! Get stupid! Get stupid!" Miggy's always sniffling and pushing his glasses up his nose, huffing his asthma inhaler, breathing through his mouthful of buck teeth.

There's a lot of me as a kid in him. Before my dad left and I started acting out all the time, I went through my nerdy egghead period where I had my hand up for every question in class. My friends were all eggheads. While all the cool kids were forming gangs, we had a stamp-collecting club. All the top nerds from school would meet up at my house, and we'd always end up fighting. I'd be pleading, "Yo, you can't fight in here. If you break anything my father will kill me." We'd wrestle and kung-fu on my parents' nuclear-orange shag carpet. We were nerds acting out in the privacy of our own home, being the tough kids we couldn't be out in the real world. Cuz out on the street we'd get our dorky asses kicked.

Miggy became the narrator of the show. He's giving a slide show about his family for a class project, and that frames the rest of the monologues. Each of the family members he talks about comes alive and I do each of their monologues in costume.

Once I had Krazy Willie and Miggy down, the rest of the family fell into place pretty quickly. The second-oldest brother, Javier, is disabled and in a wheelchair. He's based somewhat on my brother, Serge. Serge was a supersmart kid, did really well in math in school and won tons of awards, then went to study premed at Columbia University. But it's hard to come from an underprivileged background and be in that world. You're so demanding of yourself, so afraid of failure, that you can drive your brain and your body to exhaustion. I think that's what happened to Serge. While he was in premed he fell ill with osteomylitis, a painful bone infection, which crippled him for a couple of years. He dropped the premed and took up art history. Later, he worked at Dun & Bradstreet in the personnel department. He was an efficient, gregarious overachiever. Then he burned out on that and decided he wanted to be an opera singer. That didn't pan out, and as I write this, he has found his calling as a healer and masseur.

Javier's pissed about being stuck in that wheelchair. He's the most bitter member of the family, although they've all got their bitternesses. He can't come to Willie's wedding, so he has Miggy tape his message to him. It's like the opposite of a wedding toast:

"Willie, Willie . . . you're finally getting married. My condolences. You found a girl to stay with you. She must either be really ugly or really stupid. I wish you the best."

Between Javier and Miggy there's Raffi, who wants to be a famous actor. He also wants to be white, so in that way he's related to the Crossover King. He's got the toxic shame big-time. He peroxides his hair and talks in a ridiculous, poofy British stage accent. He claims Laurence Olivier as his spiritual father. "It's so hard to be Elizabethan in Jackson Heights," he sighs.

At one point he's admiring himself in the mirror—he does that a lot—and he's horrified. "I'm not black. I'm not white. What am I? I'm urine-colored, I'm actually urine-colored! . . . Well, I don't know why people insist on knowing themselves. It's hard enough to know what to wear."

The only time he even admits to his Latin heritage is to joke about it.

"If you pricketh a Latino doth he not bleed? If you tickleth a Latino doth he not giggle?"

There's some of me and some of Serge in Raffi. The wannabe actor is me, obviously. The wannabe white guy is Serge. (Sorry, bro, but you know it's true.)

Then there's the mom, Gladyz, and I'm back in drag again. She's like all the Latina coochie-mamas in the world rolled into one. Long, hennaed wig, lots of makeup, huge tits in a stretch halter top, tight spandex pants, lots of big jewelry, smoking nonstop. She believes a woman's place is in the house—and the Senate. She runs the family Laundromat. (I changed it from my real family's real estate business.) She sits in there not really minding little Miggy or her youngest son in the baby carriage as she gabs with her friends and ogles the hot guys who come in.

Gladyz has some of my real mom in her—the neglectful, self-absorbed, vain side. You can see that Gladyz, like my mom, married young and missed out on a lot of fun as she was cranking out her babies. Now she's regretting it, and wishing she was still young and sexy. She knows how much power and personal freedom she sacrificed to be a wife and a mother, especially in the Latin world.

"I never had a chance to be independent," she says to her friends. "All my life, somebody's always been on my tit. That's why they're hanging so low. Cuz people don't like their women strong. Especially Spanish women—forget about it! We're just ornaments . . . female eunuchs. We're just allowed to nurture and understand, but God forbid we should go for what we want, cuz then you're a bitch . . .

"Neñas, you know what I would like to do? You know what I'd like to do? I'd like to drink a pitcher of Yago Sant'Gria, rip off all my clothes, and run naked in the streets and hug all the ugly women and tell them that it's okay. There, I said it! I said it!"

Gladyz is my way of acknowledging how very important sexuality and being sexy are to women in Latin culture. Latin women have their own female answer to the stereotypical Latin male's machismo.

Call it feminismo. It's the same for Latinas everywhere, whether they're Puerto Rican or Cuban or Mexican or whatever, whether they're in Miami or New York or L.A. or wherever. From when they're little girls they're allowed to be way out there with their sexiness, light-years more in-your-face about it than most white girls would ever dream of being. A cousin of mine got married to an Irish guy, so you had this Irish family and a Latin family coming together at the wedding, and it was like matter and antimatter. Captain, she's gonna blow! All his sisters and all my cousin's sisters were bridesmaids, so they were all wearing the same dress. The Latin girls pulled the front down to show their tits, and dropped it off their shoulders, and hiked up the hem to show as much skin as they could get away with. Meanwhile, all the Irish girls were covered up to their chins. They looked like Muslim women or nuns. It was hard to believe they were all wearing the same dress. There's your cultural divide right there.

The dad in *Spic-O-Rama*, Felix, is like the first-draft version of the way I'd portray my dad in *Freak* and *Sexaholix*. Like my dad, Felix had his dreams of success as a young man—he was going to tour with Santana, playing the maracas. But they've been beaten out of him by life. Now he's middle-aged and bitter, a womanizer and alcoholic. He loves his wife and kids, but it's a really extreme form of tough love. He and Gladyz have huge fights all the time, just like my mom and dad before they split up. He can be really cruel and crude to his sons. He likes to tease, the same as my dad, and doesn't let up when the teasing crosses the line into truly mean put-downs.

Felix gets drunk at Krazy Willie's wedding and insults everyone there, including the bride and groom. He gives a toast that's more like a roast.

"Ah, life! Tell me, isn't it moments like this that make you think about the meaning of life? . . . What is life? Anybody! What the fuck difference does it make? The first half is ruined by your parents and the second half is destroyed by your kids. That's life!

"Now, I know the newlyweds would be disappointed if I did not speak at length about *matrimonio*. So listen up, *amigos* and *socios*, Yvonne. Willie, as I told you from the time you were yo high, and I can never tell you enough: lies, distortions, half-truths, and critical omissions are the glue to all relationships."

Then he hits on Yvonne. "Yvonne, yum, Yvonne, you look nice. There's so many things I could've done to your Bosco candy-coated thighs."

And he blows Willie away in front of everybody.

"I love you, but you're a big disappointment. I'm sorry, but you are. I couldn't make you a man. The war couldn't make you a man. What makes you think in your wildest dreams that this poor sixteen-year-old titty-bopper's got a shot?"

Nobody in the family is really surprised that Felix is being such a dick to his own son. In his taped speech, Javier tells his dad, "If I could have an orgasm, then I could have a family, and if I could have a family I wouldn't fuck it up like you did. I know you're ashamed of me. But I'm more ashamed of you.

"But don't worry about old Javier. I always got along without you somehow. I dance in my thoughts. I play basketball in my mind. And I get off in my dreams. See, Dad, everybody gets their discount dreams."

Discount dreams. That's the key to what makes Felix such a bitter, mean, angry fuck of a dad and husband. The harsh realities of the world have totally beaten him up. Like my dad when I was a kid—the would-be movie director, reduced to making ends meet and raising a family as an immigrant in Queens. My dad's relaxed a lot and made his peace with the world since then. My brother even refuses to believe how nice and affectionate my dad is with my kids.

"You have to get that on video," he says. "I don't believe it."

Luckily, neither my mom nor my dad knew that Gladyz and Felix were versions of them. There were too many brothers, it was a Laundromat instead of their little real estate empire, so they didn't recognize themselves in it. Whew. My mom eventually figured it out later . . . and she wept. And then when she saw the mom in *Freak* she was mad as hell at me. I changed their names, but it's still Mom and Dad and I'm still John, so it seemed a lot more openly autobiographical. Which it was. Years later, she's still mad at me about *Freak*. Just last Mother's Day somebody unfortunately brought it up again. She'd had a couple of drinks and started complaining.

"That's not true! That's not me!"

I said, "Who do you think it is?"

She flapped her hands. "I don't know! Some floozy you met in your travels maybe, Mr. Big Shots."

I said, "But what about the part where—"

"Okay, that part's true—but not the rest of it!"

It was Mother's Day, so I didn't pursue it. We've been having that fight for years, how much of *Freak* is true. I mean, I can understand why they're mad at me. Even though I was very careful to bill *Freak* as "a semi-demi-quasi-pseudo-autobiography," it's the first show where it's obviously John Leguizamo telling stories about his real family. I say it's my interpretation of things as I remember them, and leave it at that.

. . . Okay, I know what you're thinking. A shrink would have a field day with a case like me. As a kid, he's completely dominated by his autocratic, hyperworkaholic, womanizing dad, who abandons the family when the son's a vulnerable adolescent. The son grows up with this domineering father figure looming over him. He's always trying to impress him, but nothing he ever does is good enough. It's always good, and not so good. So the son is driven to become a perfectionist and a control freak. As an adult, he seeks the power and control over his life and his family, which he could never have as a kid. Since he's an actor and a writer, one way he can have that control, at least symbolically, is by *becoming* his family on stage. On stage, he's got complete power over them all. They do and say exactly what he wants them to.

Oh man, am I really that fucked up? No wonder my family gets so mad at me.

I mean, when you think about it that way, my shows add up to one big Freudian slip. A Freudian pratfall. I'm like the Charlie Chaplin of dysfunctional-family comedy.

The title *Spic-O-Rama* pissed a lot of people off, too. I caught a lot of shit for it. It comes from something Miggy says. He's telling about when he and Ivan were at the Fresh Air Fund summer camp and they invented a game called "spit basketball, where everybody had to spit in a bucket and the first person to get twenty-one won." Miggy beats this big white kid at it, and the kid yells, "Get out of my country, you stupid ugly spic!"

Miggy stares at him and says, "Yes, yes, yes, I am a spic. I'm . . . I'm spic-tacular! I'm spic-torious! I'm indi-spic-able! . . . Our whole families must be spic-sapiens mondongo-morphs, and when we have picnics together it's a spic-nic." He and Ivan promise each other that their lives will be "nothing less than a Spic-O-Rama!"

That story came straight out of me growing up in Queens. I grew up with a lot of white-trash kids, Irish kids, Italian kids, whatever. I didn't have a choice. The spics hadn't yet moved in in sufficient numbers to chase all the honkies away. Normally it wouldn't be an issue. We'd all just be playing together, hanging out together. But then something would go down, some kid would get pissed off about something, and suddenly it was, "You fucking spics! Get out of our neighborhood. Go back to where you came from." Things they heard from their parents, I guess, about how the fucking spics were bringing down the neighborhood. Like we were holding their arms so they couldn't paint their damn houses. Stealing their pens so they couldn't fill out a job application. Get real. People said the same shit about the fucking micks when they first moved in, but of course no one wanted to remember that.

This happened when I was maybe ten, and I remember being so shocked. Suddenly I wasn't "John"—I was "a spic."

"I'm a spic? What's that? Is that bad? We were just friends a minute ago. Now I'm a spic? Damn, why didn't my folks ever tell me about it?"

It was startling to realize that in their heads these white kids compartmentalized me that way—that they had this way of separating us and looking down on us. It was a real wake-up call. You're so hurt and angry. All of a sudden you're different, and being different is a bad thing. That's where the toxic shame starts. You're ashamed just to be who you are. You really have to fight the rest of your life to overcome and rise above that.

If you don't rise above it, you become a self-hating Latin like Raffi and the Crossover King. There's a lot of self-hate in Latin culture. Toxic shame is ingrained in you. It's this horrible, insidious self-loathing that's been built into the culture since the conquistadors, I guess. Latin people are used to it, it's just part of their whole way of viewing the world and themselves. Perfectly educated, refined Latin people think this way automatically. You have terms like "good hair" and "bad hair," and everybody just knows that good hair is straight and blond, bad hair is nappy and black. A "nice" nose is skinny and European. When I go back to Latin America I'm really aware of how deeply entrenched that kind of thinking is. All the TV shows feature the whitest-looking actors—then you go out on the streets and nobody looks like that. But those European ideals of beauty are in every level of the Latin culture. In Cuba, although blacks make up some huge percentage of the population, they're totally looked down on by the people who are more Spanish. In Mexico, Colombia, all over, the Indians are second-class citizens. The racism is horrible.

All of that went into my decision to use "spic" in the title. People often asked me, "Why did you use 'spic' in the title?" My answer was always, "Why not?"

Partly it was a shock tactic. I mean, it was a word that shocked me when it was used against me as a kid. And it was partly inspired by Lenny Bruce and Richard Pryor, the way both of them used a forbidden word like "nigger" over and over and over again as a way to drain it of its negative force. They pioneered that tactic of co-opting a "bad word" and making it harmless, like defusing a bomb. Lenny Bruce had genius bits that would shock the hell out of audiences. He'd scandalize and anger them and make them really uncomfortable—but he got them thinking. In one bit, he went:

"Are there any niggers here tonight? I know that one nigger who works here, I see him back there. Oh, there's two niggers, customers, and, ah, aha! Between those two niggers sits one kike—man, thank God for the kike!"

He'd go on like that, pretending to count all the niggers, kikes, wops, spics, chinks, and whoever in the audience. And then he'd pause and explain:

"The point? That the word's suppression gives it the power, the violence, the viciousness. If President Kennedy got on television and said, 'Tonight I'd like to introduce the niggers in my cabinet,' and he yelled 'niggerniggerniggerniggerniggerniggerniggernigger' at every nigger he saw, 'boogeyboogeyboogeyboogey, niggnerniggernigger' till 'nigger' didn't mean anything anymore, till 'nigger' lost its meaning—you'd never make any four-year-old nigger cry when he came home from school."

That's why black people co-opted the word "nigger" and started using it as a term of respect and affection instead of an insult. "My nigger! What's up, nigger?" And that's what I was up to. I'm a spic? Fine. I'm a spic. I'm spic-tacular. And my show is a Spic-O-Rama. Spicspicspicspicspic.

Not everybody saw it my way. In Canada, HBO refused to run the show because of the title. Canadians are very politically correct and touchy about words. Try using the word "Eskimo" up there, and it's like you just called somebody a nigger. "Inuit" is the proper term, they'll tell you. Not that they necessarily treat the Inuit any better, of course, but at least they know the polite term for them. Some TV stations in Chicago refused to have anything to do with the show. It pissed off some Latin groups too. They picketed against airing the show in Texas, I was told.

Fuck it. I wasn't too surprised. Political correctness was at its peak in the early 1990s. Identity politics was an extremely hot and touchy subject. A few Latin intellectuals, like in the *Village Voice*—the paper of record for PC people at the time—accused me of using negative stereotypes right at the start, with *Mambo Mouth*. The woman who wrote that about me in the *Voice* was the wife of another Latin guy who had his own very PC one-man show at the same time, and he didn't do as well as I did. Jealous much?

But there are no stereotypes in either *Mambo Mouth* or *Spic-O-Rama*. There's no *Miami Vice* villains, no drug lords, no two-dimensional Latin doorman or gardener. These people are three-dimensional characters. They've got depth and feeling. They've got whole characters and lives that you learn in the show. Stereotypes repeat common, usually false and demeaning generalities. These people are brand-new and whole. Yes, they're a bit broadly drawn, because it's comedy. But as I said before, they're not stereotypes, they're prototypes, or even archetypes.

Sure, the family in *Spic-O-Rama* is loud, vulgar, violent, over-sexed, trashy, macho, alcoholic. What do you want? They're based on my real family. Yeah, if a white guy had written the same play about a Latin family, he would've gotten his ass beat. But then again, one kid's an actor, one's a nerdy brainiac, the parents are successful businesspeople—those weren't anything like typical Latin stereotypes.

Just to drive the point home, I put a notice in the program:

THIS LATIN FAMILY IS NOT REPRESENTATIVE OF ALL LATIN FAMILIES. IT IS A UNIQUE AND INDIVIDUAL CASE. IF YOUR FAMILY IS LIKE THIS ONE, PLEASE SEEK PROFESSIONAL HELP.

A bunch of shrinks who saw the show thought this was a covert plea for help. They sent their business cards to my dressing room with *Call me* scrawled on the back.

I think that what really bothered some people was that they *wanted* to see stereotypes—ridiculously positive, "uplifting," completely heroic and unrealistic stereotypes. My characters were more real than that. They had their good sides and their bad ones.

A few people attacked me from the opposite side. They said I was playing the ethnic card. Everybody on stage was suddenly ethnic in the 90s. Everybody was a minority. The downtown stages were lousy with people doing shows about their particular minority. I'm black, I'm gay, I'm a lesbian, I'm Korean, I'm a rape victim, I'm fat, I'm a spic, I've only got one ball, whatever.

I didn't feel that I was playing the ethnic card. I was just talking about things that I felt growing up, and being Latin was a big part of that.

And remember, it wasn't cool yet to be Latin. Things were still tough for Latin people. Ricky Martin and J-Lo hadn't made it chic to be Latin yet. They were still barring the Mexican border to keep us out. It was only in the late 90s and into the 2000s, when census data showed how large the Latin population in this country had become—that Latins outnumbered white folks in California, outspent black folks in the movie theaters, and all that—that we suddenly started to get some respect, for both our voting power and our expendable income. All of a sudden you had cracker politicians like George Bush torturing Spanish in their speeches.

Now everybody wants to be Latin. And the tide ain't gonna turn back anytime soon. We got the momentum with us. All them Latin honeys cranking out that tidal wave of little brown babies. Soon there'll be all these self-hating crackers trying to pass for Latin. Ashamed to be white. Getting their hair curled and blacked. Taking salsa lessons. Trying to talk spic.

"Ay, cone-ee-o! Poon-eta! Wass happenin', pap-pi?"

*　*　*

P eter Askin was my director again for *Spic-O-Rama*. This time he got involved much earlier than he had on *Mambo Mouth*. I'd already been workshopping *Mambo Mouth* a long time when we met. But he was there from the very beginning of *Spic-O-Rama*, and he was tremendous. His enthusiasm for it was so encouraging. I need that input from other people. I can't work in a vacuum. My stage work is written to be performed and heard. It's not like writing this book, or even a movie. People have to respond viscerally to each line. Every line has to have an effect. When it's a one-man show, the director is your second set of eyes, and then the audience is your third.

That scholar, Charney, wrote about this, too. He said that jokes never read as well on the page as they come off when they're told. The audience has to participate in the telling. It's all about sitting around the fire telling a tale. It's all in the timing, the attitude, the acting it out, the setup, the delivery. The punch line isn't what's funny—

it's everything that leads up to the punch line that makes it funny. It's like the people you always found funny growing up. They were great storytellers. They got you laughing and kept you engaged. Humor is a lot like music. It's got its own rhythm, its own melody almost. The performance of it has to be precise.

So it was great having Peter to collaborate with and try stuff out on. A lot of it started with me just goofing in front of Peter. Sometimes things I thought were funny he didn't like, and sometimes he'd come up with jokes I didn't think were funny at all, but I'd try them out and people would laugh. He came up with the crazy, strobe-lit dance sequence that we used to open the show, just me bugging out, going buck-wild, getting my funky freak on. And he encouraged me to explore the darker side of the dad, Felix. That was hard for me to do.

Peter also directed the HBO version of *Spic-O-Rama*, which had to be done differently from the stage version in a few significant ways. Because we only had fifty-five minutes of HBO time, and the show was over an hour long, we decided to cut Javier out of it altogether. Which was too bad, but it had to be done. And instead of giving Miggy one long bit at the beginning, where he introduces all the other characters, we spliced him up through the video, introducing each one at a time. We couldn't do that on stage, because of the costume changes. On TV we could jump straight from Miggy to Gladyz or whoever.

We workshopped bits and pieces of *Spic-O-Rama* in little New York venues, but to open the whole show and test it out for real we decided to take it to Chicago, where I was kindly invited to perform by Robert Falls of the Goodman Theatre. Because *Mambo Mouth* had earned me some notoriety in New York, it would've been trickier to test-run *Spic-O-Rama* there. Word would get out that I was trying out a new show, and reviewers would come see it before it was really ready. Critics always want to knock you down in your next show after you've had a success. It seemed safer to go out of town, get the thing really humming, and then bring it back to New York.

It did phenomenally well in Chicago. I was only supposed to do it for two weeks, but the response was so huge I was held over for three months and moved from the small, 135-seat Studio Theatre into the 500-seat Briar Street Theatre. The entire run was sold out. Chicago has a large Latin population, and they really turned out for this. I'd say 40 percent of the audience was Latin. They were good audiences too, just as rowdy, loud, and fun as they get in New York. I got offers of sex and marriage, people gave me clothes and food. It was wild.

By the end of the run I was the toast of the town. The City of Chicago even declared a John Leguizamo Day. I was a little disappointed about that, though. It was just for that one day. I thought it was going to be an annual holiday—you know, John Leguizamo Day, like Presidents' Day or Martin Luther King Day. The banks would be closed, everybody'd have the day off and watch my movies on video. And they do the press conference announcing it at the end of the day, so you only have a few hours left to enjoy it. Not even enough time to get laid.

"Hey babe, it's John Leguizamo Day. You gotta give it up. But we gotta hurry—only a few hours of daylight left."

Between the Chicago and New York runs of *Spic-O-Rama* I took off to spend five months doing *Super Mario Bros.* Talk about culture shock. To go from this wildly successful play that I'd written and performed myself to being trapped in that boring, terrible movie. Coming off *Super Mario Bros.*, it was kind of tough to get back into the flow for opening *Spic-O-Rama* in New York. Doing the one-man shows is really hard. It's an enormous responsibility. It weighs on my mind twenty-four/seven. They don't call it performance anxiety for nothing. I still get nervous before every show, though not nearly as much as in the early years.

We originally hoped to do *Spic-O-Rama* at the Public Theater, but going off to film *Mario Bros.* screwed up the scheduling for that. Then there was some negotiating about bringing it to Broadway, which would've been awesome, but my manager Michael Bregman (who was coproducing the run with me), thought the terms we were being offered were unfavorable to me and my career. I was still young and naive and relatively new in the business, and I figured he knew what he was talking about, so I went along with it. Knowing what I know now, I find it hard to convince myself that was the right choice. To have a one-man show on Broadway, at my age and at that stage in my career—how could that possibly have been a bad thing? Then again, I am glad that it was *Freak* that went to Broadway and not this one. I guess.

Around the same time, New Line Cinema offered me a three-picture deal and he turned that down, too. I dunno. . . . As a young actor, you just sort of have to put yourself in your handler's hands. And hope they're clean.

So we opened the New York run of *Spic-O-Rama* at the Westside Theatre, where it ran for four months, six days a week, and it could've gone on longer if I hadn't called it quits. People always ask stage actors how they can possibly do the same show night after night after night for weeks or months or, in the case of a Broadway behemoth like *Cats* or *Les Mis*, even years. They always ask, "Doesn't it get awfully boring?"

I can honestly answer, at least for me doing my own shows, that no, it never does. It's always going to be interesting, every night. When you start out you're so busy remembering your lines and staging that you don't have time to get bored. But if you do a play long enough to get a little bored with it, that's when you start experimenting, finding ways to change it, improve it. It's never perfect—and since I wrote it, I can always change it. Every one of my shows changes throughout the run. I'll try something new, and suddenly solve some problem I've had with it from the start, some part that was bothering me and I never knew why. It might be a minuscule detail to outsiders, but to me it may be the tiny adjustment that cracks open a whole character. Then too, as the run progresses and I start to get a little tired up there, I'll trim. And I'll realize I always should have cut that line anyway, it was never needed. I don't miss it, and soon I don't even remember it.

The show changes depending on your mood, too. If I go on stage angry about something, it plays one way; if you're nervous that night, it plays another way. That's a great lesson many film actors who don't do theater never get to learn. Whatever you're feeling that day, that's what your character is feeling too, and it's okay. That's the essence of method acting, right there. In fact, the stage is the only place in this world where whatever you feel is okay. You use how you're feeling, you accept it and go with it and it's a perfectly valid way to approach the act of performance.

I was sure that the New York theater critics would be gunning for me after the big success of *Mambo Mouth*, but I was very pleasantly surprised. The *New York Post* critic wrote, "John Leguizamo is a force of nature, a volcano of words, a torrent of ideas. He moves a lot, too." The *New York Times'* Frank Rich, the bitch queen of theater critics, wrote an amazingly positive review. He spoke so well of me I thought I was dead. And in heaven. Still the best review I've ever gotten. He called it "hilarious" and a "tour de force." He wrote that "Mr. Leguizamo is a star, no question . . . an actor of phenomenal range." He ended by saying, "Mr. Leguizamo's huge presence and talent fill the theater so totally you feel he's everywhere at once."

Oh baby, I'm coming. I'm coming. *Aaaayyy!*

This was the same man who once called my performance "feckless." He didn't even name me when he did it, just mentioned all the other actors by name and then wrote something like "the rest of the cast is feckless." I was the rest of the cast, so he had to mean me.

As with *Mambo Mouth*, tons of artists I admire came to see *Spic-O-Rama*. I'm not name-dropping, I'm bragging. De Niro saw it and came to my dressing room to congratulate me on it afterward. Jules Feiffer said it was one of the best plays he ever saw. (Later, when I did *Freak*, he came up to me and said, "That's not so good." I was in the middle of workshopping it, and was crushed.) Mike Nichols wrote me a lovely letter when he saw it, about how talented I was and how much he liked my writing and the depth of my characters. Then he took me out to dinner, talked to me about my career plans. That's how I ended up doing *Regarding Henry*. Julia Roberts wrote me a nice note, too. Jodie Foster, Nathan Lane, Eric Bogosian, Martin Short, Tim Burton, Gloria Estefan, and a bunch of others all came.

I got more awards for *Spic-O-Rama*. Dramatists' Guild, Lucille Lortel Outstanding Achievement Award, Drama Desk Award. We kept up the run long enough for us to recoup our producers' costs, and then I quit. I dropped it because Samantha Mathis asked me to close the show and come hang out with her on the set of the next movie she was making, in Nashville.

So I went. This was definitely a case of my little head doing the thinking for my big head. Because when I got there she gave me my walking papers. I closed my play and went there to be with her, and she tells me, "You know, maybe we shouldn't be seeing each other . . ."

Dumped for River Phoenix.

Well, he got his, didn't he?

What, does that sound bitchy? Pretend I was in a miniskirt and heels when I said it. Drag queens can say anything. Snap.

I got to make another movie with Brian De Palma, and it's one of my personal faves—*Carlito's Way*. Produced by the Bregmans. I play Benny Blanco from the Bronx. They called heroin Benny Blanco for a year after that movie came out. A dubious honor I suppose. The rappers Black Sheep paid me the highest compliment in one of their joints: "I drives a Bronco like Benny Blanco."

I really found myself as a film actor doing *Carlito's Way*. At first I turned the part down because it was just another movie about Latin guys dealing drugs and being thugs (Bonnie Timmermann did the casting, natch). With Al Pacino playing a quieter, more mature version of the Scarface thing he'd done a decade earlier. I didn't want to do it.

"Yo, I'm not playing another gangster," I told my agent. "Just cuz I'm Latin, I always gotta have a gun in my hand? I always got to be a gangster? I'm sick of this. I went to NYU. I want to uplift the race."

He just shrugged and said, "Unemployment is a state of mind."

And I really wanted to work with De Palma again. And the part was so badly underwritten I figured I'd have a lot of leeway to change it, make him more real.

"You know what, let me do it," I decided. "I got nothing else going on. Let me jump in there."

I had my best time ever making a film up to then. I was working with Al Pacino and Luis Guzmán. I was working again with Brian De Palma and Sean Penn. And Sean Penn even said hello to me. Either I rated now, or he had been knocked down a few notches in life, or both.

Penelope Ann Miller was in it too. You really have to know Penelope Ann Miller to dislike her. She was the kind of girl who'll flirt with anyone in the world, as long as people are watching. We went on a date. We went to this premiere and we're holding hands. I think we got some chemistry. Then we get to the paparazzi line and she pushes me away. She's working the cameras and forgets about me. Leaves me behind. Now I can't get in anymore because she was my ticket.

I'm not bitter. Oh no. I'm just sharing.

Later, we had words on the set.

"I'm glad I don't have to act with you again," she says.

"I didn't know you had," I reply.

And it wasn't just me. A lot of people on the shoot had issues with her.

The wardrobe department got so fed up with her they started taking in her clothes a centimeter a day. Every day her outfits are getting a little tighter, a little tighter. She goes on a starvation diet. Watch the movie, you'll see she gets thinner and thinner. You can't even see her when she stands sideways by the end.

"I can't believe this," she was always moaning. "Why am I gaining weight? I keep dieting and nothing."

The crew snickered. Another example of how the crew don't play. They don't make enough to put up with spoiled people.

The script was based on two novels by Edwin Torres, a New York City judge who grew up in the barrio in East Harlem. They called him "The Time Machine" because of the stiff sentences he handed out to criminals. He's forever immortalized in courtroom lore for telling one guy, "Your parole officer hasn't been born yet." Damn, that's cold.

Pacino plays Carlito Brigante, formerly a king among Nuyorican heroin dealers, who gets out of jail after five years and wants to go straight. I guess he got to play a Puerto Rican on the same reverse-affirmative-action program that let him play a Cuban in *Scarface*.

Now, I love Pacino, he's a brilliant actor. It's a trip to watch him work. The remarkable thing about Pacino is that he really is very good, in spite of all the people who say he's very good. But his Nuyorican accent sounded like Foghorn Leghorn.

"Ah've been re-hab-billy-tated, re-loke-ated an' re-educated, yo honnah. Hoo-ah!"

He was another method actor who never talked to me when he was in character. Except to give me acting tips. He'd say, "Do less." So I did more. Cuz I'm a real Latin and I think people are always trying to trick me and mess up my game.

Pacino's one of those actors who's very different off-camera, really quiet and shy. He doesn't like being recognized. Actors work real hard to become well-known. Then they wear dark glasses to avoid being recognized. All the best actors I've worked with can't really function in real life. The shyest, most awkward and introverted people are the best actors. Pacino, De Niro, Penn. I mean, Sean Penn

Al Pacino's a great actor. And he's shorter than me.

is tough and belligerent, but he's still a really introverted, inhibited person. The more inhibited the better.

Seeing how extroverted and hyped-up I can be, you might think I'd never be a good actor. But I was extremely inhibited in my early years, too. I had to get over it, because I wanted to do comedy. You can't be inhibited and really funny. Sometimes I'm still extremely shy, and sometimes extremely outgoing. I guess that makes me extremely schizophrenic. Like my work—some serious and heavy, some wacky and wild.

Call it selective bipolarism. Yeah, I can turn it on and off at will, yo.

I was glad Pacino's short. We short guys have radar. I swear he's like five foot six, shorter than me even. But we have big heads. It makes us look taller.

Anyway, Carlito's like this cool Nuyorican tragic figure. It's funny, he's a lot like Pacino's Michael Corleone in *The Godfather III*. Just when he thinks he's out of the dope business, they pull him back in.

Benny was a small part, and so skimpily written that Brian let me improvise—and I improvised like mad. Brian's one of those directors who understands that actors are like beards—just let them grow and get shaggy, you can always trim 'em in the editing room. I improvised almost every line in the movie. Including my favorite: "You play pussy, you gonna get fucked." Can I write or what?

I love Benny's big confrontation scene with Carlito. Even if I do get my ass kicked at the end of it. When Benny says, "Maybe you don't remember me," Carlito cuts him off with, "Maybe I don't give a shit. Maybe I don't remember the last time I blew my nose either." Classic!

When Benny catches up with Carlito in the train station at the very end of the movie, I say the immortal line, "Hey, remember me? Benny Blanco from the Bronx." And put three slugs in him. Then, when Luis Guzmán says, "Let's get out of here," Benny turns to him and says (thank you, thank you), "Nah, you stay here." And shoots him too.

De Palma's fun to work with. I mean, he's not like a regular Joe who likes to hang out. He's pretty aloof, but not in an antagonistic way. He's got a warped sense of humor, which is important for me to get along with somebody. And he's not destructive, he's not out to destroy you or hurt you. Sometimes directors are too controlling, or they don't know what the fuck they're doing, and it can turn nasty. Sometimes they have their personal demons they haven't dealt with, and then you gotta deal with them on the set and it can get rough.

This was the first time a director let me improvise to my heart's content. I was like, "Wow, I like this. I like film acting." I even got to drag a bunch of my friends into it. Scenes where Benny is hanging with his crew, that's me hanging with my real friends.

After *Carlito's Way*, you can't get me to shut up in a movie. I'm always improvising and ad-libbing like mad.

De Palma gets it. He's very meticulous about the visuals, and he has an idea for the characters, but he let me play. I ad-libbed like a motherfucker. And he let me do crazy amounts of takes, too. He let me do twelve, fifteen takes sometimes. That's a lot, but he had the time and the budget. When you do small films, you get to do maybe two or three takes, four at the most. People start getting impatient with you if you're taking up much more time. But Brian could afford it, and he was digging what I was trying.

De Palma showed me how to look at the video monitor between takes, to watch what I just did. Then I could change my performance for the next take. You kind of direct yourself. It's fantastic. I do it all the time since then. It's very different from looking at the dailies. Dailies are all the rough footage shot in a day. It's a great tool for some directors—Chaplin directed himself that way. But I can't stand to watch dailies, because you can't change anything. It's too late, you're stuck with what you did, so you start looking at your defects and your limitations. How you suck is magnified. It still throws me off. I don't know how actors can watch dailies. I tried it in *Romeo + Juliet*, and I was depressed for days. But I love looking at the monitor. You can fix your performance, you can do things with it. It's like clay. You can mold yourself.

* * *

There was this beautiful Latin nymphette on the set of *Carlito's Way*. Evelyn. She was an extra, and boy was she extra. She wore dresses so tight even *I* couldn't breathe. And pretty soon she was hangin' with the homeboy.

I know. I should've learned my lesson from the Cathy days. I may not be dumb, but I'm stupid. Women should come with pull-down menus and two years of online help.

Evelyn and I became an item. Just what I needed. Another actress in my life. An actress with the thickest Puerto Rican accent you ever heard, and a voice like Spanish Harlem on helium.

I know I should've run away. I blame my ghetto roots. Screwed up my natural instincts. In nature, when you see an animal that looks dangerous, an instinct kicks in they call "fight or flight." But in Latin ghetto nature, it's fight or fuck. And then if you hook up, it's fight *and* fuck. Fight and fuck, fight and fuck, just like we saw our parents do. If we're fighting it must be love, right?

Evelyn was one twisted, self-hating Latin hottie.

"John, tell me all about myself," she'd sigh, gazing lovingly at herself in the mirror. "You know, I was the one who was gonna make it in my family. I was gonna be a lawyeress or a doctoress, right? But you know what I got on my SATs? I got nail polish. But someday, I'm gonna make it big as an actor. That's why I'm thinking of changing my name to something white-sounding. How about Visa? It could work, right? Cuz I'm almost white. I always walk in the shade, right? I got an aquiline nose. And if you look at my eyes in the right light they look hazel. Look."

I'd look at her, and there was no genetic way in hell her DNA would have given her anything but onyx eyes, cinnamon skin, and a nice button nose. And this silliness made me sad, and this sadness made me love her. I thought I could save her. I thought I could Pygmalionize her. She pushed all my perfectionist control-freak buttons. I love you just the way you are, baby. Now let me change you for the better.

I know. I may not be crazy, but I am insane.

So I started giving her these self-improvement tips.

"Number one, lower your voice to a sexy rasp. Because you're so high-pitched only bats can hear you. Two, lose the heels. It'll make me look taller. Three, 1985 called—they want their music back."

And of course she fought back. Every creation must kill its creator. Every perfectionist risks getting called out on his own shit. My sweet Latin thing turned into Girlfriendstein.

"Oh yeah?" she squeaks, and the mirror cracks. "Well I got some tips for you, too. One, you are not my goddamn father. Two, did you know that food tastes better when you chew with your mouth closed? Three, *Super Mario Bros.* SUCKED!" Lightbulbs explode all over the place. "Four, why can't you stand up for me in front of your mother? Are you still attached to her umbilical cord? Or is that her dick?"

"Yo!" I shout back. "Don't you ever talk about my mother's . . . um . . . dick that way."

"Do you know why I don't get wet anymore?" she pouts. "It's cuz your putting me down doesn't turn me on anymore."

Damn, yo. First she attacks my mother's manhood, now mine. I gotta retaliate with something really heavy.

"Well," I sneer, "as long as I can spit . . ."

Bam. Her eyes fly open. Her mouth flies open. And her legs fly open. Cuz nothing gets an actress hotter than a good, mean, dirty fight.

"Oh my God!" she screams, ripping off her blouse as windowpanes shatter all around the room. "Oh my God oh my God," she pants, unhooking her bra. "No real man could say something like that." She rips off her panties. "I don't even know if you're man enough anymore. Come over here and prove you're a man, boy."

"I'll show you who's not man enough," I snarl. I lunge. I trip over my pants, which are down around my ankles. But Little Man's homing device kicks in and guides him straight into her. "Is this . . . man . . . enough?" I pant.

"*Ay! Ay! Ay que animal!*" she screams.

And all the dishes and glasses in the kitchen blow up.

Fight and fuck, man. Fight and fuck. The bigger the fight, the better the sex.

Why do you think Latins are the fastest-growing demographic in the land?

was back in a miniskirt and heels again for *To Wong Foo, Thanks for Nothing, Julie Newmar*. Or whatever it was called. Miss Chi-Chi Rodriguez. And I looked hotter than ever. Those big lips, that juicy Latin ass. I was pretty in pink. People were beginning to talk. I'd do me in a heartbeat. Does that make me weird? I don't care. I was just too good-looking, honey. Snap.

That's why I never do anything to get me on the wrong side of the law. Never even jaywalk. Cuz you just know some prisoner somewhere, big Mr. Chocolate Thunda, has the *To Wong Foo* poster up on the wall of his cell. And he's waiting, with a box of bonbons and flowers, for the day I show up as his cellmate.

"You gonna trip up one day," he says to me, rubbing his big hands and kissing the poster. "And then you *mine*."

At least this time I had two big macho men in drag with me. Patrick Crazy Swayze as Miss Vida Boheme—and ladies' man, bon vivant, devil-may-care, blackest man in America, Wesley Snipes. As

I'd do me in a heartbeat.

Miss Noxeema Jackson. Patrick beat out Gary Oldman and Matt Dillon for his role, and Wesley was even picked over a real black drag queen, RuPaul. They both lived to regret it.

They looked all right, but I wouldn't do either of them.

Patrick spent hours on his looks. The whole crew'd be on the set, twiddling their thumbs, PA banging on his trailer door. Patrick'd be in there fussing. You know what they say. A celebrity is anybody who spends more than two hours on his hair.

Wesley didn't care. In his mind he was already on to his next action flick.

"I'm-a martial art my way into the hearts of America," he'd say.

So he didn't particularly want to look like a chick. Which I could understand, because the motherfucker had worked hard on looking tough and being tough. Works the martial arts twenty-four/seven. That's hard to let go. But I went back to my strictly vegan diet for three months, to try to get rid of all my muscle. No protein or fat whatsoever, so my body would start cannibalizing all the protein, eating up the muscles. I got all soft and girly. Little jelly rolls under my arms, round little tummy. Oh I was cute. Did I already say that?

Wesley didn't want to go that far. Wardrobe needed to hide his arms, because he wouldn't lose the muscles. I guess that's the difference between a method actor like me and an action hero like him.

Wesley was great, though. He's one of the very few action heroes who can actually act. I had fun working with him. He's got a good sense of humor and he's really bright. He beats computers at chess. Reads tons of stuff about UFOs and aliens and ancient Egypt and all that. He's the blackest man in America, a real-life action hero. And he gets a lot of women. Women by the busload, yo. I'm a family man now, so I just admire him from afar. I have a little shrine to him at home and live vicariously through his exploits. Kiss that shaved head of his and say, "You go, black conqueror."

It was another long, long shoot. Four and a half months. And let me tell you guys, four and a half months in pumps feels like four and a half years. After a while you get tired of it. It took three hours every morning to get made up and dressed. And they fucked up my eyebrows. They kept waxing them, and they've never grown back right. They waxed them too much, and now there are these permanently thin spots. When you see Patrick or Wesley next time, look at their eyebrows, they have the same problem. They're too thin. They said they'll grow back. After the third month, I was like, "Yo, it feels like less eyebrow's coming back." So I started shaving them. "You're not waxing anymore. Fuck that shit."

By the end of that movie, I was ready to retire for good as a drag queen. I had explored my feminine side as far as I needed to go. My poor little virgin feet were covered in bunions and corns from those bubblegum pumps. And I had bra burns. Word up to all you fledgling drag queens out there: buy bras that fit. Don't get suckered by the pretty little push-ups. And always wear open-toed sandals. Forget pumps, they're murder.

And then there were the gender-benders. *Ay, fo!* I don't know how trannies do it. The gender-bender is like a brassiere for your dick and balls. It flattens and hides your male equipment. They put them on all three of us—small, medium, and large. I won't tell you who wore which. Man, it was a bitch moving around in those things. But it did help us get our voices higher and more feminine-sounding. A man wearing one of those things can't help but walk and talk like a sissy.

The whole ordeal gave me a new respect for transvestites. Not to mention what women go through to look the way society says they should, I'll tell you that. Guys don't know what it's like wearing tons of makeup and walking in heels, and the wigs and the shit poking you in the head and people plucking at you and tweaking you all day long. I guess it's no surprise that Wesley, Patrick, and I could get a little bitchy.

The funny thing about dressing up as a woman on the set was the way I was treated. People would help me into a car. People were always solicitous. "Do you want something to drink?" "Is it warm enough?" They constantly complimented me on my appearance. At first it was just a goof, but then they kept doing it. Women got really touchy-feely. And they began to share all sorts of things they'd never say to a man. Girl-talk secrets. Man, I got an education. Like I found out that when girls talk about sex, they can be just as raunchy as guys, but at the same time it's gotta be romantic and sweet. So they'll fantasize about hot anal sex tied down on a four-poster bed, but only after a candlelit dinner. Other times they'd totally forget I was a guy and would start telling me things about . . . feminine issues. Plumbing and hygiene. It'd get totally TMI—too much information. Sometimes

I'd run screaming out of the makeup trailer. That's when I learned how hard it is to run in a miniskirt and pumps.

I'd like to tell you that doing drag gave me a better understanding of women, made me more sensitive to them and so on, but I can't. I don't think it really changes you. Guys are guys, women are women. I might have a better understanding now of how their feet hurt, but that's about as far as it goes. You play these characters, but when you're back in a relationship you're back to who you are. You're still a guy.

I'd done Manny the Fanny in *Mambo Mouth* for a long time, but I tried to make Chi-Chi a little different. And I had to fix the character as it was written in the script, because Chi-Chi wasn't totally jelled on the page.

So I ad-libbed like crazy again. And Patrick and I almost came to blows because of it. He went all method or something.

Early one morning we were shooting, and the movie was going over budget because we had to use a special anti-ugly lens for my costars, and shoot from lots of angles to find a good one. You'd think they'd shoot a movie about drag queens in Greenwich Village, but no, we shot in Nebraska, in this tiny little town called, um, Bumfuck I think it was. With a population of like twenty-five and everybody's your uncle-daddy. The locals loved us. They thought it was hilarious. They all got to be extras. But there weren't a lot of what you'd call amenities if you hadn't just come in from a long time alone out on the ol' prairie, where even the gopher holes started to look cute. So we were all a little on edge.

And then there was the director lady, Beeban Kidron. *Another* fucking Brit. And she was like thirteen months pregnant. She was such a control freak she wouldn't let the kid out. He's probably still in there, going to college.

"Hey Mom, pick up the pace, would ya? I'm late for psych."

So we're shooting this scene where Miss Crazy Swayze Vida Boheme turns to Chi-Chi and says, "I think they're just going to eat me up."

And I ad-lib Chi-Chi real sassy, real Evelyn, sucking my teeth and snapping, "Eat you up and spit you out like bad cooking."

Swayze yells, "Cut!" And to me he says, "Are you gonna say that? Cuz that's not the line that's written."

"Come on, you know the routine," I tell him. "I ad-lib. That's why they hired me."

"Please don't fight, boys," Beeban says. "I know it's been a tough shoot, but we're almost at the finish line. Want to feel the baby? He's kicking. Okay, let's go again. Speed. Rolling. And . . . action."

"I think they're just going to eat me up," Patrick says.

"You better get over yourself," I snap. "Cuz you're a dinosaur and the only love you're gonna get is from a paleontologist."

Cut!

"Why don't you just say the line?" Patrick growls.

"Make me," I say.

And he says, "I'll punch you in your face."

"You must be PMSing," I say. "Beeyatch."

We're squaring off, and Beeban's moaning, "Oh, please, can't we be mature about this? My water's breaking."

"No, let them settle it," Wesley tells her. "They can take it. I got your back, John."

Patrick swings. And I swing. Both of us in Frederick's of Hollywood. I'm in hot pants. He's in fuck-me pumps. And the crew's going, "BITCH FIGHT!"

They break it up before we can start pulling each other's hair and scratching each other's eyes out. They talk to him on one side of the set and me on the other.

"Yo, we gotta work together," they're telling me.

"I ain't working with him no more. Fuck that shit. I'm walking off. I don't need this shit."

And he's saying the same thing.

We finally calmed down. Still, we'll probably never work together again.

Until the next time.

I wasn't too satisfied with the way the movie came out. It was sentimental when it should have been hilarious.

The thing is, if you're a director you have total control in the editing room. That's where you make your final decisions. So while you're shooting, you should let your actors try things out and get a variety of takes. Get everything. You don't know what's going to work, so why not let the actor have his choice? Who gives a fuck? You have final control. You do multiple takes so you end up with a bunch of variations to choose from. You gotta play as much as you can in the time you've got. It's like jazz, you gotta improvise your ass off. Because you don't know what's gonna really work. And if you get a variety of takes—loud, quiet, wild, boring, too much talk, no talking—then you have a range of material to work with in the editing room. I guess some directors don't know that.

One cool thing about making that movie was getting to meet Julie Newmar. Oh man, what a goddess. What a dish. She's the blue-plate special. I couldn't believe what a sexy woman she was at sixty. If I was going to do a woman older than my Moms, it'd be Julie.

I got a Golden Globe nomination for Chi-Chi, which was very nice. The old ladies on the committee liked me. And the committee members who were in solitary with the poster on their walls.

And I got into the Academy, so I could be an Oscar voter. I learned pretty quickly the three rules of Oscar voting.

Rule number 3, vote for your friends.

Rule number 2, vote against your enemies.

And rule number 1, vote for yourself.

Unfortunately, *The Adventures of Priscilla, Queen of the Desert* beat *Wong Foo* into the theaters, and when we came out it was a little like, "What's this? Another drag-queen movie?" We were supposed to shoot at the same time they were, but I was doing another film, and so was Wesley, so we kept pushing *Wong Foo* back, and they got out in front of us.

It's never good when two very similar movies come out almost simultaneously. Sometimes it's just a coincidence. Sometimes a studio will have a film in development for a long time, and then they hear another studio is doing a similar one and they rush theirs out to try to beat them into the theaters. And other times the executives will see a movie doing well and they think, "Oh, I want one of those," so they come up with their imitation.

I got to work with Wesley again almost right away on *The Fan*, where he's a star baseball slugger and I'm his agent. And it was nice to work again with Tony Scott, who'd directed *Revenge*. I had a small part, but a solid one. In the end it got trimmed down a bit, because Tony went gaga over Robert De Niro's performance as the bad guy, and as De Niro's part got bigger, mine and Wesley's got smaller. It was supposed to be Wesley's movie, but De Niro kind of gobbled it up.

De Niro is the super method man. He was playing a knife salesman, so he was coming to the set with his hands all bandaged up from playing with knives all night.

De Niro is another one of those shy actors. He doesn't talk much. Going out to dinner with him is like "So how's the family? How about them Knicks? You a basketball fan? What's your next project? Can you lend me a million dollars? Don't answer right away."

Ellen Barkin was in that movie. That bent nose, that twisted face. She looks like whoever was sculpting her had a seizure toward the end. It's sexy as hell. All you think about is doggy-style when you're with her. She tried to steal all my lines, but I didn't care because she's so hot.

Once, we were talking about our careers and she said to me, "I fucked my way to the middle."

I love that.

And De Niro was brilliant. It's no wonder Tony totally had a man-crush on him and cut the rest of us back. That happens sometimes. The director falls in love with one of his stars, and the star's part grows. I saw it happen in *Summer of Sam*. Sometimes the movie suffers for it, because it wasn't written that way and the finished product can come out feeling unbalanced. Other times it works.

*   *   *

My agents finally talked me into doing a TV show. But I did it my way. *House of Buggin'*, the first all-Latin half-hour variety show on TV. I starred, and Michael Bregman and I were producers, and I did a lot of the writing and chose the cast, which included homies like Rosie Perez, Luis Guzmán, Guillermo Diaz, Jorge Luis Abreu.

I hired my mother, my brother and my best friend Derek to work for me. I made Derek a producer and writer, even though he'd never done anything like that before. I got my brother to be my assistant and my Moms to be my accountant. We Latin people gotta keep our families around to remind us where we came from.

Yeah, I know there were deeper things going on. Ever since my dad left us when I was a kid, I'd felt like it was up to me to take his place and be the man of the family. I had to look out for my mom and my younger brother. It just took me a long while to be in a position where I could really try to do that. At first I was just a kid and a fuckup. Then I was a teenager and a fuckup. Then a starving young actor and still a fuckup.

House of Buggin', the all-Spic predecessor of *Mad TV*.

Now I was a successful actor and a bit less of a fuckup, and I thought I could finally try to be the man in the family. And as a special added bonus, I got to stick it to my dad. Prove to him that pursuing my acting dream hadn't been the stupid waste of time he always said it would be. And show him that the family could get along without him, cuz we had me to take his place.

Oedipus wasn't Greek, you know. He was Latin all the way, baby.

My Moms got into it right away. She was happy to have her successful, famous son take care of her. She always did like to handle other people's money.

"I'll take good care of your money," she promised, in a way that made me instantly suspicious. "And if I steal, at least it's your mother and not some stranger. Tee hee . . ."

Serge was a lot more dubious about the whole thing. Looking back, I don't blame him. Serge was a really bright guy. He'd graduated from Columbia. Gone to work for that big Wall Street firm. He'd grown up being dominated by my dad, and then by me, and now he was out on his own, making it in the world. He'd been my "assistant"—AKA "slave"—the whole time we were kids. No wonder he had major doubts about going back to that. When I asked him to give up Wall Street and come work for me, it must have sounded a lot like I was asking him to do my homework for me again.

"You're going to pay me?" he asked suspiciously. "What, like a loan I have to pay back?"

"No, stupid," I said. "It's a job."

"Is it a salary, or by the hour?" he wanted to know. "Cuz I need benefits. Medical too."

"Keep it up," I said. "You're gonna need medical. With dental."

He finally caved and came to work for me. Little brothers are such suckers.

I got other Latin guys involved. Jellybean Benitez, the great New York DJ, did the show's theme music. He's done the music to a lot of things I've done, stage and screen. We are not real family, to the best of my knowledge. But who knows. My dad got around in his younger days.

House of Buggin' replaced *In Living Color* and ran for thirteen episodes. We did some crazy, hilarious sketches, and poked a lot of fun, and pissed some people off. I reprised my drag queen routine, gave the Japanese guy his own talk show. There was the sketch about a cosmetic service for illegal aliens that would cover up their Latin looks so they could evade the INS. The spokesperson was basically Raffi from *Spic-O-Rama*—a Latin faygeleh who tries to pass for white by peroxiding his hair and talking like F. Murray Abraham. We did one about a priest who got turned on hearing people's confessions. That got us picketed by the Catholics. Don't ever, ever mess with people's religion or politics.

Another sketch won us an Emmy nomination. It was a *West Side Story* spoof, updated for the 90s. We shot it in Hell's Kitchen. We did a lot of remotes and location shooting. It was part of what made the show different from most sketch-comedy shows. This *West Side Story* gang of dancing, singing spics, like the Sharks only even queenier, real fairies, led by me, runs into a real, modern-day Latin street gang, led by Luis Guzmán. Like the Latin Kings, only packing more firepower than Iraq. Me and my gay homeys dance and comb our hair and challenge them to a "rrrrumble." They pull out all their Uzis and Glocks and threaten to pop some caps in our tight little asses. We go all sissy and run away. Luis and his crew are high-fiving and gang-signing when suddenly another rival gang shows up—the cats from *Cats.*

"Man," Luis sighs, "I *hate* the theater district."

That joke may not have played too well out in the boonies, where folks might not know that the theater district is what used to be the Hell's Kitchen ghetto back when—oh, forget about it, Oakie. There were a lot of jokes on that show that probably flew right over your jimmy-cracked-corn head.

Doing *House of Buggin'*, I understood for the first time the effect I sometimes had on my fellow actors, making them insecure and cranky with my crazy ad-libbing and other antics. There was this one actor on the show, David Herman, who was always upstaging me. I couldn't keep up with him, because I had too many responsibilities. He was always faster and funnier, and it was killing me. He was murdering me. It got to where I could only watch my own show if he wasn't in a sketch.

"Fuck! I hate being the producer and having too many roles. I can't excel in anything because I don't have the time. I just throw myself in and wing it. He has the time to think about every role and every laugh. Fuck!"

Oh man, it was eating me up. I knew that I should just relax about it. I knew that when you put together a show like that, with a great cast you picked yourself, part of the gig is giving them all the opportunity to show their stuff. You're the man, you're the headliner, it's your show, but you don't carry the whole thing yourself. You can't. You gotta share the spotlight. Like the way Jack Benny never minded being upstaged. He was always playing the straight man to Rochester, the great black comic actor Eddie Anderson. Half the fun of the show was Rochester's running commentary on what a doofus his boss was. Or the way Ray Romano would just sort of lay back on his show and let the rest of the cast, all phenomenal comic actors in their own right, get a lot of the laughs.

But I didn't *want* to share the spotlight. It was all about *me.* I'd think, "Yeah, but Jack Benny was just a straight man. He was a conduit. I'm no conduit, man! I'm a comic genius. I'm the fireworks! Everybody loves Leguizamo! Fuck sharing the spotlight."

So I started to do the same things to David that other actors did to me. I tried to scare him, I tried to whittle his part down, cut him out of sketches. I did everything I could to trip him up and stop him from standing in my light.

And wore myself out in the process. Between producing the show, and the inevitable fighting with the network to keep it smart and edgy, and writing and doing my own bits, and constantly competing with one of my own cast members, I exhausted myself. And that's when I realized that jealousy and rivalry are destructive. You're just letting your insecurities get over on you, and it ruins your work. I learned to let the people around me excel. Let them help me carry the burden. You don't have to do it all. When you figure that out, you relax and your own acting becomes so much better, because you're not trying too hard anymore. You do your part, and the rest of the cast does theirs, and everybody does better.

So, for instance, a few years later when I did *Undefeated*—which I wrote the original treatment for, coproduced, directed, and starred in, thank you—I surrounded myself with great talent and relaxed. I was happy that everybody excelled. I Jack Benny-ed it. You learn to focus on what's best for the final product, and in the end that's going to serve you better. It took me a long time to reach that level of maturity, but I got there. As long as you don't stand in my light when it's my turn to shine, we're cool.

The Fox network, unfortunately, didn't dig the all-Latin cast I assembled for *House of Buggin'*. You could do all-black shows, but I guess all-spic was still a little ahead of the curve commercially in the mid-1990s. Fox wanted me to fire most of the cast. I wouldn't. So they fired me instead. And then fired most of the cast. They kept the format, the writers, one of the directors and one of the actors, and turned it into *MAD TV.*

So that's how *MAD TV* got its start—as the de-spic-ized version of *House of Buggin'.*

I was pissed. I told my agent that I felt like going to the press and denouncing Fox as a bunch of racists.

"If you don't have anything nice to say," he advised me, "go on a talk show and say it anyway."

He was like that. My agent did for show business what the Boston Strangler did for door-to-door salesmen.

So I went on Jon Stewart's show and mooned Fox TV. They slapped the station logo over the appropriate place on my anatomy.

I had to fire my family. Without the show, I couldn't carry them. What a humiliation. I felt like such a failure. The fact that I knew my dad was out there somewhere thinking the same thing didn't help.

Serge took it philosophically.

"That's all right," he shrugged. "I always knew it wasn't going to last."

Thanks, bro.

Meanwhile, my mom kept spending my money, living off my fame like Jackie Stallone. Only I didn't have Sly Stallone's budget. But my mom was living like I did. Throwing my money around. Not saving for her old age. Assuming I'd take care of her. Put her up in a seniors home.

"You're right," I told her. "It's gonna be the one where the staff are all out on work-program day passes from the state pen. They'll feel you up every day."

"Oooo," she smiled. "Before bingo or after?"

So I had to downsize my mom. Because she's into retail therapy. Shop shop shop, until you feel better. Maxed out all her credit cards. I had to commit euthanasia. Put a tourniquet on the hemorrhaging.

Also, a weird thing happened between me and Derek while we were making *House of Buggin'*. It was a hint of things to come, but I was oblivious to it at the time. Because we were friends, right?

"Look, you've got to make me the executive producer, because then I can protect you," he said to me. "I need the power to be able to protect you."

"All right," I said. "That sounds right."

At the same time, it sounded kind of wrong. He was a producer— why couldn't he look out for me from that place? But he wanted to be the whole show and have all the power. It just sounded kind of odd. But then I thought maybe I was paranoid.

It happens when you get successful. You also get kind of paranoid.

Then again, you know what they say about paranoia.

eanwhile, Evelyn and I were still fighting and fucking, fighting and fucking. So we did what all couples in my family do when they have conflicts they can't possibly resolve. We got married.

We did it during the *Wong Foo* shoot. Flew down to Vegas. We got married in the Elvis Chapel, but not by an Elvis. We were couple number fifty-four. They chose us a song, some sort of Christian salsa waltz or something.

Evelyn was in rare form that day. My little Bride of Frankenstein. Even at our wedding she couldn't help but go off when some fan approached me wanting an autograph. That always made her jealous, being an aspiring actress and all. She was always saying, "You're holding me back."

And I'd say, "No baby, I want you to do well. Just not better than me."

This other couple had just got hitched, and the guy asks me for an autograph. Evelyn gave him the dirtiest look, then turns to his new bride and snaps, "How could you marry him?"

Then she turns on me and whines, "This is my moment! Why you gotta make it about you all the time?"

The other groom's glasses shattered.

And then it turned out that Derek, my best man, had forgotten the ring, so she got pissed at him. He ran back to the hotel to get it.

In the ceremony I made this beautiful romantic speech, and when it was Evelyn's turn she just kind of said, "Well, I just kind of want to have fun."

"What? You wanna have fun? What is this, a ping-pong game? This is not a ping-pong game."

I guess there were clues everywhere. I just didn't pick up on them. She was just so fucking raw, she never held anything in. But that's what I admired about her and what I fell in love with, this little Latin lunatic who was like a tornado, who would say whatever the fuck was on her mind to anybody, anytime, anywhere. It was incredible. There was no filter. I thought that was so beautiful, like watching a hurricane on the Weather Channel. Mad respect. I wished I could be that ballsy. We all wish we could be that fucking honest all the time.

But it does wear you down. There's a reason why people have filters—so society can function. You can't be that raw all the time. It really beats on the people around you. It's no wonder there's always fighting in the Middle East. You have these whole countries full of people who hate one another all crowded up together, always griping and snapping and complaining at one another, it's no wonder they blow up. My solution, separate them all with really wide NSZ borders: No-Snap Zones. Make them wide enough so that even if everybody in every country gathers at the border and shouts their shit at the people across the way, they can't hear each other.

I could have used my own NSZ to protect my fragile ego from Evelyn. I can't handle the truth. That's why I'm an actor. I make my living in the Land of Make-Believe. I have an ego like a robin's egg. You keep zinging me with the undiluted, unvarnished, Latina head-snapping deadly calculated truth, I'm going to shatter. When Evelyn and I got married, I should have gotten two pieces of paper: a marriage license and a restraining order.

My family showed up for the wedding, and they added a few other levels of Latin drama to the affair. Oh, it was a scene. I don't want to think about it now. I'll tell you about it later.

Evelyn and I took a place in L.A. I still kept my place in Manhattan, but I was making all these movies, spending so much time out in L.A. anyway, it seemed like the smart thing. But I discovered again that I hate California. Everything about it. Even going out to dinner sucks. The people you go out to eat with make you feel like scum. They only eat health food. Like cottage cheese and carrot juice. For dinner. I'd retaliate by ordering something real New York.

"Give me a bacon cheeseburger and a plate of cigarettes."

And the actor with me goes, "Oh, I'll just have a Perrier and a motivational cassette."

Grr.

I met up again with Steven Seagal doing *Executive Decision*, the action flick about terrorists who take over a commercial airliner and a team of commandos has to get in there and stop them. It wasn't a Steven Seagal flick. He only had a small, weird part in it. It was more of an ensemble thing featuring me, Kurt Russell, and Joe Morton, my old Oberon from the Public Theater.

To get us all prepped to act like a military team, they sent us for a couple of weeks of training at Fort Bragg, North Carolina. We worked with Navy Seals and Green Berets. It was like a boy's dream to have all this hardware to play with. It was like living an Israeli arms dealer's fantasy. We were shooting sawed-off shotguns, MP-5s, 9-mms, 38s. We shot off tons of ammunition—on the government's dime, your tax dollars at work, and each round is really expensive. Sorry. We went through basic training, only they were a little softer on us than they'd be on real recruits. I mean, we were only actors after all. Wouldn't want anybody going, "Fuck this, I'm quitting. I'm gonna go do a comedy."

And we partayed. Those mufukkas can party hard. You can't even come close. Drink you under the table. And then kick the shit out of you for not being man enough to keep up. Boo-yah! And the stories they tell are wild. They've lived so much life, killed so much, seen so much raw experience—they live life on the edge, so they compress a lot in a small amount of time.

So one day we had this drill where we were all playing commandos practicing overtaking this villa. Kick in the door, toss in the fake flash bomb, storm the joint, the whole thing. We're all gathered there, and Seagal comes striding in, acting all stiff and butch.

"I'm in command," he announces. "Anybody doesn't agree, this will be you."

And he comes running at me, puts his elbow in my chest and shoves me across the room, slamming me up against a wall. Seagal's maybe six-five, and I'm just under six feet tall . . . well, way under. Five-eight. In heels. And I wasn't expecting it, because he'd been such a nice guy when I knew him a few years earlier.

I hit the wall, and I'm fucking pissed. I wanted to say, "You run like a big fat girl." Because he does. Watch one of his movies sometime. If you can stand to. Runs like a big fat sissy doing double dutch.

But he'd knocked the wind out of me, and all I could do was gasp, "Why? Why me? I was supposed to be on this side."

From that moment on I was like, "I hate this mother."

I don't know what his trouble was. Maybe he was pissed that he suddenly gets killed like a quarter of the way into the movie. He's in this tube attaching a plane—the "remora"—to a passenger jet at twenty-thousand feet or something, and the tube erupts and he falls to earth.

As originally scripted, he was supposed to die in a different, even messier way—his head was supposed to blow up from the sudden change in air pressure. But Steven wouldn't let his character die like that. He said it was ignoble for Steven Seagal to die that way. He actually wanted to die holding the two jets together, like Superman. He wouldn't leave his trailer until they changed it for him. Just sat in there and sulked. The big fat sissy. So they changed it for him.

Now I'm thinking I don't want to be in this stupid movie anymore, and I try to get out of it to go do *Tin Cup*. A nice, civilized golf movie. I could show Kevin Costner everything I'd learned about staying out of his light. It was coming down to a contest between me and Cheech Marin for the part, and even though the studio thought maybe I was too young for it, it was a possibility.

So I kept begging the producer of *Executive Decision*, Joel Silver, to let me out of the movie.

"Please kill me, man, just let me die. I could blow up. Let *my* head blow up, please! Let me go, man."

"No, John, you gotta stay in the movie."

"Come on, man, do me a favor, just let me go. *Tin Cup* is going to be so much fun. I could rock it. Please."

"John, man, you signed up to do this. Once you finish this one, you can go on to something else."

I lost out to Cheech anyway. God bless him. The bastard.

So I'm bored and unhappy, and to amuse myself I start ad-libbing like crazy again. And that's how me and Kurt Russell got it on.

You ever notice that Kurt Russell and Patrick Swayze look like they were separated at birth? Couple of square-headed Hollywood leading men.

And here I am ad-libbing all the time, just goofing. Kurt Russell did not like that. He didn't know how to react.

"Man, stop improvising," he'd say. "Why you got to fucking improvise all the time? Just say the lines."

At first he tried talking to me like an older brother—an older, more experienced actor, helping me out. But I was too arrogant for that.

"Yo, man, that's what I do, that's my thing. I don't even want to do this movie. I want to be in another movie."

I don't think that went over very well. I guess I was being a bit of an ass. Ya think?

Anyway, I kept improvising, and it kept making him mad. One day I went too far. I did an ad-lib that in retrospect I can see was pretty stupid and childish. It was a scene where we take off his shoes, because we don't want to make noise as he crawls around at the top of the plane.

And in this one take I went, "Whew! Man, they're gonna find us just from that fucking odor from your feet!"

He went off.

"Your ad-libs make me fucking sick! You have no confidence in the script, so you dance around it like some fucking fag. Be a man and say the line. Say the line!"

And I go, "Why? So I can be as wooden as you?"

"I'm the star," he growls. "People do what I say."

"Yeah? Like what?"

"Like if I want to do this—" And he shoves me. "—I can."

"Oh yeah? Well if I want to ad-lib like this—" I shove him back. "—Who's gonna stop me?"

He pushes me again. I push him back. And we go on like that till lunch.

After lunch, we start up again.

Okay, not really. What really happened is that he stormed off the set.

The crew was like, "Oh shit . . ."

I was like, "Oh shit," too.

So Kurt Russell and I did not get along. I just kept ad-libbing where I was gonna ad-lib. You can see some of the animosity between us on the screen. My line survives in the film. I tell him, "Whew! Hope they don't find us by the smell."

And then a funny thing happened when we had to do the press junket for that film. He was really nice to me. But I was furious. I'm from New York—if you've crossed me, I'm not gonna pretend to be your friend later. I wouldn't shake his hand.

I guess that wasn't very politic of me. I didn't know how to be diplomatic or political, I just did what I did.

The longer I'm in the business, the more people I never want to work with again.

Until the next time.

* * *

And Evelyn and I are still fighting too. But we're not fucking so much anymore. I got her to throw me a mercy fuck on our first anniversary, like for old times' sake, but she just lay there while I humped like a jockey.

"Could you move a little?" I beg her.

"I told you I'm not in the mood."

"But come on, baby, even people who don't fuck fuck on their anniversary."

"Now look what you made me do. You made me lose my place in the book."

"Come on, baby," I plead. "Can't you at least fake it?"

And she goes, "What do you think I've been doing?"

"Well then you suck as an actress," I say, disgusted.

"Well maybe if I had a bigger part," she says, flipping the page.

I may be stupid, but I'm not retarded. By this point, even I could tell where this relationship was heading. And it wasn't up.

I auditioned for Baz Luhrmann for four hours to get the part of Tybalt in *Romeo + Juliet*. Baz is very meticulous about auditions and casting. The competition was between me, Benicio del Toro, and somebody else.

I didn't want to be Tybalt, I wanted to be Mercutio. He has the best speeches, and I felt I could make him funnier than he'd ever been. But Baz had determined that he wanted Tybalt to be Latin and Mercutio black—he already had his color-casting done. Still, he let me audition for Mercutio. He let me do the speech any way I wanted. I had no voice left by the fourth hour, because he had me screaming and yelling and then holding it back and then letting it rip. It's amazing how much he can get out of an actor. He's so in love with the moment and the vibe that you're like, "Yeah, yeah, baby, that's what it's always been about—just a vibe. Let's see what we can do, let's experiment. There are no limitations."

I ended up playing Tybalt. Then we had a two-week period in Lower Manhattan, rehearsing with all the cast and videotaping everything. And that's when my method approach got me into yet another fight.

When you're working on a character you obsess like a maniac. You may not actually "become" that character in your everyday life—although some actors do—but it does preoccupy you like a mother. You have conversations with your girlfriend or your friends and your mind's not really there, you're thinking about the scene for tomorrow. You just can't get your mind off of what you're doing, especially if it's a hard character. You find yourself speaking in the character's accent, walking the character's walk, whatever.

I guess I carried Tybalt a little too much into my regular life, and it got me into a fight on the street.

I was out walking my dog near my brownstone in Alphabet City. Derek was with me. We were going to play basketball. I was going over my lines in my head—I was better at Shakespeare by now, but it was still hard, man—when this guy like half a block behind us yells at me to pick up after the dog.

I always picked up after the dog. I was just preoccupied.

I called back to him, "Look, I'll pick it up later."

"I said pick up after your dog *now*," he yells.

I say, "Hey, I want the block as clean as you, but I forgot to bring a bag. I'll come back and pick it up later."

He shouts, "Punk."

I shout, "Asswipe."

He shouts, "Pussy."

I shout, "I am what I eat. Fag."

That was not smart. He starts barreling down the block toward me. I wasn't wearing my glasses or contacts, so I couldn't see him too well. And now he's getting bigger . . . and bigger . . . and bigger. He's way over six foot, and built. He looks like The Rock.

"Oh fuck."

But I can't back down now. He's made me mad, and I'm in full Tybalt mode, all cocky and shit. I pull myself up as big as I can get and go swaggering down the block toward him.

So we meet halfway, and I look up at him. And up. And up.

And I forget all my street skills, everything I'd learned about street fighting when I was growing up. Like the first rule is, if it's time to get it on, you don't stand there and talk shit with the dude. You sucker-punch him. You always want that element of surprise. You want first-strike capability.

But I forgot all that. I'd lost all my street instincts. I'd been living too cushy. I'd become very white. You get money, you get white. I mean, I'd catch myself walking down my block in Alphabet City thinking, "Oh, I gotta move. Too many Latin people in this neighborhood. Gonna lower the value of real estate."

So the two of us come face-to-face—well, my face to his pecs— and he hadn't lost any of *his* instincts. *POW.* He sucker-punched me right in the mouth.

I guess he didn't realize he was punching out John Leguizamo, Star of Stage and Screen.

Or maybe he did, and he just didn't give a shit. Maybe he wasn't a fan of my work. Maybe he paid money to see *Super Mario Bros.*

So he clocks me, and then Derek does a really stupid thing: he yanks me back, just when I'm taking my first swing at the guy. So all I punch is air.

Then Derek lets me go. And the guy nails me again.

I go to land my right again—and Derek, my friend, my homey, my backup, grabs my arm again.

"No, man, come on, don't fight."

I'm struggling to get my arm free. "Dude, what are you doing?" And that's when the guy punches me for the third time.

That was the end of the fight. Big Guy 3, Little Latin Guy 0.

Some Latin brothers who watched the whole thing go down started giving Derek hell.

"Yo dog, you supposed to have your homey's back. Man, you jump in there. You don't hold him down so the enemy can assault. Yours is yours."

And then they stroll off, laughing and snickering among themselves.

"Damn, you see how he beat up Leguizamo? That shit was hilarious."

"Thanks," I mutter. I spit blood and wiggle a loose tooth.

They were right. That's the way I grew up. That's what they taught me my whole life. "Yo man, you got my back? You got my back?" Something happens, you jump in. You always gotta jump in, no matter what happens. You jump in for your friend. You don't try to break it up. You don't hold him back so the other guy can beat on him.

Well, Derek was Jewish. What do Jewish guys know about street fighting?

"You want to go to the hospital?" he asks.

"No, man, we're gonna play basketball, man."

So we walked the rest of the way to the court and shot some hoops, and the whole time I was shaking so badly I could barely hold the ball. It's that fear and rage and adrenaline that pumps through you after a fight. Blood dripping from my mouth to the court.

The guy had split my tongue, my tooth was loose, and my lip swelled up. I could barely talk. I go to rehearsal, and I sound like Sylvester the Cat.

"Oh that thizth too too thzullied flezth zthould melt and zthaw and reztholve itzthelf into a dew."

Baz thinks I'm just trying out a different voice.

"That's very interesting, John. But annoying. Could you try it straight now?"

"I am trying it zthraight."

So that's what being too method got me. It got my ass kicked. That taught me a fuckin' lesson. Method schmethod. All it ever does is get me into trouble.

* * *

I loved working with Baz on this movie. I called him the Marsupial, because he's an Australian with a bit of a paunch. Baz is crazy Australian, but not like Crocodile Dundee or that guy who wrestles alligators. He's not a hick, throw-another-shrimp-on-the-barbie Australian. He doesn't sound like that, he sounds almost British. He's very educated, very intellectual. Comes from money. Very knowledgeable about literature and movies. He was an actor at first, but it didn't work out, and everybody says it was for the best that it didn't. Then he did *Strictly Ballroom*, first as a play, then as a movie. And that launched his career.

Baz called *Ballroom, Romeo + Juliet,* and *Moulin Rouge!* his Red Curtain Trilogy. They're all ultralavish, really stagey and theatrical musicals. He and Catherine Martin, his wife and production designer, got the idea watching Bollywood movies in India. Baz demands a very special kind of performance. It's not the naturalistic sort of approach all American actors are trained in. It's almost operatic. Everything has to be BIG and LOUD. It's all high comedy or high tragedy. It's definitely a return to an older, premethod style of acting. It's more Greta Garbo than Marlon Brando. Baz has this idea that emotionally it makes things more real than your average "realistic" movie.

You can see in all three films that Baz has a hyperactively fertile imagination. He has a million ideas. Yet it's wonderful how he lets you be a part of the whole process; from the costumes to the sets to the scenery, you're involved. He just opens up everything to you. Even though he wasn't exactly mentoring me, I took him as inspiration for the kind of artist I wanted to be.

"We have a theatrical contract," he would say. "Don't censor yourself. Don't edit. Let me be the safety net. Look at Mister Camera. Be more theatrical. Bigger."

We went to shoot in Mexico City and Vera Cruz. And while I'm down there, I hear from Evelyn that she wants to leave me. Says she needs to find her own path and follow it her own way. Says that's why she didn't come with me to Mexico, because she didn't want to be tagging along behind me. I was done arguing with her. She'd worn me out.

We'd had one of our big fights right before I left. I'd been out late hanging with some of my friends, and when I got home she was waiting up and spoiling for a fight.

And at the height of it she squeals, "I'm gonna sew up my pussy so you can't fuck me no more. And then your dick'll wither and fall off and then you'll have a pussy and then maybe one of your friends'll wanna fuck you."

She actually said that. I couldn't write a line like that.

So she calls me in Mexico and tells me, "I'm leaving cuz you make me miserable. You make me feel like your name's always in capital letters and my life's in lowercase."

And I say, "That's not true, baby. I want you to do well—"

And she hangs up.

So I was bumming. Leo DiCaprio saw it, and decided he had to cheer me up. He was really good about it, even if the way he went about it was really . . . bad. Oh man, we went crazy. Crazy crazy. Mad crazy. The wildest parties, strippers, hookers, getting into fights in clubs. I thought *Casualties of War* was a crazy shoot, but this was crazier. And because the majority of the cast was younger than I was, I felt challenged to act even crazier than they were. A lot of stupid male nonsense. We would have parties, just the guys playing poker and talking shit, while strippers danced on our table. And there were some adventures with the hookers that were videotaped, two on one, voyeurism, all that. Thank God for certain people's careers those tapes were erased.

I was with this stripper/hooker, and I asked her, "You ever make it with another woman?"

"Why don't you work on satisfying one woman first," she says. "Then we'll graduate."

It wasn't easy dragging myself onto the set the next morning, I'll tell you. But we were all supposed to be rough and ready youth in the film anyway, so I suppose it was method whoring.

The locals got pretty wild themselves sometimes. At one point a gang of banditos kidnapped our makeup man, Aldo Signoretti, who'd worked with Fellini. They sent Baz a ransom note demanding $300, which is a lot of money in Mexico. It was surreal. Here we were, making this gangsta-style version of *Romeo and Juliet*, and real gangsters are fucking with us. Baz had to send a crew member to meet with them on the street. They drove up in a car, he handed over the money, and they threw Aldo out as they drove away. You know the old theater saying, "Break a leg"? Aldo did.

Leo was amazing. I was really impressed by the type of guy Leo is. He's such a pretty boy, and you always have some disdain for pretty boys. You never think they merit their success, because so many non-talents get their jobs in the business just on looks. But he was cool. I was amazed to find out what a down white boy he is—rapping, hip-hopping, and he could breakdance, too. Leo DiCaprio popping and locking. I was like, Damn! And he likes hanging out with a rough crowd. He's not a prissy kid at all. He looks so delicate, but he's an animal. Girls know about the sweet-faced pretty boys. We're the ones you gotta look out for, right *mami?*

Brian Dennehy, on the other hand, is exactly the tough cookie you'd expect. I think he was drying out at the time, so that made him a little edgy. He'd have long waiting periods in his trailer, and then they'd send some hapless production assistant to get him. One time they sent the PA for him and he was like, "If you knock on my door one more time, you're gonna have to get an ambulance, cuz they're gonna have to dig so far up your ass to remove my foot."

Miriam Margolyes, who played Juliet's nurse, is a funny-ass lady. Funny, Cockney, crazy broad. She farted once just to make us all laugh. "There, that'll teach ya!" A raunchy, crazy broad.

I tried to ad-lib some. And believe me, it's hard to ad-lib in iambic pentameter. Baz let me do it. He filmed it all—and then he cut it all out. You just don't ad-lib Shakespeare. It's like the eleventh commandment. Thou shalt not fuck around with Shakespeare. But I came up with some good lines anyway. I went through a lot of Shakespeare, found some really funny lines and some really serious ones, and I figured I could just throw them in, just to embellish a little. Why not? What the fuck? Baz was cutting lines out—why couldn't I add some back?

All the young American actors had problems with their speeches. You can definitely see it in the movie. The British ones, of course, rocked it. They're the only ones who can do Shakespeare correctly. They're schooled in it, they grow up with it.

You should have seen the looks on their faces when I was doing some of my ad-libs. "Yo, verily wilst I poppeth a cappeth in thine ass . . ." Things would get real quiet on the set, all the Brit actors just staring with their mouths open. It felt like I was back at the Public.

Baz pushed all the actors to be more extreme in their performances. I had a creative battle with him on it, trying to hold my performance back a little. He kept pushing me for more, and I kept pulling back.

At the same time, I worked hard to make Tybalt believable as the gunslinging spaghetti-western type he was supposed to be. All those scenes of him twirling those big pistols of his, doing those cowboy tricks like flinging one over his shoulder and catching it—that's me. No stuntman inserts, baby. I did it myself. I got applause from the crew I was such a badass. I practiced for three months in my hotel room. I kept dropping them on the floor, and these were heavy pistols. Once I dropped one on my foot, and that thing hurt. I was hopping around my room, cursing. The people in the room downstairs complained to management. From then on, I'd stand on the bed to practice. Three months I worked on it.

When we did the big fight scene on the beach, the one where Tybalt kills Mercutio, Baz even got Mother Nature to overact. He heard that a hurricane was blowing into Vera Cruz, and while the whole rest of the town was boarding up windows and dragging the children indoors, he rushed the crew down to the beach to shoot the scene with those dark hurricane clouds looming behind us and the wind blowing sand in all our eyes. Right after we finished the scene, the hurricane slammed the beach and blew the whole set away.

I loved most of the movie when I saw it. I loved the energy, and the idea of making it for kids, getting teenagers to appreciate Shakespeare. Critics who didn't like the movie hated the way Baz took Shakespeare and made him modern, all hip-hop and MTV and gang-

My method acting in *Romeo + Juliet* got me beat up.

sta. But they were forgetting that in his own time Shakespeare wasn't making high art for the elite, he wrote for the masses. Theater was a popular art-form in the 1600s. For like a century after he died, literary and theater snobs wrote him off as a hack. It took a hundred years for them to "rediscover" him and realize how great his work was. I think all Baz was doing was returning *Romeo and Juliet* to its populist, mass-audience roots. As he put it to an interviewer, he wasn't making Shakespeare "groovy for the sake of being groovy." He made a considered artistic choice to MTV-ize Shakespeare. He modernized the look and style of performing Shakespeare, so that it wasn't a museum piece, and by doing that, I think he made the story and the emotions much more accessible and real to audiences today. I thought it worked brilliantly. And obviously an awful lot of young people in the audience did too.

If I have a critique of the film, it's not about what Baz did. I do think there are limitations to what some of the young actors were able to do in a medium they're not accustomed to. Shakespeare's tough, especially for young American actors. Baz maybe was using some people who weren't quite seasoned enough.

Although it's not just a question of age. If you go back and watch Zeffirelli's *Romeo and Juliet*, Olivia Hussey rocks as Juliet, and she was only sixteen or so. Not to dis anyone, but I can't help thinking what it would've been like to see Olivia Hussey and Leo doing it together. That would've been awesome.

I came back to New York, because Evelyn was in L.A. threatening to divorce me, and I was afraid she'd start yelling at me and rupture an eardrum. I was supposed to push the movie with the media, so I went on David Letterman's show. I had my choice between Letterman and Leno. When you reach a certain level of celebrity you can do both, but at my level I had to pick one. I picked Letterman.

Another brilliant career move.

The producers overcoached me. See, the talk-show producers conduct what they call a preinterview with you. They ask you a bunch of questions, and then they script the actual interview based on your answers. They're looking for your best stories and they want Dave to be prepped, so he can be real funny pretending to be spontaneous.

Right before the show, the producer, who must've heard about my reputation, warns me, "Don't ad-lib out there. Dave's not feeling well. Don't test him too much. He's not in the mood. And whatever you do, don't like hit him or pat him on the back or the neck. He has an injury. Could go into spasm."

So now I'm all paranoid. And Dave keeps the studio really air-conditioned. It's like the Antarctic. He believes comedy is funnier in the cold or something.

I go on, and I'm freezing. My nipples are erect. Now I know why Letterman likes having all those models and actresses on the show. And I panic. I'm not funny. I'm talking when he's talking. Not talking when he's not talking. When I do talk, I'm speaking too fast. I'm white-knuckling the armchair. Babbling about how my wife started to divorce me while I was shooting the movie.

Letterman asks me, "So why is she divorcing you? Did you cheat on her?"

And I blurt, "Are you kidding? I'm so loyal. Even when I go out with my mom, I don't look at other moms."

Dead fucking silence. It's as quiet and cold in that studio as a morgue.

I haven't been on his show since.

☆   ☆   ☆

It was only maybe a week after I wrapped *Romeo + Juliet* that I went to do *The Pest*. I was working like a maniac, and I'm sure that was part of what killed my marriage.

Well, that and the fact that my wife was a fucking lunatic human tornado.

But when I go back to L.A. to shoot *The Pest*, Evelyn's now surprisingly friendly—because she wanted to have a part in the movie. She still wouldn't hang with me, though. We went to get marriage counseling from three different mediators, and she yelled at all of them. L.A. is a weird place, because the therapists all know your movies and suck up to you. That fed her anxiety and rage.

"He was just kissing your ass!" she'd yell at me. Then we'd fire that one and go on to the next.

It was no use. The marriage was over and we both knew it.

The Pest was me and Derek venturing to conquer Hollywood. We cowrote, coproduced, and cobombed. If you've seen it you know. I have to take a lot of the blame. It was my vehicle, my Jerry Lewis movie, a chance for me to do a lot of characters and shtick and clowning. It was supposed to be a zany, wacky, crazy, madcap comedy. In the end, it was mostly just crazy.

Derek and I wrote the treatment together. He'd never written anything before.

"Think up a good beginning," I told him. "Then think up a good ending, and finally bring the two as close together as you possibly can."

When I saw he hadn't written anything after a while, I made him a deal.

"If you write it in three days, I'll give you $3,000."

So he wrote it on a dare. And it wasn't bad. Still, it needed a lot of work, so I gave him tons of jokes and rewrote a lot of it.

Then one day he told me, "I don't think you should get a writing credit, because people will think you wrote the whole thing."

That sounded kind of true to me—but kind of weird, too. It was definitely a dissonant chord. But he was my friend, and I could see how much it meant to him, so I let him take the sole writing credit.

I wish I could say he pulled it off, but the script never did get right. The characters never became three-dimensional the way I hoped. I was able to write some funny bits for myself that worked, but the whole structure in the third act just falls apart. It ends up being about nothing.

I had a lot of talks with Derek about it.

"Dude, the third act's not working. It's so shallow. It needs a speech." He wouldn't fix it. I kept saying, "Dude, you gotta fix it, you gotta change it." He never did.

The story was simple. Retarded, even. Pestario Vargas is this crazy Miami cat. He's always got a scam. And they're always going wrong. He winds up owing $50,000 to the Scottish Mafia. It was funny on paper. So he takes a *Most Dangerous Game* bet with a loony Nazi hunter, who chases him all around with a high-powered rifle.

That was about it for plot. The rest of the movie is me goofing. Doing my wacky dances, playing characters like a rabbi and a Japanese karaoke guy. I do a lot of running around. I must have run six marathons shooting this movie.

Oh, and in one scene I take a dump. A long, long dump.

The Pest was not, as they say, well received. It was hardly received at all. It came out when *Star Wars* was rereleased, which didn't help, and it wasn't advertised well, and it bombed. It does great on video and DVD, but who cares?

Kids seem to love it. People come up to me and say, "My child loves it. It's one of his favorite movies."

I'd be like, "Lady, I wouldn't admit those were my kids."

Too bad there aren't more eight-year-old movie critics. The critics murderlized me. One wrote, "John Leguizamo has basically one joke, and he's it." Another said, "Obviously, someone must have told Leguizamo he's a comic genius. Whoever did that isn't his friend."

Hello, Derek?

Gee, it took me all those years to realize I had no talent. But now I couldn't quit, because I was too successful.

Between my failed marriage and this failed movie I was feeling really down. And it was lean times for me financially, too. I had points in a lot of the movies I made. I was supposed to see a percentage of the profits. What they call a backend deal. I learned why they call it that. That's exactly where you get it. In the back end. I was getting zilch, *nada culo*.

"You have too much talent," my agent explained.

"What does that mean?" I asked. "That's like saying, 'You're so talented we don't want to work with you.'"

"Thank you for making it easy for me," he smiled. "Remember, you don't give me 10 percent of your salary. I give you 90 percent of your salary."

"When I die I'm gonna get cremated," I told him, "and I'm gonna have them throw 10 percent of my ashes in your face."

I had rehired Serge to help me out while making *The Pest*. Now, with no money coming in, I knew I had to face the music and refire him. Only this time he quit before I got the chance.

"I'm out of here," he said. "I no longer want to be your assistant. You make me miserable. You make me feel like your name's always in capital letters and my life's in lowercase."

Oh man. I hate déjà vu.

"Come on, Serge, don't go. What are you gonna do without my money? Who's gonna put up with your sloppy work?"

"I'm going to become an opera singer," Serge said.

Wow. Well, never mock other people's dreams.

Even if it is your little brother. And he's obviously competing with you.

CHAPTER
14

So Evelyn and I got divorced, and my movie bombed. I was feeling so down it gave me courage to call this hot little white girl I'd met. I figured what was the worst that could happen?

Teeny was in the business, but she wasn't an actress. I may be retarded, but I'm not a complete masochist. She was a production assistant. We'd met on a movie set a couple of years earlier, when she was doing costumes. She seemed really cool, really smart. It was like a five-minute thing, and I was in the midst of my madness with Evelyn at the time, so nothing happened. But she must have registered somewhere deep in my brain, because now I remembered her and really wanted to get to know her better.

So I called her. Teeny was in New York and I was still in L.A., but I asked her for a date and then flew cross-country to see her. We went out on a beautiful summer Sunday afternoon. Just walked around the East Village, watched kids playing in the public pools. Just talking and getting to know each other. It was obvious she'd been damaged by her folks, just like me. A perfect match.

I fell for her right away. I thought I had finally met my true love. But she was too smart for that. She wasn't gonna let me bum-rush her into anything heavy.

"Look, John, maybe you should get to know me first," she said.

"Does that mean you have to get to know me too?"

"Relax," she smiled. "Maybe I'll like you."

"Anything's possible," I shrugged.

"I've worked hard on myself so you don't have to," she went on.

"I've worked hard on myself too!" I said. "Does it show?"

"All I'm saying is, if you could just be there for me sometimes when I need you, then we're golden. So let's play it by ear. Whatever happens happens. Okay?"

Her coolness turned me on even more. I had always thought I can't get it up unless a woman treated me like shit.

"I celebrated my thirtieth birthday the other day and my mother told my father that I was a failure," Teeny once said. "And I asked her, 'How could you say something like that?' And she said, 'I didn't know it was a secret.'"

My soul mate.

Pretty soon I got up the balls to tell her I loved her.

"Teeny, I lo—"

"Don't," she said. "You're in love with the idea of being in love."

"Maybe I am screwed up," I admitted. "I think it's cuz my brother used to make monkey noises when he masturbated."

"That's so weird." Teeny laughed. "My sister used to bleat like a sheep."

"See!" I said. "We *are* soul mates."

"I don't wanna marry you," Teeny said.

"But I lo—"

"John, grow up." Teeny laughed.

And believe me I wanted to. A woman who calls me on my bullshit but is sweet when she does it. What the fuck happened? Did God give me a coupon?

I went back out to L.A., and soon Teeny joined me there, and we set up house in the little bungalow I was renting in Echo Park, which was as far across town from Hollywood as I could get. It was like our little love nest, with a swing on the porch and avocado trees in the backyard. We couldn't get enough of each other. We locked ourselves up in the bedroom. We wanted to be together all the time. To explore every facet of each other's minds, bodies, souls. Nothing was off-limits.

It was paradise.

*　*　*

And then I went straight to hell. Well, to Hollywood, which is only about a block away. To film *Spawn*. Where I play the fat, flatulent clown from hell.

I loved the comic book *Spawn*. Spawn was the first black super-hero. I was looking forward to playing a comic book character. I'm not good at being me—that's why I have to act. It's why all actors are actors—so we can spend as much of our lives as possible pretending to be other people. So we don't have to face ourselves and fix ourselves and grow up and all. We're just kids in long pants. So playing a comic book character was perfect for me.

Who knew what torture making that movie would be? *Spawn* was definitely the most physically taxing movie I'd made so far. The fat, flatulent clown from hell was literally a pain in my ass.

Did you see that movie? Can you imagine being in that costume? Every morning they put me into that fat suit, it was like I was wearing a big medicine ball. And then a mask that fit over my whole head and face, right up to the eyeballs and lips. Plus contacts and sharp fake teeth. It was like being in a giant condom. I know I can be a dick sometimes, but this was ridonkeylous.

It took like four hours every morning to get me ready, so once they got me into it I couldn't take it off. They glued on the prosthetic mask, sticking it to every pore. It itches, but you can't scratch. After a while my face actually started to blister from it, and calluses formed around my eyes. And it got hot as hell in there. I was sweating bullets. I sweated maybe thirty pounds off.

I got paid a lot for it—2 million dollars and a two-year production deal. *Wepa!* All I can tell you is I fucking earned it.

Developing titanium buns as the Clown from Hell.

Michael Jai White, who played Spawn, was going through the same agony. And he wasn't used to wearing contacts like I was, so even his eyeballs hurt. Michael was fucking miserable.

After *Wong Foo*, I was used to painful costuming. Still, the first day I almost flipped out.

"Shoot, man. You gotta shoot right now. Because if you don't shoot, I'm gonna tear this shit off. I'm about to lose my mind in here, man. I'm freaking out."

There were days I told the producer, "I'm walking off. I can't take it, man."

The producer was, like, "Dude, we're so close."

"I'm outta here. I'm so fuckin' sick of this costume."

To make matters worse, I did the whole part squatting down. The clown is a short little fat guy, so I had to make myself shorter than I already am. At first they tried to rig various prosthetic devices that would give the illusion, like these bent stilts that would go up inside my pants and end in a seat I could balance on. But everything they invented constricted my movement and put me off-balance. In the end, it was easier for me to squat. I squatted, and even squat-walked, through the whole shoot.

By the end of filming I had titanium buns. I could have bent steel with my buttocks. Not that that's anything to aspire to. But you never know. It's always good to have a skill to fall back on. If my acting career tanked, I could get a job in a freak show. The Mighty LeSqueezemo. Bends Steel Bars in His Ass.

Sometimes shooting a scene would go on so long that I just couldn't hold the squat anymore. My legs would be shaking and then they'd give out and I'd involuntarily pop up to a standing position. Pop! Cut! More like a jack-in-the-box than an evil clown.

I was squatting in that costume for sixty days. Sixty days of that torture. Long days, too. I had to leave my house at four a.m. And then it was either do as much as you can every day, or spend more days doing it. Michael and I were both, like, "No, let's get this over with."

Spawn got screwed because the studio couldn't decide whether to make it for adults—like the original comic book—or for kids. At first it was going to be R-rated, then the studio decided it should be PG-13. And we heard rumors that the studio didn't believe that a black superhero could carry a movie for a general audience. It went through a lot of rewrites and editing, and the story suffered from it. It's still a good movie, and it's dark and grungy and nasty, but it should've been a lot darker and grungier and nastier.

The Clown was a huge part. It was a tour-de-force role, and I ran away with it. I took it seriously. I'd prepped by reading all the *Spawn* comic books the film was based on, then I actually took classes at a clown school in L.A. I took tumbling lessons, juggling, mime, all the clown techniques, looking for inspiration. Because you always want to invent something new. You don't want to keep going back to the well of things you already know. And you don't want to spend too much time watching other movies either, because you're only going to repeat behavior other actors have done—and probably repeating their clichés, too.

Once again, I ad-libbed like crazy. The character was funny as written, but I still felt I needed to update him and punch him up. I do Jimmy Stewart and Schwarzenegger impressions. I bust some squatted hip-hop moves. A lot of the funkier, more contemporary lines in the film are mine.

And he has some great lines. Performing at a child's birthday party, he says things like, "What an adorable little girl. Aw, look at her. Can I keep her? No, of course not. No pets allowed."

Before Spawn realizes that he's died and been resurrected, he asks the Clown to take him to a hospital.

The Clown goes, "A hospital? Have you looked in a mirror lately,

Burnt Man Walking? Even the entire cast of *ER* couldn't put you back together again. How can I put this to you? You're pushing up daisies. You're in permanent naptime. You're fertilizer. Is any of this sinking in? You're dead. D-E-D dead."

When the Clown takes Spawn to the cemetery where his body is buried, he says, "This is where old folks go after Florida, son."

I took the Clown as far as that character would go. Did I mention I ate live maggots on a pizza in one scene? I pick off the anchovies first. The Clown hates anchovies. Is that mad method or what?

Spawn was the beginning of the end of a certain phase in my movie career. I used to love to do characters that were so other than myself. Loved proving I could do the outrageous costumes and physical transformations. The drag queens, the clown from hell, two different genies in *Arabian Nights*, Toulouse-Lautrec in *Moulin Rouge!*

But I feel like I'm done with all that now. I don't have to prove I can act anymore. *Empire* was the beginning of the next phase of my career, where as often as I can I play characters who are real and closer to me. I'll still do some of the silly stuff, but now it's to earn enough bread and acquire enough power to do what I want. A big part of my salary from *Spawn* would go into producing movies I liked. Sure, I'll do a silly voice for *Ice Age*, but you're gonna pay me a fortune for it, and that's going to help fund my next film.

*   *   *

When Serge quit, I had to hire a new assistant. If you're just being an actor, you don't need an assistant. But I was acting and producing and writing, doing a million things, movies and TV and stage, and you can't be in all places at once. You need somebody to help you keep it all organized or your life will fly off in fifty directions.

I had one assistant for a while who was too good. He was amazing. He was so good I found myself totally dependent on him. After a while I couldn't do anything for myself. I started to feel really retarded. I could barely turn my computer on. He ran my whole life. It was too much.

Serge was better for me—he wasn't that good. Now I needed to replace him before I went off to do *Spawn,* and I met this girl Athena.

That's not her real name. I can't use her real name. I have a restraining order against her.

"My name is Athena," she told me. "Like the man/woman goddess who sprung from Zeus' head. My father was in Desert Storm. He taught me how to make car bombs using ordinary household items."

"Well, um, that's just great," I said. "I hear there's all kinds of good bomb recipes on the Internet."

"I also carry a very small handgun," she added.

I said, "Hired."

I think it was the only time in my life that I've been scared into giving someone a job. Another genius business move.

Athena turned out to be a complete psycho stalker bitch lunatic maniac. The clown from hell hires the assistant from hell. It was a total *Single White Female* scene. She started to imitate Teeny. Dressed just like her. Got her hair cut and dyed to look just like Teeny's. Started wearing the same clothes and shoes as Teeny. And when she signed for packages or whatnot, she started signing "Mrs. Leguizamo." Which was doubly creepy, because Teeny and I weren't married.

But she wouldn't *do* anything for Teeny. Like if I asked her to run an errand for Teeny, she wouldn't do it. You could see her grinding her teeth and thinking, "I'll fetch his coffee—but none for his girlfriend."

Once, I sent her out on an errand just to get her out of the house.

A placebo errand. Then I ransacked her handbag. I knew I was invading her privacy, but fuck, this girl was Desert Storming mine. I found a bunch of index cards she'd written notes on. One was quotes from a book on psychological-control techniques:

1. *Use the diminutive of his name. Call him "Johnny" to make him feel subordinate.*

2. *Pat him last when leaving, to make him feel inferior.*

And that afternoon, when I told her she could go home, she said, "Okay, Johnny. See you tomorrow." And patted me on the shoulder.

"Yep," I said, and patted her arm.

Two can play this mind-game crap, bitch.

"'Night," she smiled, and patted me again.

"See ya," I nodded, and patted her again.

"Well, I guess I'll be going," she said, and she reached—but I jumped back.

"Would you get going already?" I said.

"Okay," she shrugged, "Johnny."

She did have a sense of humor. Like she'd always joke, "I had a dream last night that I killed you. Ha ha."

She told Derek that she could kill me and commit the perfect murder and get away with it.

"Well now Athena," Derek said, finally watching my back, "nobody can commit the perfect murder. Everybody slips up. Everyone gets caught sooner or later."

We were all weirded out by her. People started staying away from me because she was so creepy. Meanwhile, she swore all the guys were in love with her. She started dating these much younger dudes on the sets of my movies. But she'd creep them out, too. She was a very strange woman. But she was brilliant. She could run the shit out of everything I needed her to run.

It took me a year to figure out how to fire her, but I finally hit on it.

"Athena," I tell her, "you're too good for this job. It makes me feel bad. You're wasting your talents."

And she says, "Poop."

I go, "Excuse me?"

"You heard me!" she yells. "That's a lot of poop."

I lost it. I'd been putting up with her madness, and tiptoeing around my own assistant for a year. I stood all I could stands, I can't stands no more.

"Listen, you manipulative psycho," I yell back, "I don't want you poisoning my life anymore with your fucking sad antics. You're fired."

"You can't just throw me away," she counters. "An assistant isn't a toy. I could have made your life so perfect. I could have helped you."

"I'm counting to ten for you to get the hell out of my house," I said. "If you're not out I'm calling the police and having you put away. One . . . two . . . three . . ."

Athena is crushed. She starts picking up her things, sobbing.

"Ten," I say. "And give me my keys, you won't need them anymore."

She turns at the door, roots for the keys—and then hurls them at my face with all her might. They whoosh past my face and bury themselves like knives in the wall by my head. *CH-CHUNG.*

She slams the door on her way out. I run to the alarm and set it. Then I start examining the office. I unplug the fax machine—she may have wired a bomb to it. I lose contact with the world at large, but at least I am alive to tell about it.

Next thing I heard of Athena, she was working for a television series. Well, people do fail up in this industry.

Actually, she'd written herself a glowing recommendation on my stationery, and forged my signature.

Whatever. She was their problem now.

Still, her malignant freakazoid spirit continued to haunt me for a while. Like I had the bitchingest time with any equipment I'd had her buy for the office. They wouldn't give me the warranties, because she had signed for it all in her name.

*   *   *

Well, at least Teeny and I were rocking. We had our families meet that Christmas in New York. I made it a costumed Christmas party. I wanted as many layers of camouflage on my family as possible.

But of course they found ways to embarrass me, even in disguise.

First, my mother comes dressed up all orange and smelling like a fish.

"*Besitos todo el mundo! Feliz Navidad!* Merry Christmas!"

I grabbed her arm.

"Mom, what the hell are you wearing?"

"*Papi*, I'm trying to impress them. I'm lox. Smoked salmon."

"Mom, go home and change."

"Don't be silly. Serge, help me. My schmear is slipping."

We lit Hanukkah candles for Teeny's parents. My father instantly blew them out.

"Dad, what the hell?"

"Sorry, *mijo*. I thought it was my birthday."

"You people are mortifying me," I groan. "Why can't you be like her parents?"

And then Teeny's father comes over to me and says, "Hey, You're-gay, we took these pictures in Cancún. Boy, do we love Mexico."

"No offense, *vato* sir, but I'm not Mexican."

"Whatever," he shrugs. He puts his arm around my shoulder and leans toward me, all conspiratorial-like. "My daughter tells me that she loves you," he murmurs martini breath in my ear. "What's it gonna take to make you disappear? Fifty? A hundred? Here's a hundred-dollar bill. I bet you never seen one of these before."

"You'd have to talk to my agent," I say, wriggling out of his hug. "Why don't we ask Teeny what she thinks."

"She's just a child," he tut-tuts. "Look, you seem like a smart guy. You must know it's not gonna work. I'm trying to spare you some heartache. She's gone slumming before."

"I'll take my chances," I say through gritted teeth.

"You think you're different?" he growls. "You think you got big *cojones*?" He pronounces it "co-joanies."

And then he lays this big, wet martini kiss on my cheek.

"Actually I do too, son," he says. "You got the balls to marry into this family, then you're man enough for me."

I was like what the—? But that was how it was with me and Teeny's dad. Not quite a love–hate relationship, cuz I don't think he really hated me. He was just being a dad and overprotective of his daughter. It developed into a grudging respect sort of thing. In spite of himself, he sort of dug that I was a rebel and so brazen in my shows. He told Teeny I reminded him of himself in his younger days when he was Meyer Lansky's accountant.

When I heard that about him, I liked him better too. Original Gangsta, yo! In some ways he reminded me of my Pops, tough on the outside but with a tender core somewhere way down deep inside. Like one of my mom's pot roasts.

Still, from the stress of being around both our families at one time, Teeny and I had a big fight that night.

"Why are you trying so hard to get my family to like you?" I accused her. "I gave up a long time ago."

"You don't want your family to like me because they don't like *you*?" she fired back. "Do you know how sick that is? You could try a little harder with *my* family, you know."

"You mean act whiter?" I put on my fake British voice. "Oh, Teeny, shall I reserve box seats for the symphony, or should we winter in Gstaad? *C'est ce que tu penses, mon petite chou-chou?*"

She whacked me. Then she calmed down a bit and said, "Look, let's stop trying to change each other. That's all I want. That . . ." She paused and gave me a very serious look. ". . . and kids."

Kids! All my panic alarms went off.

"Kids? We don't need kids. We got me."

"But John, my clock is ticking."

"Well put it on snooze."

She whacked me again.

"Look, I'm sorry," I said. "Your clock is telling you to have kids, mine is telling me to go to sleep. Good night."

Whew. A narrow escape.

But I knew I'd only bought myself a little time. And the more I considered it, the less terrifying the idea became. Well, slightly less terrifying. After all, I loved her and she loved me. She was the woman of my dreams, my soul mate, my life partner. Maybe it was time for me to settle down and become a daddy. Why shouldn't we have kids?

So I went to Teeny and said, "I've been a stubborn jerk. Look, I've been thinking a lot, and despite our differences, I really wanna try. I hope you do too. I mean, maybe it's time to settle down and have kids someday before I become an old guy like my father—fat gut, using those tired playboy pick-up lines everywhere. 'Hey, tell me about yourself. Come on, be different. Say yes.' So let's . . . um . . . go for it."

Teeny smiled and touched my cheek.

"I think I heard an 'I love you' in there somewhere," she said. "Which is good, because I'm pregnant."

After *Spawn* I was sick of movies. I started to write *Freak*, my third solo performance, because I'd had enough of Hollywood, I'd had enough of movies. I'd done a whole string of them, one more or less right after the other, and most of it was empty. American movies are so shallow. I felt like a hooker. Making random calls. I wanted to do something creative, because I was feeling *very* uncreative. I was making good money and beginning to acquire the kind of status that let me take the parts and make the movies I felt would be more fulfilling, but it still wasn't enough. I needed to do things that would rock my world, shake my soul.

So I decided to take some time off from them and go back to writing my own stuff for the theater.

I ended up taking two years off from movies.

And Teeny and I moved back to New York

full-time. I'd been living for two years in L.A., and I know that had an effect on me.

I was still very resistant and wary of it at first. I'd seen so many friends change when they went off to Hollywood. Really funny, cool people who went out there and became paranoid hustlers. Everybody's hustling in Hollywood, and everybody's afraid. People don't say "How are you?" in Los Angeles. They say, "What are you doing? What are you working on?" What happened to the human being? There's no humanity in that. Everything's work. Everybody's in the business, and everybody's paranoid of what they say to everyone else, so everybody's always lying. When everybody you talk to is also in the business, you can't really say the truth anymore. You don't know who could be listening. God forbid you should speak your mind and say anything negative about anybody. They might be your boss on your next project.

And it's still weird to be Latin in L.A. In the rest of the country, all the white kids wanted to be Ricky Martin or Christina Aguilera. But in L.A., it's still so segregated. People in Hollywood still only deal with Latins in the service areas—their nannies are all Latin, their valets, the chauffeurs, the gardeners. That's all they see you as. It's so weird—they won't let you upgrade but then they let you raise their babies.

Gradually, I did learn how to make and have friends out there. It's a totally different culture from the East Coast. I started to understand that in L.A. you have to book your friends. In New York, you bump into people on the street, you meet interesting people all the time. In L.A., you don't meet people. You make appointments. L.A. people are awkward in social situations. They're only comfortable in their cars. I figured out how to hang out more with friends, mostly people from back East who'd moved out there. And Teeny introduced me to a bunch of her friends, people she'd met a few years earlier when she was working in Hollywood.

Not bullshit Hollywood types, though. Just nice folks who happened to live in L.A. Teeny didn't like the oily movie-industry scene any more than I did. She found the parties and premieres a giant bore. I only dragged her to the bare minimum of things I felt I had to do for my career. Then we'd run back to our little love nest in Echo Park. We were both much more comfortable there.

And besides, I had work to do. I came back to New York with Teeny and wrote *Freak*.

Freak was much harder to write than the others had been, because it was the most open and personal. It came much closer to being the straight-up truth about my fucked-up childhood and family. It was going to be much more nakedly me, John Leguizamo, exposing his life in front of a bunch of strangers. An emotional enema. I had been able to hide behind the characters in *Spic-O-Rama*, even though they were close to my real family. But *Freak* was going to be a lot closer. I knew it was going to be really hard and painful to dig into those personal experiences, but I had to do it. I had to exorcise these memories that had been hounding me for years. But it all had to be funny, too. Even though there would be a lot of brutal and awful stories, it had to make people laugh. Cuz that's what I do. I don't write tragedy, I write comedy.

Teeny couldn't get over how hard I worked on *Freak*. I'd be working on it when she went to sleep at midnight, and still at my desk when she got up the next morning. That impressed the hell out of her. She'd grown up pretty well-off, and a lot of her friends had led pampered lives where they got everything in life handed to them and never missed their beauty sleep. She hadn't spent much time around a poor spic from the ghetto who was obsessed with making it and had to do it for himself.

Freak started out as a collection of little vignettes, scenes, and sketches. I had been entering them all into a big document on my computer—thoughts, scenes, a line, a note, a wordplay, whatever. Then I started sorting them out, figuring out what I was trying to say. I started putting them together with Derek, who was going to direct instead of Peter Askin this time. Peter was off directing *Hedwig & the Angry Inch*.

In *Freak*, I hang out all the family laundry. All of it. My mom's girdles, my dad's leopard thong, Serge's skid marks, my cum-stained Fruit of the Looms. All of it. The crazy grampas and grandmas, the faygeleh uncle. You know that cartoon strip, *Family Circus*? With the cute little round-headed white kids and all? This was the Leguizamo Family Circus. Pinheads and all. And it wasn't cute. But it was a whole lot funnier.

I fictionalized and fucked with details, to protect the guilty. Especially me. But if the facts aren't all true, the rest of it is, you know?

Freak was not the original title. First I was thinking it'd be called *Full Frontal*. Cuz of the way I was exposing myself. Then it became *Freakazoid*, then eventually just *Freak*. Because ultimately it's about feeling like a freak, like you're outside of things and different from everyone else. A show for all the freaks in the world.

I mean, look at me. My father used to call me his "little abortion that got away." I guess I've always felt like that, like I didn't fit in, like I wasn't even meant to be here. A freak.

I still don't fit in—but I like it now. And that was part of the point of the show.

Freak is basically my story, from being born in Bogotá to my first stage-acting gig. About how my family joined the miserable, huddled masses coming to Queens, where my folks worked "twenty-eight hours a day, fourteen days a week" struggling to make it in America. About me and Serge growing up in apartments so puny they wished they were projects. How my mom put up for years with my dad's drinking and his evil temper and his chasing other women and his failed get-rich-quick schemes, like his plan to become "king of ten-ements," the Latin Donaldo Trumpo. Until she finally rebelled and stood up to him. And he reacted the only way he knew how—he tried to beat it out of her. Which started the divorce, where he got every-thing, and me, Moms, and Serge were basically thrown out on the street. And I came to Manny Hanny in search of fame and fortune. And started a career in theater instead.

My crazy Gramps is in it, stuck in his wheelchair and always ask-ing me to cut off his life support. "We were keeping him alive against his will," I say. "Because my Pops wanted him to live long enough so he would suffer what he had made my Pops suffer."

There's my two grandmas, the nice one and the evil one. We called the evil one Grama Dulce, not because she was sweet but because "her fingers were always sticky even though she never ate any candy."

And Uncle Sanny, "what you'd call a triple threat: Latin, gay, and deaf." One of everybody's favorite parts of the show is when Uncle Sanny shows me how to sneak into Broadway shows during the in-termission. He called it "second-acting." You mingle outside with the smokers during intermission, grab a program, sneak inside, and take an empty seat. He and I saw the second half of *Chorus Line* that way, and I was amazed that one of the dancers was named Morales.

"There was a Latin person in the show," I explain. "And she didn't have a gun or a hypodermic needle in her hand, and she wasn't a hooker or a maid, and she wasn't servicing anybody, so it was hard to tell if she was Latin . . ." And that's when I decided I was going to be on stage someday.

When I had a ton of stuff assembled, I read it for friends. Because I'm writing for the stage, I need to read things aloud, hear people's responses. I'd invite people over to my place, get them all drunk, and perform it for them. Then they give me notes. My friends and family have sat through some long, long readings. The first time I read *Freak* it was three and a half hours. Epic. My entire real life didn't feel as long as that reading. Poor people. I feel sorry for them. But fuck it, I needed to purge. Wouldn't even let them get up to pee. And it was hot that day. Harsh.

Then I did some public readings at PS 122, and people went nuts with their comments. One woman really accosted me.

"You only do eight characters. And it's all about males and their penises. And you don't do enough voices or characters. I do thirty-nine characters in my show."

So she was some kind of performance artist. The crowd turned against her when she said that. Other people had some interesting notes. They felt that the whole story was between me and my father, and I was like, God, I don't want it to be about that. But I knew they were right. People kept saying, "You could be darker and deeper." I just wanted it to be really hilarious. And every time I read it, the audience kept pushing me to be darker and darker.

Except for my mom and Serge. When they came to one of those public readings, they freaked. They still hate me for that show. They still attack me for *Freak* every chance they get.

"How dare you," my mom said, crying. "Please don't put me in your show. Just tell them you sprang from air, like bacteria." She was depressed for a month afterward.

Serge was livid. "I'll never forgive you. Telling everyone my grandmother was an alcoholic. She wasn't an alcoholic. She could quit any time she wanted to. And how dare you say I'm fat?"

"Because you're fat," I said.

"You can't use my name," he insisted.

I realized he was right, so I called him Poochie. But I left him fat. Cuz he was.

Luckily, my family has a price tag. I bought their love back at

Christmas. And every Christmas since. Xbox, plasma screen, whatever it takes. That show has really cost me.

In the end, though, *Freak* really is all about me and my father. I'm like Luke Skywalker battling through three episodes of *Star Wars*, only to find out that my enemy was my own dad. My dad is my Darth Vader. With an accent. May the Schwartz be with you.

There's a central scene where I describe how the only time he was even remotely nice to me was when he'd get drunk and sit out on the fire escape, and sometimes I'd sit out there with him. I'd love being out there with him, but I'd be wary and on my guard the whole time, because you never knew when he was going to jump back over to the Dark Side and start beating you again.

"Having a good time?" he says to me. "You enjoying this? Good, cuz I'm gonna take it all away from you. Then you'll really know how miserable life can be."

He drinks some more and gets sloppy and says, "C'mere, I love you. What are you cringing at? Afraid of a little affection? I'm your father, you little faggot. Come on, give me a kiss. You kiss me or I'll punch the shit out of you."

So I kiss him, and he snaps, "Not on the lips, you little freak!"

That was hard to write and hard to perform, but the big final blowout between him and my mom was even harder. After fifteen years under his thumb my mom had begun to emancipate herself. She went to college, she started going out and having fun on her own, and he couldn't handle her being independent. It was all right for him to be out all the time, getting drunk and screwing other women, but she was supposed to stay home and be his slave. Like any normal Latin family.

One night he blew up. They had a huge fight in the kitchen. They're wrestling on the floor, he's choking her, she's screaming. And I can't stand it anymore. I grab a big butcher knife and go after him.

"If you touch my Moms or anyone else in this house ever again, you're a goner," I warn him.

We struggle and he takes the knife away from me.

"I hate you!" I scream at him.

That puts an end to it. For the first time, his whole family has fought back. My father puts on his coat and hat.

"I'm sorry, *mijo*," he says to me. "I didn't mean to hurt you. I'm not a cruel person. I hope your son never looks at you how you're looking at me. You know, John, I came here to work. I didn't come here to crawl. But I didn't care, 'cause all I ever wanted was milk for my kids and beer for me. And always remember, in life there are no do-overs or repeats. So if you don't do what you want, you'll end up like me."

For the first time I saw my dad as he really was: a child. I was so moved—until he added, as his parting words of wisdom, "Your mom's a *puta* bitch."

My dad didn't see *Freak* until it was actually in performance. Because he and I weren't speaking again when I was writing and rehearsing it. Because he'd totally screwed up my and Evelyn's Las Vegas wedding.

It was a Latin family thing. I had my mom there, of course, but then my stepmom, my dad's second wife, whom he married after he and my mom divorced, came too. My stepmom was a big mentor in my life, despite me and my dad not getting along. She showed up even though I didn't invite her. I felt like I couldn't, partly because my mom would be uncomfortable with it, but more because my stepmom and my dad didn't get along. They weren't together anymore either, see. He was on to his third wife. Whom he brought to the wedding. And she wasn't cool with the second wife being there. So the third wife threatened to leave, and my dad threatened to leave with her.

Are you following this? I told you, it's an es-tended family thing.

So my dad throws one of his fits, saying that if my stepmom stayed he and his new wife were leaving. This was maybe five minutes before the ceremony.

"Dad, you can't do this to me now," I begged him. Oh man was I pissed. I already had Evelyn acting out. I didn't need two Latin drama queens screwing it all up. Or three, if you count the third wife. "Can't you just deal with it?"

"No," he says. "I have to leave."

So I had to ask my stepmom to go. I was furious with my dad and his wife. Instead of just dealing with the situation, they had to make everything horrible, minutes before the wedding.

Then, at the reception, my father was supposed to walk out with my mom—act like the groom's happy parents, just for a few minutes. But when she went to take his arm he pushed her hand away. I have it on videotape. He wouldn't play along at all.

So I didn't speak to him for a while.

And then he shows up for *Freak*. It's been a few years since we've even spoken. I'm in the dressing room after the show, greeting people. I'm talking to Mike Myers, when I see this seething face in my peripheral vision. Twitching and frothing. It's Pops. And he's furious.

"How dare you," he growls, in front of everyone.

I drag him out into the alleyway. And there, among the garbage cans, we have a confrontation just like the one that ends the show.

"Why must you drag your family in the mud and shit?" he's seething. "Why can't you make things up, like other writers? Don't you have any imagination at all? You call this creativity?"

And I let him have it—everything I've wanted to say to him since I was eight years old.

"You were never there for me," I tell him. "You never played ball with me. You wouldn't even pay for my college. I want my child support. Now. I want reparations."

And my father starts to cry. It was a shocking moment. I had made my father cry.

In the end it brought us closer. We've dealt with each other better since. And he's good to my two kids. He actually likes being a grandpa.

I think it helped that I just gave up. I just stopped expecting him ever to be the kind of father I always wanted. And that made things easier between us.

You feel so much better when you give up hope.

* * *

So I took *Freak* to Broadway, and it was a huge hit. With audiences who were actually under fifty years old, and not in wheelchairs, like most Broadway audiences. A lot of them were kids, Latin kids,

Hirschfeld was out sick, so I got a Norkin.

Look, Pops! I won an Emmy!

on dates. Coming to see me, Johnny LeGreasemo from Queens. On Broadway. All alone. Doing what I like to do best—cracking jokes, showing off for the girlies, and talking about myself.

Did you know the 7 train runs all the way from deepest, darkest Queens straight to Times Square? I'm living proof. Only in America. Home of the freak, land of the depraved.

Freak did very well, and people were digging it, so I did it for as long as I could take it—six months. I got nominated for a Tony for best performance in a variety or musical.

Spike Lee came to see it, and that's how I got what turned out to be the lead in *Summer of Sam*. And when it was time to get a direc-

Lots of stars came backstage when I was doing *Freak*. This is Forest Whitaker.

tor for the HBO taping, he was my first choice. He let me go into the editing room, which was great. I'd been in the editing room before for *House of Buggin'* and a little bit for *Spic-O-Rama*, but on *Freak* Spike gave me a whole week in the editing room, nine hours a day. I learned so much from Spike.

Freak was also the dissolution of my friendship with Derek. We had been friends since *Mambo Mouth*. He was funny and we had had a great time together. Then he became power mad. That's how I saw it, anyway. It started with him wanting to be the executive producer on *House of Buggin'*. Then there was the writing credit on *The Pest*. Which he probably regrets now.

Then I let him direct me in *Freak*. We were hanging out together a lot, and I thought we'd have a great time. And if I'm having a great time I'm crazy creative. My experience from the movies was that when directors allowed me to be me I usually did my best work. Any time they tried to control me or shape me or mold me I gave my worst performances.

I know how that sounds. I have issues. Problems with authority figures. I want to impress them, but I don't want to be controlled or bossed around by them. It all goes back to my childhood, obviously. When you're the son of a guy like my dad, it can really Puck you up for dealing with authority. And then I chose acting for a career, which is like choosing to remain a perpetual child, playing dress-up and acting the clown—or the clown from hell—your whole life. And what are directors if not surrogate parental figures?

It screws you up in your friendships, too. Since I'm so driven, I can become competitive and weird even with my best buddies. In retrospect, I can see how letting my best buddy be my director was just asking for trouble.

Derek was all right at directing, even though, once again, I was letting him try something he had no experience in. He had some skills. He just didn't have it all. When we were doing the show in San Francisco, a lot of people kept saying that it wasn't working, that it had a lot of problems, the staging was bad, and so on. That sent all my insecurities and anal-perfectionist-overachiever instincts into overdrive. So without Derek knowing, I flew in the director of the Steppenwolf Theater in Chicago to see the show, and he gave me tons of notes. I fixed the show behind Derek's back, when he was away. Then we got this great producer, Gregory Mosher, who used to run Lincoln Center, and he started directing me on the weekends. It all made the show much better—but it all put a strain on my friendship with Derek.

We had our big blowout in front of a restaurant one afternoon. He was late meeting me and I used it as an excuse to confront him.

"This is the tenth time you're late," I said. "You're fired."

He laughed sarcastically. "That's funny. I'm the reason you're here, remember? You think everybody has to kiss your ass. You don't take responsibility for anything."

He was the reason for my success? I was so pissed I shoved him. He shoved me back. We stood there staring at each other for a second.

"This is how you thank me?" I said. "I get you this job, and you don't even say thanks. You're like a fucking mushroom, living in my shadow."

"Right," he says, still all sarcastic. "Thanks, Santa Claus."

"Come on, Derek," I plead. "You're like my brother."

"Fuck you," he says, and walks away.

Suddenly I remembered that fight I was in, and how he didn't get my back.

Cutting my ties with him wasn't as easy as that. When I did *Spawn*, part of my salary was set aside to create a production company. I made Derek my partner, without asking him to invest a dime. Because we were best friends. That was the biggest business mistake of my life.

When I told him I couldn't work with him anymore, he threatened to sue me. And that's when the lawyers told me that he owned 50 percent of the company.

"He owns half the company? But he didn't put any money down."

"You signed the agreement," my lawyer said. "You don't have any leverage."

I felt like the stupidest man alive. I had no fuckin' business sense. I'd signed that contract without really reading it.

So I talked to Derek again.

"Yo, we've been friends, man. I stuck out my neck for you lots of times. Dude, you can't do this. It was all my money."

In the end we settled. He took 35 percent instead of 50. And I started a new company, Rebel Films. We haven't seen or spoken to each other since. It's like sometimes you break up with a girl, and you run into her a few years later and enough time has passed that you've forgotten all the things you despised about each other, so now you can be friends. And other times it's so bitter and awful and painful you never want to see each other again. You'll cross the street, move to a different city, just to try never to bump into her for the rest of your life.

It was a sad awakening for me. Derek and I had been really close. But business really does screw up relationships. And so does success. I think Derek watched me become famous and successful—and he helped me do that, no question—and now he wanted some of the spotlight for himself. He even started dressing like me. It was very strange. It was like he wanted us to be the new Jerry & Dean, a comedy duo. And as much as I loved and respected him, I didn't see that happening. I was having a hard enough time trying to be a successful comedy solo.

Not that I'm totally innocent in this whole sad affair. I could have paid better attention to what was happening. But I was a workaholic and had no support group outside of my friendship and partnership with him. I talked to him about everything. I had no other perspective. All his friends even became my friends, because I had let go of all my real friends. His friends weren't theater people, which was fun, because actors are so annoying.

So now I had a hard time asserting myself with him, standing up to him, separating myself from him. It was really painful. I finally learned that lesson: don't hire your friends, dumbass.

Still, looking back across my fiascoes with Derek, and Serge, and even the psycho bitch assistant, I had a spooky thought.

"Shit," I said to Teeny one night, "is my mom the only person in the world who can *stand* to work for me? Am I that big a dick?"

"Well," she replied slowly. I could see her considering a joke about my dick size, but she let it pass. "You are very driven, and you do expect people around you to work as hard as you do."

"I know I'm a control freak," I confessed. "I know I have trouble letting other people hold the reins."

"Except when it comes to cleaning up around the house," Teeny noted.

I let that pass.

"And I'm a perfectionist. Maybe I drive people nuts with my nit-picking over minutiae?"

"Well, it sounds like you did drive Evelyn kind of crazy with trying to make her over into the wife you wanted her to be, instead of loving her for who she was."

"But she *was* imperfect," I said. "I was just trying to help."

Teeny raised an eyebrow.

"You're also an exhibitionist," she went on. "You do get jealous about sharing the attention with anyone. Remember that guy on *House of Buggin'*? I mean, no wonder Serge wanted to be an opera singer. He wanted a bit of the spotlight too, you know."

"So maybe I overreacted about Derek?"

"You can be sort of an egomaniac sometimes," Teeny said. "Was it really so awful of him to want to bask a little in your reflected glory?"

I suddenly remembered what I'd said to Derek when we'd had our big breakup: "You're like my brother." Shit, he *was* like Serge—a surrogate Serge! I loved them both, and I wanted to look out for them both and have them work with me—but that really meant they would both work *for* me. But like Serge and Evelyn had both said, it would still always be my name up there in lights and capital letters, and theirs in small print. They could have a little corner of my spotlight, but that was as much as I was willing to share.

"Oh man," I moaned. "So it is true. My mom is the only person in the world who'll work for me. And look at how much I have to pay her!"

"And another thing," Teeny continued.

"Enough about me," I said, cutting her off. "Let's talk about your flaws now."

"Hold that thought," she said, jumping up.

I sat there mulling it over. About what a perfectionist control freak workaholic exhibitionist egomaniac I was. I thought about it for a long time, waiting for Teeny to come back so I could tell her all her flaws. I waited and waited, and finally realized she'd snuck out of the house.

So I was left with only myself to criticize. Which I hate. But I forced myself, and came to a stunning insight:

It was all my dad's fault. I thought about all the psychology I'd read about the sons of autocratic-dictator dads like him, and it all fit. It's no wonder I'm so screwy.

Whew. What a catharsis. I felt much better. I could stop blaming myself for my faults.

I could blame it all on him.

The falling-out with Derek did force me to realize I don't take care of my friendships as well as I should. It happens to guys when they reach their forties. Especially if you're ambitious. You've got your work and career, you've got your woman and kids who take up all your free time, and you become isolated from your friends.

I reconnected with a couple of my best old friends, and they were all going through something similar, working their asses off, cutting themselves off. It's an American thing. We're all waiting to retire at sixty-five before we really live, and that's insane. In Spain and Latin America, people hang out, they talk, they spend time with family and friends. They appreciate quality time. They work to live. In America, people live to work.

It's strange to look at where I am now and where I came from. It's just so different. When I used to go back to the old neighborhood and talk to friends, they'd be like, "You talk weird. What's wrong with you?" You start changing. You start moving away. You feel like you can't connect. When I played Victor Rosa in *Empire*, I really identified with his story. Because he's a smart, driven guy from the Bronx who makes good and starts hanging out on Wall Street, exchanges his old friends for all these sophisticated white people downtown, and when he goes back home he's an alien in his old 'hood. Franc Reyes, who wrote and directed it, was from the Bronx, and he'd gone through the same thing.

At least now a couple of my friends from high school are successful too. We're driven guys, we all have kids, we're all trying to make it. We understand one another and have good times together.

It helps to surround yourself with people who are just as fucked up as you are.

A fter *Freak* I did *Summer of Sam,* and it was the best time I ever had making a movie. It was so much fun. I love Spike Lee. Spike's the kind of guy who says nice things about you behind your back. We had such great chemistry together. When things sucked, he held his nose, like I stunk up the screen. And if he loved it, he'd pump his fist. He's not a very emotive guy in real life, but when he's working he gets so into it. He loves when it's raw and real, and we got to improvise a lot.

At last, a movie I could personally relate to. Spike called it his first whitesploitation movie. I think of it as Spike's *Tale of Two Cities.* Summer of '77, the best of times and the worst of times for New York City. You had the big blackout and the riots. David Berkowitz and the Son of Sam murders. The war in the music clubs between the disco crowd and the punks. The Yankees in the World Series. Plato's

Retreat, swingers' clubs, and the grindhouses on Forty-second Street. Studio 54 opened its doors that April. Coke and pills everywhere. Remember the movie *Escape from New York*? It was supposed to be science fiction, but it looked like real life. New York, the city God made and then forgot. It was a jungle, broke, broke-down, funky, scummy, sexy, gritty, dangerous, drugged-out, and fun as hell. The jungle may be full of death and decay, but it's also teeming with life. You can't have one without the other.

When New York started cleaning up its act and being colonized by yuppies in the 1990s, a lot of old-timers would look back to the late 70s as the city's heyday. That was the real New York City, the fucked-up, crazy, exhilarating city we all loved and hated. By the end of the 90s, it was just another boring, safe, clean American city, Oshkosh by the Sea. At least until 9/11.

Not that I was ever in Studio 54 or Plato's Retreat. I was thirteen in the summer of '77. What I remember most about Son of Sam was that he was targeting couples in their cars on Lover's Lane in Astoria. We used to ride our bikes over there at night, check out the older kids necking and humping, hoping to see a flash of tit or something behind those fogged-up windows. With Son of Sam on the prowl, we had to decide if that was worth risking our lives for. A thirteen-year-old boy shouldn't have to make that kind of decision.

I clearly remember the night of the big blackout. I was at home in our apartment in Elmhurst. Everybody in the neighborhood was leaning out their windows, screaming and yelling. It was like a big block party. I hung out on the fire escape, yelling to people out on the street.

"Yo, wassup? How you doon?"

No looting or rioting in Elmhurst. Everybody was cool.

I loved the *Summer of Sam* script by Victor Colicchio. Spike also worked on it, and Michael Imperioli, who has a cool little part in it

and later scored hugely as Christuhfuh in *The Sopranos*. I got deep
into my character, Vinny the hairdresser. Pretty ironic. The story's by
an Italian guy who played Puerto Ricans in movies. Now I'm a Puerto
Rican playing an Italian in his movie. Holy shit, I crossed over! I figure I was on the Al Pacino exchange program. If he can play Latin
twice, I get to be Italian once.

There's so much gnarly sex in *Summer of Sam*, it should have
been G-Spot-rated. Vinny's a tortured sexaholic. He's a little man
with a little dick, which his wife, Dionna, reminds him of when they
fight. He's got this tall, blond beauty of a woman at home. Played by
tall, blond beauty Mira Sorvino. But he can't get it up with her because he's wracked by Italian Catholic guilt from fucking every other
woman in sight. He's a sex machine. He's fucking all his clients at
the hair salon, his boss (Bebe Neuwirth), even Dionna's cousin from
Italy. He drives her cousin home, fucks her in the ass in the car, then
meets up with Dionna, who can smell her cousin's pussy on his
breath.

Busteded.

He can't do all that nasty stuff with Dionna, because she's his
good Catholic wife. So he does it with everyone else. As long as he
ain't married to them, he can treat them like hos.

The night Vinny's screwing Dionna's cousin in the car, David
Berkowitz blows away a couple of lovers in a car nearby. Vinny completely loses it. He thinks it's a sign from God. He tells his good friend
Richie (Adrien Brody), "I think God's telling me that I'm gonna burn
in hell if I don't stop cheating."

That's from the script, not me ad-libbing. I'm Catholic, but not
that Catholic.

Spike let me ad-lib like crazy, so I gotta admit there's at least a
little of me in Vinny. Me cheating on Cathy, me fighting with Evelyn. The more wild ad-libbing I did, the more Spike liked it. Like the

scene near the end where Vinny gets into a big fight with his boss and I pour a cup of coffee over Bebe's head. That was spontaneous. Luckily it wasn't hot.

Or the scene where Vinny just jumps on top of Dionna and bangs her really fast and hard. You know, that happens in long relationships. The sex gets old, it loses all its romance and mystery. You just jump in there and bang away and get your rocks off, then you roll off and light a smoke. Wham bam, and not even a thank you, ma'am. That was my idea. That's how Vinny would do Dionna, quick and impersonal, so he wouldn't have time to feel guilty and conflicted about it.

Getting to have those really hot scenes with Mira Sorvino was kind of trippy, because Teeny was pregnant at the time. Mira is really beautiful. And really smart. And really talented. She's a great package.

People always ask movie actors if it's sexy doing the sex scenes. Sometimes it is, sometimes not. It depends on how you're feeling that day, how you feel about the other person, the type of scene it is. Like the orgy scene was hot to do. It was the kind of movie where the girls were not auditioned—they were measured. Nasty. Because it's a group thing, with a whole bunch of you naked and pretending to have sex, you don't feel like the focus is just on you. You can get into it easier.

When you feel like everybody's staring at you it can get uncomfortable. I'm not a porn star. I don't get off on everybody looking at my dick.

And you feel bad for the actress. All of a sudden the set is full of guys trying to see her tits or whatever. Funny how the entire crew, people you can never find on normal days, all show up on the set for the sex scenes. The craft-service people, gaffers, everybody turns thirteen. Directors usually try to close the set and work with as small a crew as possible, but people still show up.

But you do get turned on sometimes. I've gotten wood. Which can be embarrassing too. If you're a porn star you're proud that you can get hard with a lot of people watching. A Dirk Diggler with a love muscle as long as his leg will march around that porn set all day showing it off. For me it's more like springing an unintentional boner in the showers at the gym. I feel like I should apologize for it, like the owner of a dog that's humping somebody's leg.

"Sorry. Down boy. Roll over. Play dead."

For me, it's most arousing when (Teeny, skip to the next page please) it's just you and the girl and a tiny, essential crew. Then it's more relaxed and intimate, and you can find yourself actually getting into the sex. And of course if you're the actor you ask for a lot of takes. Directors tend to be good about that. They want you to enjoy it.

"How did you feel about take fifty-six, John?"

"I dunno. I think I can do better. I don't feel like I really nailed her. It."

"You want to give her-it another go?"

"I guess. Anything for the picture, right?"

Yeah, sometimes directors are like Heidi Fleiss, enabling horny actors and their dirty desires.

The worst sex scene I've ever done was with myself. The jerk-off scene in *Spun*, the speed-freak movie that came out in 2002. It was disgusting. My character jerks off to phone sex. I tried to talk the director into cutting it. Then I was supposed to be butt-naked, but I refused.

"No way, man. No way I'm gonna be in this movie if I have to get naked and jerk off for the camera."

"John, you have to do it. That's the way it's written."

"No way, man. It's repulsive. I don't want to be naked."

We ended up compromising. I jerk off with a sock over my joint. I remembered that from a roommate I had in college who used to jerk

I stole *Summer of Sam* from Adrien Brody, but we're still friends, I think.

off into a sock because he thought it was "cleaner" to do it that way. At least it made the scene funny.

Mira and I had a great time doing the dance sequences. We worked really hard on them. You can see from all my shows and a lot of my movies that I love to dance. I don't need an excuse to get my freak on. Dance is such a big deal in Latin culture. The Hustle I knew a little from growing up. My people invented it, after all. In fact, the couple who invented it taught me and Mira. We would go to their club on Monday nights and dance all night. Teeny came a couple of times, I brought my cousin and my stepsister, who loves disco. Mira did really well—for a white girl. A lot of people don't know this, but the Travolta *Saturday Night Fever* thing was the white-boy version of what was really going on in the clubs. Nobody really hustled like that. That bus-stop thing? That was like ballroom Hustle. You should have seen the way my people did the Hustle. It was like ballet and gymnastics and sex and poetry.

Vinny was supposed to be a secondary character, but he turned into the lead. Adrien Brody's Richie was supposed to be the main character. The weird thing was, Adrien had just done *The Thin Red Line* and was supposed to be the lead there, too, but Terrence Malick kept giving Jim Caviezel more lines, and cutting Adrien's lines, moving him into the background.

And then it happened to him again in *Summer of Sam*. Spike and I were having such a great time, and Vinny just sort of ate up the picture, shoving Richie into a supporting role. Adrien started to feel like something weird was going on. He was really hurt. I mean, after a point you're wondering, "Is it me? Why does this keep happening?"

I felt for him. I was excited for myself, but I really liked Adrien. He's good people. I would have been crushed if I was in his situation. But he hung in there, and eventually he got his Oscar, so there you go.

I still love *Summer of Sam*. That was one premiere I was happy to go to. I'm Latin, so I always bring all the family to everything. Cousins, uncles, aunts, brothers, and sisters. Like fifteen people. It's not that we're that close. It's just that we like to travel in big groups. Cuz we're afraid.

When Teeny got pregnant, I prayed for a daughter. I was scared of having a son. I wasn't sure I wanted to carry on the curse of the Leguizamos. I was terrified I'd fuck up my son the way my dad had fucked me up and his dad had fucked him up.

We decided to do natural childbirth at home. No hospital gown, no drugs. Teeny got a Brazilian wax, because she knew I was gonna videotape it. I'm playing with the camera, zooming in, solarizing, and she's squatting and grunting. I'm staring at my favorite part of the female anatomy, my safe haven, through the lens . . . and I see it being ripped open by this eight-pound *thing*. This beast crawling out of her insides.

And all I can think is, "Damn! Next time we have sex I'm gonna have to bang the hell out of the sides for her to feel me at all."

I was still hoping for a girl. I was chanting for one, rooting for one like a cheerleader.

"G to the I to I-R-L! G to the I to the I-R-L! Go *mami*, go *mami*, go *mami*."

I see the head pop out.

"Look, Teeny, it's got the face of a girl. Keep pushing."

A shoulder pops out, and then the other.

"Honey, keep pushing. Don't be afraid of making rude noises."

"I did drugs all my life," Teeny is groaning. "This was not the time to quit."

"Be ready to catch the baby when it comes out," the midwife tells me.

"What? Look, I'm no Mike Piazza."

"Just do it," Teeny hisses.

So I get in position and Teeny gives one last, hard push . . . and this little baby slips out into my hands. This tiny, bloody little . . . human being. My baby. I made this thing. It's all hot and gooey. And it's a girl.

"Teeny, it's a girl!"

"Calm down, Mr. Leguizamo," the midwife is saying. "Here, cut the umbilical."

"What? If I'm doing all the work, what the fuck am I paying you for?"

You have to wait for it to stop pulsing before you cut it. I'm watching the heart beat in it. Ba-bump . . . ba-bump . . . ba-bump. And as soon as I cut it, my daughter was so present. Stared right back at me. Me and my little Boogie.

So Teeny and I are a mommy and daddy. And that new baby was like a sponge sucking every breath of fresh air, all the time, all the spontaneity out of our lives. No sleep, no sex, *nada*.

It wasn't that I wanted to have sex all the time. Teeny was just so tense I felt that she needed it. I used every trick in the book.

"Here honey, I brought you aspirin."

"But I don't have a headache."

"Ah-HA!"

"John, I've been with the baby all day. I just don't feel very sexy."

I give her my biggest, saddest, most imploring eyes.

"All right," she sighs, lying back on the bed. "But hurry, before she wakes up."

Trust me, I don't mind being hurried. It saves me the embarrassment of apologizing later.

But she's just lying there.

"Come on, Teeny, you gotta get into it a little," I whisper.

"But she's looking right at us," she says.

"Just pretend she's blind."

"Oh, that's so sad," she moans. "Now I can't anymore."

I roll off her.

"You know," I grumble, "I'm starting to feel like I'm getting replaced around here. Like I'm Number 2."

Teeny pats my cheek. "No you're not. You're Number 3. I'm Number 2."

But I finally got in there. And Teeny got knocked up again really quickly. And eleven months after Boogie appeared, God cursed me with a son. Little Bubba.

Yeah, you read right. My kids were born eleven months apart.

Latin twins.

What do you want? I couldn't wait. I was horny.

* * *

So all of a sudden I'm a dad with these extra mouths to feed and extra asses to wipe, and I'm thinking, "Dude, you better get out there and make some money." Besides, since I wasn't getting a lot of sex at home, I figured maybe if I went and made a movie I'd get to live vicariously. And if you tell Teeny I said that I'll poppeth a cappeth in thine asseth.

So I did *Moulin Rouge!* And it turned out to be a huge turning point in my life and my career. Not in a good way. After the success of *Freak* and the great experience I'd had doing *Summer of Sam*, the debacle of *Moulin Rouge!* was a total shock.

A studio head at Fox called me and said Baz was doing this movie. I met with them, and they really schmoozed me about how it was going be an Oscar-winning part. But there was a problem. I was signed up to do *Shaft*. John Singleton and Richard Price had written a big part for me in it and everything. When I got offered *Moulin Rouge!* I had to make a choice between them.

It reminded me of the time I turned down a big part in *Philadelphia*. I could've played Tom Hanks' lover. I decided he wasn't cute enough. So I went and did *Super Mario Bros.*

My thing with *Shaft* was what they call a play-or-pay contract—I'd have to buy my way out of it. I decided on *Moulin Rouge!*, and the producers of *Shaft* sued me. Rightly so. They used the same high-powered lawyer who'd sued Kim Bassinger over not doing *Boxing Helena*. Which scared me, because she lost that lawsuit. But luckily, where she was supposed to play the lead in that movie, I was just supposed to be the villain in *Shaft*, so the movie wasn't hanging on me. It was a great role and a really hard one to turn down, but Fox dangled that Oscar carrot in front of me and I jumped. I used the rhythm method and pulled out.

Working for a Hollywood studio is like fucking a porcupine.

A hundred pricks against one. They offered me a choice between Toulouse-Lautrec and the Narcoleptic Argentinean.

"I'm not going to be the sleeping fucking Argentinean! How many lines can a narcoleptic Argentinean have?"

But then he did have a great song, that big tango number, and it was a dance sequence I could've tore up. Still, I thought Toulouse was gonna be the part. I met with Baz about it.

"He's the heart of the movie, John. He's the heart, the soul of the picture. Just come to Australia and we'll work on it."

He gave me a stack of books on Toulouse. I pored through them, underlining key passages. Read his diaries and letters, looked at his photographs, studied all his paintings and the criticism of his paint-

Pretty much captures my mood during the entire shoot of *Moulin Rouge!*

Moulin Rouge! is the film where I look shorter on screen than in real life.

ings. If you're doing a historical figure, you can't really create it out of the air. I need to be inspired.

I felt I understood Toulouse. A dwarf who never got a break. He suffered from a lot of physical impediments, because his parents were first cousins. His shins were so thin that they snapped when he was very young. When they saw he wasn't growing properly they tried to stretch him. His father was an athlete, so weak little Toulouse was an embarrassment. He also had a very high-pitched voice, and spoke with a lisp, and drooled. People would later ask me why I made him sound like Daffy Duck, but that's how he spoke. I wasn't just doing another of my goofy voices. His parents were also wealthy and didn't have to work, so when Toulouse went out to work in the world it was a further embarrassment to them.

Oh, and another reason I knew I was right for the role. Despite being a dwarf, Toulouse was so well-hung the ladies nicknamed him The Tripod. When I read that, I knew I was made for this role. I could do it standing on my head. My *other* head. (When I told that to Michael Musto of the *Village Voice*, he had a hilarious response: "I guess no one was too loose for Toulouse.")

Even though the studio knew they wanted me, Baz made me audition for the part. He wanted Toulouse to have this very toffy British accent. So I locked myself in my hotel room, studying tapes of Jeremy Irons in *Brideshead Revisited*. I hired a speech coach to work on it with me. I wasn't worried about getting the lisp. I could do that in my sleep. But I worked really hard to get the British accent perfect. If I hadn't gotten on the wrong side of F. Murray Abraham, I coulda gotten him to help.

I auditioned for two hours on my knees, which is how I get most of my roles. This was at the Chateau Marmont in L.A. Two fucking hours on my knees in front of a video camera, with Baz pushing me to try everything bigger, louder, more extreme.

"More, John. Now with the lisp. Now without the lisp. Now make him more English."

And I nailed it. I beat out two really fine (and really British) actors for the part, Rowan Atkinson and Alan Cumming. I was very proud of that.

But then when I read the script, I wasn't so sure about that. The part was awfully small. No pun intended. But they kept telling me not to worry, it would grow. Still, I had shafted the *Shaft* people for this. And Spike had a really cool part for me in *Bamboozled*. I would've loved working with Spike again. And then I had to turn down a part in *Blow*, too. I turned down a lot of work to be in *Moulin Rouge!*, and then the part didn't grow.

In fact, it started to shrink.

"Baz, I don't even have a song in this movie. I'm not singing. I'm not even doing a dance number. Everybody else is. You know, I hate to be the fucking whiny little bitch . . ."

I whined to the producers, too.

"Yo, I'm turning down crazy shit to be here and nothing is happening. I don't understand what's going on. I been Bamboozled! Shafted! This Blows!"

Baz said, "Read those books, John. Find lines, find dialogue. We'll use it all."

I continued to bug and annoy everybody.

"Look what I wrote. You gotta give me a song. Everybody else has a song. I don't wanna whine anymore. Shut me up, please. I'm starting to hate myself."

And Baz finally did just that—he gave me a song just to shut me up. And the song I sing became the theme of the movie. "There was a boy / A very strange, enchanted boy . . ." They did a whole reshoot to make it the signature of the movie. I sang it pretty fucking well, too.

I ended up writing Toulouse's big speech, too. I took it from Toulouse's letters. The scene where he tells Christian, "Christian, you may see me only as a drunken, vice-ridden gnome whose friends are just pimps and girls from the brothels, but I know about art and love, if only because I've longed for it with every fiber of my being." I wrote that scene, and Baz put it in the movie. It completely explains Toulouse and his relationship to Christian.

Unfortunately, it comes practically at the end. Toulouse is totally missing from the middle of the movie.

I don't understand what happened. I don't really care what happened. It was just a really crushing career moment for me. One of the darkest moments I've had. To have come from doing *Summer of Sam* and *Freak* and have all these other big projects offered to me, and then to spend almost a year of my life on this skimpy little role.

I left for Australia when my daughter was four days old because they said they were ready to shoot. I get down there and they're not shooting for two weeks. I'm thinking, "What the fuck is going on?" And then Baz's father dies, on what was supposed to be the first day of shooting, so there's another postponement. Baz had this thing printed on the tags we all wore to get onto the Fox lot:

The show must go on—it's a matter of life and death.

And I'm thinking, "Yes, and at whose expense every time?"

Then Jim Broadbent's wife took ill and we had to postpone further. Then Nicole Kidman broke a rib rehearsing. (She ultimately broke two ribs and a knee doing this movie.)

And now I'm praying, "Oh God, please don't prolong this movie anymore."

And then I watched as everybody else's parts grew while mine shrank. Which bugged me even more.

"Oh my God, how the fuck is this happening to me? Have I been that much of an ass all my life? This movie is killing me."

I felt it was some Catholic punishment meted out to me. So I tried to follow Adrien Brody's example and rise above it. I put all my free time to good use. I saw a lot of Australia, learned a lot about the Maori and aborigines. Racism in Australia is really severe and harsh. Australians are very generous people. It's like America was in the 50s. But with the same racism. I saw how the aboriginal people are really getting the short end of the stick there. They're in ghettos, just like black folks here. I went to the Maori and aboriginal festivals, and they're doing hip-hop and breakdancing and playing the blues.

The funny thing is that despite all that, white Australians are really good people. Very warm, very friendly, very relaxed. "No worries, mate," is their favorite thing to say, and they mean it. It really made me wonder how they could just turn off that one section of their brains and be so racist, because they're so big-hearted in every other way. I don't know if it's hypocrisy or schizophrenia.

I loved to hear them speak. They have really cute slang for everything. Breakfast is "breaky." Costume is "cosi." They call you "runt" all the time, especially if you're an American male. And under six feet tall. They have all these sayings that reminded me of how American Southerners talk. "That's as slippery as a butcher's penis." "I was hornier than a five-dicked dog." "It went off like a bucket of prawns in the noonday sun."

When it became obvious that I was going to be stuck in Australia for a long, long time, I flew Teeny and Boogie down there. I was not going to be away from my family for all that time. And I wrote like a motherfucker. I started writing *Sexaholix*, and I started writing a couple of screenplays, including *Undefeated*. Because I knew that spending all this time on this tiny part was going to hurt my career. If you miss your opportunity when you're hot, you lose out.

And I was right. I came back to the U.S. after a year and I was cold as a shark's balls. I had no movies coming out because I hadn't banked anything. I had to rebuild from scratch.

But when we were working, we worked like maniacs. Baz was given an enormous budget for *Moulin Rouge!*, like four or five times what he'd had to do *Romeo + Juliet*. He had a lot of money and time to burn, and he did. Those lavish, beautiful sets designed by his wife, Catherine. Those costumes. The giant cancan number.

And oh my God, the crazy camera angles. There are as many as twenty-seven angles in some scenes. Which means you had to do the scene over and over and over and over. I mean, I love doing multiple takes. But a lot of angles, I don't know about that. They reset the cameras, you do it again. And they reset the cameras again. And you're like, "We gotta do this scene again?" You're married to making the same movements, over and over and over again, so that they can cut between them. You're not acting anymore, you're just repeating. You lifted your hand over here, you have to do it again, on the line. It becomes rote. It kills all the feeling. Though it did make everything look grand and operatic.

Now, Spike knows how to shoot. He puts two cameras up, shoots the scene from two angles at once, and then he can marry those two shots however he wants.

But Baz can whip you into a frenzy. He can make you believe. And he gives it everything he has himself. Which is good, because he demands an awful lot. After *Spawn, Moulin Rouge!* was the most physically painful movie I've ever made. I played the whole movie on my knees. They created this weird amputee prosthesis for me, with moveable ankles and little feet on the end. I had to go to the outback of Australia to have it done. The people out there speak the most extreme Australian I heard. It's a foreign language. It's not English. It's not even Cockney. People would mumble something at me, and I'd go "What?" And they'd mumble it again, and I'd say, "*What?*" You begin to wonder if you're just stupid. And so do they. You can see them getting annoyed with you.

Come to think of it, I couldn't understand a word Ewan McGregor said to me, either. Ewan is a nice guy. But in his normal speaking voice he has a Scottish accent that's as dense as a twenty-pound haggis. His accent makes Bob Hoskins' Cockney seem crystal-clear.

"John, na heath na moor na angus na hoot mon."

"*What?*"

I couldn't understand him unless we were both drunk.

So I'm out in the middle of fucking nowhere, sitting in my underwear with all these people walking in and out, and I've got my legs in

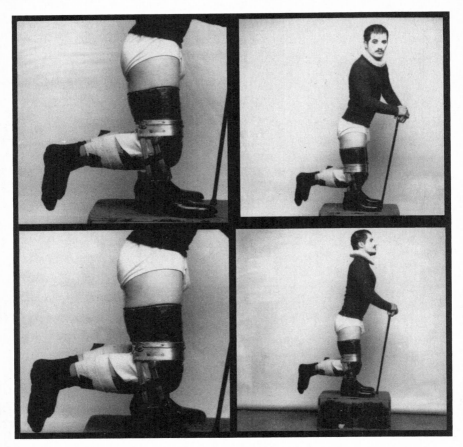

I played all of *Moulin Rouge!* on my knees. And I don't mean metaphorically.

this goo up to my knees to make the mold of my legs for the prosthesis. Which, when it was built, was really heavy plastic, because it had to be able to take my weight. They'd strap me into this contraption, kneeling, and I had to learn how to balance on it and walk by kicking each leg forward. Seen from the front, it really does look incredibly real. From the side, you could see my real legs hanging out the back, but they just erased that digitally in postproduction.

Of course, I had to be taken out of some dance sequences, because I couldn't move. Then again, being down that low all the time,

I got to peek up Nicole Kidman's skirt. Let me just say the curtains match the carpet. We were almost intimate. And we're still close. Her publicist talks to my publicist all the time.

I gotta say Nicole was cool to work with. She's really thoughtful and generous. When we had some of those long, really grueling days on the set, like sixteen-hour days, Nicole would bust out the caviar and champagne for the whole cast. And that was a big cast. She threw a big morale party after one especially long and painful week, too.

So there I am, on my knees every friggin' day, and the inevitable happens. My back gave out on me. I was writing at the computer one day, and suddenly I was paralyzed.

"Teeny, I can't move. I can't move. What the fuck happened? Is it something I ate?"

I went to see Annette, the physical therapist who was working Nicole's broken rib. "Your back is totally compressed," she explained. It was from kneeling in that contraption all the time. My back couldn't handle being forced into that unnatural pose day after day after day. She showed me stretches I needed to do to keep my back flexible. She saved my life.

That was the longest movie shoot of my career. And even when it was a wrap our job wasn't over, because then we had to do a lot of press-junketing for it. Because everybody knew this movie was going to be huge, win a lot of awards and shit. So Fox fired up an enormous publicity juggernaut for it. We all went to Cannes, where it played on the opening night of the festival, and they rolled out the red carpet for us. The biggest red carpet in the world. More like the Red Sea.

Doing the Cannes-Cannes for *Moulin Rouge!* Oh my God, what a media zoo that was. Not even a zoo, it was more like a media jungle, with thousands of autograph hounds and paparazzi all around us, acting like wild animals in a feeding frenzy. Elbowing each other in the throat, knocking each other's cameras to the ground, screaming

Doing the Cannes-Cannes for *Moulin Rouge!*

at us, slavering, gnashing their teeth. Sometimes when you're watching celebrities on the red carpet outside one of these events you'll see them get this funny look on their faces, like they're scared shitless? They are. It's fucking spooky having all those people screaming and pointing things at you.

And then, just to add to my pain and humiliation, it seemed like practically everyone else involved in that movie, from Nicole down to the grips and caterers, was nominated for an Oscar. Except me. I went to the awards ceremony, because that's what you do when you're part of a movie that's got that many nominations. But going to the Oscars without a nomination is like going to the prom without a date.

Harvey Weinstein avoided me the whole night. Because I'd said a crazy thing at his friend Hillary Clinton's birthday party at Radio City Music Hall, which was also a Democratic National Committee fundraiser for the Gore-Lieberman campaign. Harvey, *Rolling Stone*'s Jann Wenner, and some other big Dems in the entertainment industry had organized it. Michael Douglas; Bette Midler; Harrison Ford; Crosby, Stills & Nash, and other celebs came onboard, and Harvey asked me to speak, so I did. I just said the wrong thing.

"It's an old New York legend that Jews know how to satisfy their women," I told the crowd. "That's why it's gonna take a Jew [Lieberman] to lick Bush."

Hillary was aghast. The whole crowd was suddenly carved out of stone. Republicans cited me as an example of what a terrible influence the entertainment industry is on the children of America.

Harvey got over it eventually. They invited me to a 2004 fundraiser for the Kerry-Edwards campaign. I had a bunch of new dirty Bush jokes I was going to tell, but this time Whoopi beat me to it. I just said that I didn't believe a lot of Latin people were for the Republicans. Latins for Republicans is like roaches for Raid.

The whole *Moulin Rouge!* experience was so painful for me in so many ways that I can't watch the movie. I just can't watch it. It hurts. Teeny can't watch it either, because she was there with me, suffering through the whole thing. I love Baz, I still do. I'm sure some of it was beyond his control. I'm sure he didn't screw me on purpose. I'm sure it wasn't that I sucked so bad that they had to cut me out of the movie. I know that—because there wasn't enough there to cut out. The *New York Times* wrote, "John Leguizamo was completely wasted . . ." I was, like, "No shit."

For the first time ever, people on the street were telling me, "You look taller than in the film." I was afraid I was going to get typecast as the little-people actor. Play Hobbits, jockeys, elves the rest of my career. The life story of Hervé Villechaize.

But it made me grab my balls and say I'm a man.

"I'm not gonna let this shit ruin me," I told Bubba. "Your granddad's been crushed many times in his life, and he came back. You watch. I'm gonna rise above it too."

And my baby son smiled. It was a crooked smile. Almost a sarcastic smile.

And then he crapped his diapers.

Oh man, me and my son. A typical Leguizamo father-son relationship. A beautiful standoff.

With two little kids in the house I started to feel really ignored by Teeny. Just watching her breast-feed Bubba made me jealous. My son was getting tit all the time, and I wasn't getting any. It wasn't fair.

Teeny was always too tired for sex. She always had an excuse now, and his name was Bubba.

"You're hiding behind our son," I pouted one night when I wasn't getting any as usual.

"What is *that* supposed to mean?" Teeny asked.

I got up and started to get dressed.

"Forget it. Don't sweat it. I'm just gonna go out and hang with my friends. I'll holler at you."

Teeny sat up.

"John, grow up. You're always running away from him. Now who does that remind you of? Hmmm?"

"Leave my father out of this," I grumbled.

Teeny jumped up.

"You know what? *You* stay here, *I'm* going out. No offense, but if I don't talk to another adult soon, I'm gonna scream."

She got dressed. On her way out the door she smiled and told me, "Don't wait up."

And she was gone. It was a milestone in manhood: my first night home alone with my kids.

Boogie was an angel, sleeping peacefully. Bubba, on the other hand, was wide awake.

"Hey, little man," I say to him. "We're two guys alone together for the first time. We'll watch a little TV, have pizza. Here, have some beer."

And the little prick gets colicky on me. He cries one of those piercing screams that make you wanna rip out your ears. I pick him up in my arms, the way I've seen Teeny do a thousand times. I'm walking around, cuddling him, bouncing him, all that. And he just screams and screams.

"Holy shit," I say. "What the hell's going on? I fed you, I shared my beer with you. I know you can't talk, but what the fuck do you want?"

He just lies there in my arms and makes this horrible, angry face and blows raspberries at me and starts screaming some more.

"Oh, you think you can take me?" I say to him. "I see how you're trying to take Teeny away from me. Every time you breast-feed you put your little arm around her. Don't think I haven't noticed."

He quiets down a second and gives me a look. I realize it's the same shifty I-grew-up-in-New-York-City-too-motherfucker look I have.

"Wait till you've got children," I warn him. "I put a curse on you. *Sofrito cuchifrito que se joda un poquito.*"

And his eyes and his mouth fly wide open and he lets out another ear-shattering scream.

Now I'm bugging out. I have no idea what to do. Teeny's not there to take over like she always has.

So I call the only other person I know who's been in this mess before.

"Put him down and get out," Pops says to me. So I lay my son in his crib. "Close the door." I tiptoe out and shut the bedroom door behind me. My son's in there screaming his lungs out.

"Okay," my dad says, "now break open a bottle."

"He just ate."

"Not for him, *stupido*. For you."

So I pour myself a mild sensation.

"Pops, I don't know if I'm cut out for this fatherhood business. I haven't finished growing up myself yet."

"So now you finally appreciate all my hard work to raise you," my dad says. "You're lucky you had me as your father. I was never my father's favorite. No—and I was an only child. My father was afraid of his father, and I was afraid of him, and I wanted the same for you. But today kids talk back to you before you get a chance to say anything. You gotta kick ass from the start, or they'll ruin your life, take your dreams, and wreck your peace. Oh, Jesus Christ, I hated you Johnny. I hated you and loved you and wanted to kill you. You son of a bitch, I love you. Call me any time. Bye."

My Pops, king of mixed messages, going through male menopause.

Well, I knocked back my drink, rolled up my sleeves, marched back into the bedroom, and had it out with my son. I explained to him what was what. I told him in no uncertain terms who was boss around our house.

Him, Boogie, and Mommy.

We've gotten along fine ever since.

* * *

I came back from my tour of duty in Australia a changed man. I wasn't the naive, generous John Leguizamo of old. Now I was the bitter, angry, gonna-take-everything-for-my-damn-self John Leguizamo. Not gonna play any more games, no more Mr. Nice Guy.

The first thing I had to do was just get myself in some movies, get back to work, back on the screen. And I took whatever I could get. I did *Empire* and *Collateral Damage* and *What's the Worst That Could Happen?* and *Spun*, bam bam bam. I had to work, I had to rebuild.

That's why I decided to start directing, too. *Moulin Rouge!* completed the mental journey that had begun with *Spawn*. I wasn't going to let this happen to me ever again. No more clown suits. No more getting down on my knees. No more being at someone else's whim. I decided I had to take things into my own hands. At least that way, if things fuck up it's my own fault.

Still, at first I was throwing myself at anything, just to get back into the game. Went back to Mexico to shoot *Collateral Damage* with Arnold Schwarzenegger. And who was my character? A Colombian coke dealer. *Miami Vice*, supersized. As usual, I worked on him to make him more of a human being, less of a stereotype. He's a coke dealer who dreams of becoming a rap star. But I got all the Colombian people mad at me anyway because it was a stereotype. Writing letters to the Latin papers. I was excommunicated as a Colombian.

Arnold's a good man. He has a great sense of humor and he's a lot more gregarious than you'd have any reason to guess from his movies. He said crazy shit on the set. I don't want to blow up his spot, but it's true that he talked some wild shit to the ladies. I heard him tell one woman in the costuming department, "Your fingernail polish is pink. Are your nipples the same color?"

If I said something like that I'd get slapped. But he got away with it—most of the time, anyway—because they knew he was just kidding around. And because he's, you know, Ah-nold.

He'd say funny things to all the rest of us too. Once he was walking around without a shirt on, and we were all agog. The man is an awesome physical spectacle. He's not that tall—like five-ten—but he's wide as a Hummer. He's like three normal guys standing next to each other. He sees us gawking and says, "What are you all staring at me for? You bunch of homosexuals!"

I mean come on, he's from Austria. They're not known for the subtlety of their humor.

He came to Mexico with his personal gym-on-wheels, this giant trailer packed with weights and equipment. He let me train in there, but it was too demoralizing. All the machines were set to his weight, like five hundred pounds to my usual thirty-five.

"Thanks, man, but I can't work out in this gym. It's too depressing."

What's the Worst That Could Happen? is one from that period I'm not proud of. *That's* the worst that can happen to you—watching that movie. Totally off-the-rack formula Hollywood comedy, just another Martin Lawrence vehicle. I knew this movie was going to suck as we were making it. You can tell it's not going to be good if you're not having a good time doing it, and I was having a terrible time. It was a whole different type of terrible experience from *Moulin Rouge!* There, I was working with a genius, and what was demoralizing was not being able to have a big enough part to really make my mark in it. My part in this movie could not have been small enough. I would have been happy to disappear altogether.

For one thing, my character was awful. I made him funnier, ad-libbed a lot, and got to make him more interesting. But there was a problem, something that was keeping me from ad-libbing the way I wanted to.

That something was Martin Lawrence.

"John, it's already funny," he told me. "We don't have to make it funny. Don't add another line."

I knew what he was doing—cuz it was what I'd done back on *House of Buggin'*. He didn't want me to compete with him for the spotlight. Keeping the other comic down. His name in capital letters, mine in small print. I guess it was my penance.

I like *Spun*, though. Three completely fucked-up days in the lives of a bunch of speed freaks. I think it's a good little just-say-no-

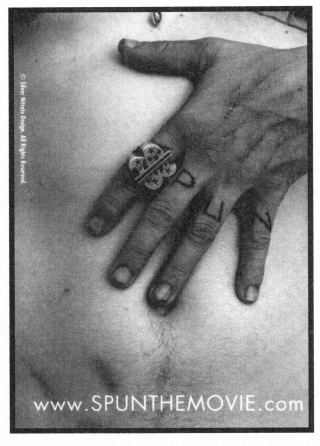

www.SPUNTHEMOVIE.com

Spun featured my most disgusting sex scene . . . so far.

to-crank movie. Everybody in the movie is bugged out. Everybody fucks up.

The cast was incredible. They put themselves way out over the edge. Mickey Rourke is sleazy as hell as the pervert cowboy who cooks up the shit. Of course, Mickey Rourke is sleazy as hell in real life, too. Mad ups to Mena Suvari for looking so ugly and scuzzy, with the green teeth and everything, and for taking a constipated dump on camera. I give props to everybody in that movie. Eric Roberts for playing a screaming queen, Deborah Harry for playing a bull-dyke phone-sex worker, Chloe Hunter for doing basically her whole part butt-naked and tied to a bed, Brittany Murphy and Jason Schwartz-man, all of them really put out.

I guess in the end that's why I agreed to jerk off into a sock. I didn't want the rest of them to think I was a pussy.

CHAPTER

19

B ut *Empire* . . . *Empire* brought me back. It saved my life and was the movie that really restarted my career. It did remarkably well for a small, independent film with a budget of maybe $3.5 million. Compare that to *Moulin Rouge!*'s 40 or 50 million. Less than a tenth of the cost. And it's a great film. It's crazy what you can do with no money and a strong story.

Though it only played on maybe eight hundred screens nationwide, which is very small distribution, it did extremely well. During the Christmas season of 2002, it performed better, percentage-wise, than the James Bond movie that was out at the same time. It became the highest grossing Sundance film of 2002.

And that was with a screwup in the scheduling. Originally it was slated to come out in February of 2003, but a hole appeared in Universal's Christmas schedule, so they rushed it into theaters. And when that happens, you're the redheaded stepchild. You don't get the stories in the magazines, because they don't have time. There was really no time for publicity. They did buy a lot of advertising, by independent film standards, but at Christmas time "a lot of advertising" isn't enough. What would be a lot of ads in February just gets lost in the Christmas movie blizzard. You need to spend crazy money to stand out. You gotta be schmearing it across the sides of buses and all over the subways, buying billboards in Times Square, all that. There wasn't time or money for that.

But despite everything, the film did well in the box office. And it got me tons of favorable notice. I was back, and the offers started pouring in again, and I could take charge of my career, pick and choose my projects.

Empire is the kind of realistic, character-driven story I like best. Franc Reyes, who wrote and directed it, is like me, a Latin guy from the 'hood. Only his neighborhood, the South Bronx, made my Queens look like Westchester. The gangstas he grew up with were *real* gangstas. The girls in his neighborhood could probably kick the shit out of the toughest hoodlums from mine. Franc wrote his life into the script. It's not his personal story, but it's based on a lot of people he grew up with, friends and family.

Some people compared *Empire* to an old Jimmy Cagney gangster movie, but that's a really shallow view of it. On the surface, I suppose the lead character, Victor Rosa, could be seen as just another gangster, just another Latin drug dealer from the ghetto. But he's no stereotype. Even though he does Latinize a line from *The Godfather* when he says, "Keep your homies close, but your beef closer." No way is this *Scarface* or *Miami Vice*.

I really wanted to play Victor. But at first they were just offering me the part of his best friend from the ghetto, Jimmy.

"No way. Give me the lead."

Empire brought me back, baby.

They said they had somebody else already cast for Victor.

"Well, take him out and put me in."

Then I got involved in casting the whole thing. I worked really hard with my manager and agent to get A-list actors interested, because the original actors were more like a B-movie cast. God bless them, but I had bigger plans for *Empire*. It was going to be the best movie I could help it be.

I went for the dream cast. I called around to people who knew and respected me, and a bunch of them came onboard. Isabella Rossellini, another Italian playing Latin on the Al Pacino plan. Peter Sarsgaard, Denise Richards. And Fat Joe as Victor's rival Tito. We got him in there to keep it real and, you know, add some weight to the proceedings. Then I convinced Franc to let us use the Spike and Baz method of workshopping a lot. He was cool about taking the best improvs from those sessions and working them into the script. Which made it a better movie all around.

I ended up being a co-producer on it. Even helped get investors, who are usually these rich business guys who want to be in show biz. Suckaz. How do you become a millionaire in show biz? You start out a billionaire.

I spent time hanging out with some drug dealers to research the part of Victor. I grew up with a lot of gangsters in my neighborhood, and I thought they were cool as shit. But I never did any of the runs with them, I just hung with them. They taught me how to rap to girls and how to fight. We played handball and basketball all day, smoked some doobies, but that's as far as I went. Somehow my parents' fear of drugs limited me just to smoking weed, while everybody else was doing acid, coke, PCP, angel dust.

For researching Victor, I hung out first with a Dominican couple in Washington Heights, a poor and mostly Latin neighborhood on Manhattan's way-Upper West Side, and then with two Puerto Rican brothers who were dealing heroin in Alphabet City. It took a few weeks to get them comfortable with the idea. We spent a lot of time in restaurants just talking while they sussed me out.

I did everything with those two brothers. Watched them pack the heroin into nickel and dime bags. Went with them to store their dope and their wads of cash in different people's homes in the neighborhood, spreading it around so if they got busted or ripped off they wouldn't lose too much from any one location. They used all sorts of normal, poor Spanish folks' homes in the neighborhood—even a French professor, a sanitation worker, like that. These people got taken care of for providing the service.

Victor explains how it works in the film:

"I keep my money in nine places. An apartment that belonged

to some old woman who can't afford to live there, bodegas, a blind man's place, a principal's office, all over. I pay their rent, give them some grocery cash, and in return they keep it safe for me."

I went out to Jackson Heights with the brothers to pick up their supplies. We went into a lot of bars where they'd be resupplying, and people would recognize me and start schmoozing me. It was bizarre. I got offered a lot of coke in the bathrooms of those bars. As reward for my good work on the screen, you know. Fortunately, I guess, coke is not for me. I'm already wired enough.

They showed me what the undercover cops look like. If you see a parked van with the windows all blacked out, that's the cops, because blacking out the rear window is illegal in New York. That kind of scared me. I started to worry about getting caught up in a bust. Because I couldn't use the I-was-only-doing-research excuse. That was played out when Winona Ryder got busted shoplifting. I wasn't afraid at first, but the more I learned about what I was doing with these guys, the more I got scared.

But they're impressive people, these two. They were kids, eighteen, nineteen years old, and already they'd been shot and arrested. They were so charming and bright, and great businessmen. They had maybe forty people working for them, a whole hierarchy worked out with promotions and raises and a 401(K) program. They take care of your family if you get shot and go to the hospital or get arrested. A complete system based on loyalty and payback.

The Washington Heights couple was very ambitious, very together about their entrepreneurial trip as well. They were putting their kids through the fanciest Upper East Side schools. They'd go and film the school plays, just like all the other parents. When the husband got arrested and put behind bars on Rikers Island, I went to visit him. He told me there's more drugs in there than on the street. The violence in there, people getting their throats cut and such, scared the hell out of him. He'd gotten popped because they got careless—they started using the heroin they were dealing, the classic dealer's downfall. You use, you lose.

In a lot of ways, their story was very similar to the story of the couple on whom Abel Ferrara based his movie *R-Xmas*, which I was going to star in for a while. Abel's a genius, but he's also a maniac. He's brilliant, but he creates a lot of chaos around him, and I couldn't deal with the disorganization. I'm too anal. I helped out with *R-Xmas* for a while, just trying to create some order. I started typing into the computer, fixing the script.

I'd say, "Yo, Abel, the structure's a little loose, a little sloppy."

He'd start riffing on the spot, making up new dialogue out of his head, brilliant ideas. I was so impressed.

"What would she say here?"

He'd go, "Well, she'd say . . ." yadda yadda, and it was hot.

Abel's one of the true characters of American filmmaking. He walks this world like Nosferatu. He looks like a bum. Hunched over, hair a mess, nails black, and he speaks in this guttural growl. He'd say, "You wanna beer?" Then he'd look in the fridge and there wouldn't be any, so he'd go around to all the open bottles and cans lying all around the place and pour all the dregs into a glass and hold it out to me. With those black nails.

"No, man, thanks. I don't drink."

"Really? When did ya quit?"

"Just now."

From then on I'd bring beers with me when I went to work.

In the end I couldn't commit the time to help him get that movie together. I had to go Catholic on it—I pulled out before I shot.

Oh how Abel yelled at me when I said I wasn't going to do it.

He flew into such a rage. And as usual, it was brilliant. I'm going to remember the things he screamed at me and use them in a movie someday.

We shot *Empire* in only twenty-two days. Which in one respect was plenty, because we were on location a lot of the time in the most dangerous neighborhood in the world, the South Bronx. It was okay during the day, kids playing in the streets, kind of nice. But as soon as the sun went down it was the O.K. Corral. I ran to my trailer and hid between takes at night. I'm not kidding. And I had three bodyguards to escort me back and forth. There were shootouts, catfights down the block. There was a sniper on the roof. The drug dealers came and threatened us, told us to get the hell out of the neighborhood because we were bringing in too many cops. I'd run to my trailer, turn out all the lights, and hunker down on the floor.

Audiences loved *Empire*. Latin people especially loved it to death. I got a lot of kudos for it, which really pleased me. In retrospect I was really glad I'd done Victor instead of the drug dealer role I was supposed to play in *Shaft*. In *Empire* the drug dealer isn't just in the script so that Samuel L. Jackson can kick his ass. He serves a larger purpose and tells a cautionary tale. Victor is this ambitious, driven guy who, because he's in the ghetto, turns to drug dealing as the most viable route to success. *Empire* raises the legitimate question of who's the bigger criminal and has the worse impact on society—the drug dealer in the Bronx who turns to crime because of his environment, or the Wall Street scam artist who rips people off for zillions simply because he can? Like one character says, if Victor had been born anywhere but the Bronx, he wouldn't have been a drug dealer, he'd be the CEO of a Fortune 500 company.

I played Victor against the usual stereotype. No cheesy movie-Latino accent, no hideous outfits. Because I'll tell you, the dealers I met weren't like that at all. They were sharp, organized, savvy. None of that *Scarface* crap.

But even with a movie like *Empire* you're going to hear from the Culture Police. The same kind of people who didn't like *Mambo Mouth* and *Spic-O-Rama*. The same ones who bitched about *The Sopranos* perpetuating bad Italian stereotypes. *Empire* was written and directed by a Latin man, produced by and featuring lots of Latins. And there's a certain segment of any minority community, usually the intelligentsia, who expect you to project only positive images of *la raza*. Like they think phony, all-positive stereotypes will cancel out the negative stereotypes.

But it doesn't work that way. Stereotypes are stereotypes, and the truth is the truth. *Empire* has a lot of truth in it. I'm proud of it. Fuck 'em if they didn't get it.

But I gotta eat. And so do my kids. And I wanted to make some money I could pour into Rebel Films, cuz I had plans.

So I did another big Hollywood film. And I made some of the craziest money I ever made, for being in a film where you don't even see my face. No makeup, no costumes, and I don't even interact with any other actors. Just me, alone, with a microphone, doing a wacky cartoon voice. Back to where I started on the 7 train.

I did the voice of Sid the Sloth in *Ice Age*, Fox's blockbuster smash hit of 2002. And I loved it.

What do you want? I never grew up. It's criminal that I'm a daddy. My kids should be looking after me. I love cartoons, comic books, animation, Japanese anime. I learned a lot of my comedy from Bugs Bunny. Watching those cartoons is a big reason I became a comedian. I wanted to be as funny as Bugs. Mel Blanc, who did Bugs and a million other cartoon voices, is the Brando of voiceovers. So when I got the opportunity to start doing some voiceovers myself, I leaped.

I started right after *Freak*, doing all the voices for a story in Rosie O'Donnell's series of cartoons for HBO. Then I did the voice of Rat #2 in *Dr. Dolittle*, which I thought was so-so. Then I did *Titan A.E.*, which bombed.

Then I did Sid in *Ice Age*, which was a giant success.

Voiceovers are a trip to do. The first time I did it I was so confused. You go into a recording booth by yourself. You slap the headphones on. Then you just stand there.

I was like, "You gonna show me the cartoon? Oh, no cartoon. So where are the other actors? Oh, no actors either. So I'm doing this alone? Reading the script by myself? Oh. This blows."

But then I realized how freeing it is. By the time I did *Ice Age*, it was so much fun for me not to be dealing with other actors and their problems, nobody saying no. No actor egos, no entourages, no hissy-fits, no sitting around in makeup. You just do it and do it till it rocks. That's the way I love to work anyway. I figured out that even though you're alone in the booth, you have to act out the scenes. If your character is supposed to be running, you run. If he gets hit, you bang yourself in the head. Whatever. That's how the voice comes to life.

I researched Sid sort of like I would any character. If a sloth could talk, what would it sound like? I must have tried out thirty different kinds of voices, but none of them felt right.

Then I bought some documentaries of sloths from the Discovery Channel. I'm watching them, and I notice that they make no noises at all. And they hardly move. Paint dries faster, and more entertainingly. Watching a pair of sloths mate is like watching the entire history of natural selection. Two hours of sloths silently mating and foraging and I thought my VCR was broken.

"Damn, there's no sound. And it's stuck in slow motion."

Near the very end of the tape, the narrator talked about how sloths store food in their cheek pockets. Eureka. If they could talk, they'd sound like they have their mouths stuffed with food, right? So I came up with a voice for Sid that was kind of a modified Sylvester the Cat slur, like thizth.

I called Chris Wedge, the director, and said, "Hey, lithzen. Ithz Sthid. I found it. Sidzth talkin' to you."

He loved it. And the rest is filmmaking history.

Ray Romano took the opposite approach. He figured that even though he was playing a woolly mammoth, it was a woolly mammoth that thought and spoke like a human, so why not use a normal voice. Later, he told an interviewer, "You know John. He's just showing off."

Love you too, guy.

They recorded me doing all my Sid lines first. Then they gave Ray my recorded stuff, and he did his Manfred part to my voice. Then I rerecorded my lines, and then he rerecorded. It sounds weird, but it works. I'd hear his lines and come up with ways to tweak mine, sharpen the jokes. Then he'd hear my responses and come up with ways to tweak his bits. Then they added Dennis Leary to the mix, and he recorded his lines as Diego the sabertooth tiger to our voices. By the end of the process, it totally sounds like conversation.

Only then, when they've got all the voices down, do they actually draw the pictures. They draw to the emotional cues in your voice. That's how they get it so accurate and lifelike. It's exactly the opposite of the way I always thought it was done. It's a v-e-r-y slow process. Sloths fuck faster. *Ice Age* took four years.

There's another reason I love doing voiceovers. Unless I'm mistaken—and I could be, since it was my agent who told me this— my deal for *Ice Age 2* made me the highest-paid Latin actor in the world.

Go Johnny! Go Johnny! Get stupid! Get stupid!

Hey, don't hate me. I've got two kids.

Ice Age and Empire rocked the movie theaters. I felt like I was back, big time. I was a success and making crazy paper. But I was still a workaholic. My Pops beat that into me good. It doesn't matter how well you think you're doing, you still gotta work. Forty-eight hours a day, fourteen days a week.

When you grow up poor, success never seems quite real. You keep expecting The Man to show up. He'll look like the Boss in Cool Hand Luke. A mean peckerhead in reflector shades.

"You there, Le-goosy-ammo. You enjoying all that fame and fortune, boy? Good, cuz now we gonna take it all away from you."

"Yassuh Boss."

I decided I had reached the point in my film career where I could take complete charge. I wanted to direct.

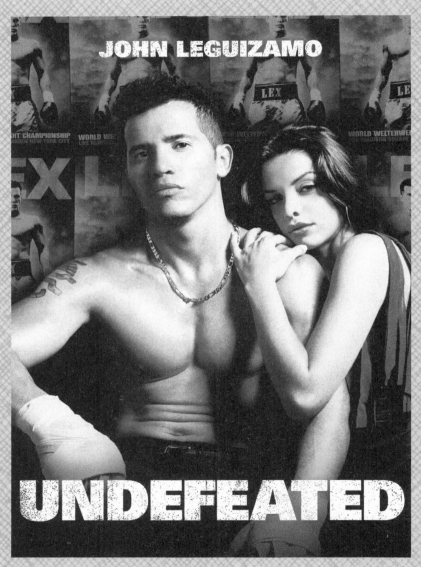

JOHN LEGUIZAMO

LEX

UNDEFEATED

I produced, directed, wrote, starred, catered, and posed.

I know it's a cliché. Everyone wants to direct. What were Mother Theresa's last words? "I wanted to direct . . ."

I'd been wanting to do a boxing movie for a long time. I've boxed now and then, sparred a little, and I loved it. So while I was in Australia with all that time on my hands I wrote a boxing movie.

And it sucked. Fight pictures are one of the most cliché-ridden genres of them all. Fight pictures and gangster movies. It's hard not to fall into all the traps. You really have to resist the impulse to do another *Rocky*.

I knew there was an interesting story in the Faustian bargain young fighters have to make. Fighters are almost all from poor backgrounds. They're almost all black or Latin. If you come from that sort of background and you want to be a champion, what would you sacrifice to make it? And if you do make it, how much are you willing to pay to stay on top?

That's the movie I wanted to make, but I just couldn't get the script right. So we brought in another writer, Frank Pugliese, to work on it. He went through lots of drafts before we got it down.

Originally we called it *Infamous*, but it was later changed to *Undefeated*. And HBO picked it up and let me direct and produce it with Kathy DeMarco, my partner at Rebel Films. And I starred in it, too. By the time we were done, I did everything but cater that movie.

Even with all of Frank's input, there's still a lot of me in the lead character. Lex Vargas is a Latin guy from Jackson Heights. When his dad dies, he and his brother are left running the corner bodega. But Lex is a good fighter and he knows he can be the champ and rise up out of the neighborhood. Then his brother is killed in a robbery, and Lex is left with the store. He has to make a choice: live the rest of his life behind the counter, or go for his dreams.

He goes for it. But as he becomes more successful, he finds it

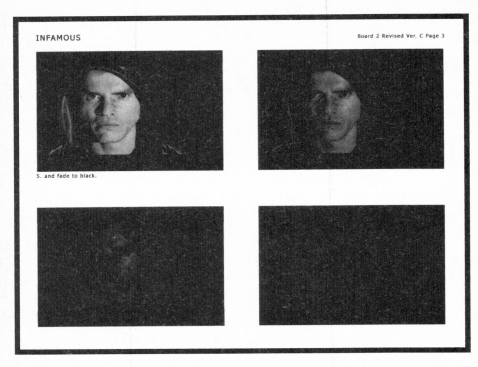

INFAMOUS

Board 2 Revised Ver. C Page 3

5. and fade to black.

I loved the enigmatic ending of *Undefeated*.

harder and harder to keep up his friendships with his old gang. He sells out his trainer and everybody from his old life to get fame and power. Then he realizes what a lonely journey that is. But he still doesn't want to go back to being poor and unknown.

So how does he balance all that? Those are things I've dealt with a lot in my own life. I felt a real connection with this character. Lex meets a hot Latin girl who's at the start of her own career and just as ambitious as he is. He wants to be the world-champion boxer, she wants to be the next J-Lo. Like me and Cathy, or me and Evelyn. But not me and Teeny, thank God.

It's a pretty classic fight-movie problem. He's forced to decide between throwing a big fight, which will make him a ton of money, or sticking to his principles and maybe killing his career. The new spin I put on it is that it's Lex, not his manager, who suggests throwing the fight.

Lex knows from the start that he wants to be a champion. I wasn't so organized about it in my life. It wasn't like I was dreaming of becoming a movie star when I was a kid. I just wanted to have fun, tell jokes, impress the girls. I didn't start studying theater seriously until I was in college. I knew by then that I wanted to be an actor. That helped me channel and focus everything I had.

Otherwise, I don't know what I would have become. I studied psychology. Maybe I would have been a social worker. But even that's aiming for the stars where I came from. My friends all became doormen and cab drivers and sanitation workers. A lot of them joined the marines. There was a point where I was going to sign up too. Thank God I got cold feet when I got to the recruiting office.

"What can I do for you, son?"

"Oh, uh, nothing, Mr. Huge Imposing Bullet-headed Sergeant, sir. I, um—this isn't Elegant Lady Nail Salon, is it? Silly me. Ta-ta."

What I'm saying is that wanting to be a comedian and actor saved me, the way wanting to be a champion prizefighter saves Lex. But you pay a price.

I had some real-life boxers in mind as models for Lex. There's a little of Macho Camacho and Cesar Chavez in him, and an early draft I abandoned was based on the controversy surrounding Bronx fighter Luis Resto and his manager Panama Lewis. I decided that story was too dark. Resto is sometimes called the "dirtiest" fighter in recent boxing history, and both he and Lewis got banned from the ring for life for doing things like removing the padding from his gloves.

In the end, Arturo "Thunder" Gatti, the explosive welterweight with a career of really dramatic highs and lows, was probably the biggest inspiration. I met him briefly. I also got to meet Angel Manfredy, who beat Gatti once, and Micky Ward III, the latest in a long line of

Great White Hopes. Nice to see there was still one Irish boxer out there representing for all the white people.

I wanted to make sure we portrayed Lex as a smart guy. Because all the boxers I met were sharp. They usually aren't punch-drunk palookas. There are more Muhammad Alis than Michael Spinkses. Smart, funny, humble—the coolest jocks I ever met. And they're all true gentlemen. There's a classiness to boxers you don't see as often in other athletes. I guess because you go at it alone, all the time, and you have to be the best you can be. Every time you go out there in the ring you could be beat down. I guess that's what makes them so humble.

A few months before *Undefeated* aired, I flew to Las Vegas to do joint promotions with Fernando Vargas, because HBO was going to premiere the movie on the same night that Vargas was fighting Fitz Vanderpool. Vargas was only twenty-five, but he was smart and savvy. He ad-libbed some funny bits with me. They had the two of us do the press conference together like two fighters would—Vargas v. Vargas, cross-promoting. We did a funny thumb-fight, then sat together to watch his nemesis Oscar De La Hoya fight.

Unfortunately we had to leave out a lot of fight-world details. Like the things fighters will do to make their weight class. Erik Morales once weighed in at 128 instead of 126 pounds. He had an hour to lose two pounds. He used enemas, diarrhetics, a sauna—and they drained a pint of blood. They had to carry him back to the scales, but he made his weight.

Gatti was always fighting his weight too. He once came in a pound over and started to strip naked, right there in front of the press. Gatti is very well-hung. Let's just say all the Thunder isn't in his right hook. All the female journalists in the joint started squirming and fanning themselves with their notepads. All the guys looked away in shame.

"I am not a man. I do not have a penis. It's just a large clit."

We did not have a huge budget to make *Undefeated* with—maybe 8 million dollars, when all was said and done. So to make the caliber of movie we wanted to make meant that a lot of extremely talented people really had to dedicate themselves to it. I was so gratified and honored by everyone's commitment.

We shot most of it on location in Jackson Heights, and some in Manhattan. My cinematographer Enrique Chediak and Kathy Aric did the location scouting. Unfortunately, the film industry in New York is in such a bad state that people like Kathy can't find work. And they're not allowed to work out of state, because the unions in other states freeze them out. But she found us amazing places to shoot. Like a bar with a giant aquarium in the men's room. That's a gay bar in Chelsea. I never would've found that spot. If you know what I mean.

What?

Man, you wear a wig and hot pants a few times in your career, everyone thinks you're gay.

We auditioned a lot of people, and got some great actors to be in the movie. Robert Forster (the white guy in *Jackie Brown*), a real sweetheart, and Omar Benson Miller, Nestor Serrano, Clifton Collins. . . . The whole cast was great to work with.

I worked my ass off, pretty literally, to get in shape and train with real boxing pros to make my fight scenes as authentic as they could be. Marty Jaramillo was my trainer. I grew up with him—he's from Flushing, and a friend of the family. He trained the hell out of me to get me in physical condition. He got me boxing coaches—Devon Cormack and Hector LaRoca, who trained Gatti.

For the first three months I worked just a few hours a day with Marty on building up my physical strength and stamina. Even that was killing me at first. And then we really got down to it, training me to look and move like a real boxer. We trained at the famous Gleason's

Gym in the old waterfront and warehouse area of Brooklyn they call DUMBO (Down Under the Manhattan Bridge Overpass). I would start out the day training with Marty at another gym near my apartment in Manhattan, work out maybe an hour with him, then run a little bit, then get on my bike and ride over the bridge all the way to DUMBO. I'd train and choreograph the fight scenes there until three p.m., then ride my bike home. So it was nine a.m. to four p.m. nonstop physical activity, every day, for four months.

By the end of that I was in ridiculous shape. I was able to do inhuman feats during the shooting. Forget bending steel bars with my buttocks. By the time we were ready to shoot I could crack walnuts with my eyelashes.

Because of our small budget, we had to shoot all our big boxing match scenes in one long day at Madison Square Garden. I had to do all three rounds of one fight, fifty punches per round, plus scenes from two other fights. We just couldn't afford to book the Garden for more than one day. Plus we could only hire two thousand extras, which wasn't nearly enough of a crowd, because the Garden seats twenty thousand. We had to fill in with a lot of cardboard cutout people. My most loyal fans. They'd sit through anything. Too bad we couldn't create crowds digitally, like they did for *Gladiator*. We didn't have an $80 million budget. This was a Rebel Films production. We had to squeeze every nickel.

And I boxed for real. None of that phony movie-boxing stuff that you can tell is fake. We were connecting with our punches. It's as close to *Raging Bull* as I could make it. Maybe their scenes are a little more poetic than ours, but I got hit a lot. There was one moment when I dipped when I wasn't supposed to and the other guy clocked me. I saw lightning, and little Amanda Parsons birdies circled my head again. I was so pissed—at myself mostly, but also at him, and everybody else in the place.

"John, are you all right?"

"Don't talk to me."

Crew started hovering around.

"John, you okay?"

"Don't talk to me. Everyone get away from me." I was either going to cry or go nuts. Or both. I wanted to quit right there, and fire everybody else too. I needed a few moments to gather myself.

We also kept practicing another punch, where he'd hit me with an uppercut. You never see uppercuts in fight movies—and I found out why. It's impossible to choreograph correctly. It's too painful for the guy taking the hit. He kept snapping my head back, and I couldn't relax my neck enough to go with the blow.

After a while of trying, the other fighter said, "I can't do this to you anymore, man."

The stunt man who was coaching me on it agreed.

"It's not looking right, and if you make it look any more right it's gonna be dangerous."

Toward the end of the day I snapped from all the pain and humiliation. I uncorked a jab to the other fighter's chin, which jerked his head back and made his eyes water. I didn't do it on purpose, but I still felt vindicated.

"Hey, I can hurt him, too. It's not just me who's a pussy."

But I took a lot of hits. And screwed up my rotator cuff in one shoulder throwing punches. I hated boxing by the end of that movie.

Still, it was fascinating to direct and star at the same time. The director in me hated the actor. And the actor in me was always trying to get over on the director. For a long time I had sort of directed myself in other people's movies anyway, studying myself in the monitor between takes. But it was a whole new experience to be directing *other* actors while I was acting myself. I'd step out of Lex's head and go into director mode, which meant getting into the other characters' heads. Then I'd have no time to get back into Lex's character. It burned me out, but it worked—maybe because Lex and I were pretty close in the first place. *Undefeated* debuted on HBO in the summer of 2003 and I loved the final product. I still do. I'm very proud of *Undefeated*. I love the montage in the middle of the movie where we show Lex spiraling downward. We didn't want to have montages in it at first, because that's another 1940s fight picture cliché— the spinning newspaper headlines, the magazine covers, the pages being ripped from the calendar, all that. But you have to let the story tell itself and go where it wants to go. *Freak* had done that—it wanted to be much darker and more personal than I wanted it to be. I just wanted to be funny, but the show wanted me to dig deeper and ex-cavate more painful moments in my past. You have to listen when the story is telling you where it wants to go. *Sexaholix* did that too. You have an idea, and you have to shape it, but if you try to exert too much intellectual control over it you're going to ruin it. So when it became clear in the editing process that *Undefeated* needed that montage, we had to go back and shoot some new scenes for it and dig up some footage that we didn't think we'd use.

I also love the abrupt, enigmatic ending. Enrique came up with that. I hated the original ending: a horrible, smiley-face postfight scene where Lex is hanging out with his friends again and it's clear that he didn't throw the fight. The way it ends now, you don't know what he's going to do. It's a very European ending. When we tested it for audiences, they were divided about it. Half of them loved it, and half of them hated it. Which I figured was good.

We were hoping for another Emmy nomination, but we were up against some amazing competition that year. The art of making mov-ies for TV has come so far. HBO in particular has raised the bar really high. In 2003 you had things like *Normal*, William H. Macy in *Door to Door, Live from Baghdad, My House in Umbria*. Tough crowd.

Producing, writing, acting, and directing your own film is either pure egomania or the best way to follow your artistic vision. Maybe it's both. Whatever else people think of it, I'm proud that *Undefeated* succeeds in showing that Latin people aren't all just about ghetto stories. We can be successful. Because if you're Latin, you can't just be *good*—you gotta be ridiculously entertaining. You basically gotta do it all yourself. Write it, direct it, produce it, cater it, watch it, pay admission, and like it.

I don't know, maybe all those hits I took made me punchy. Because at the same time that I was making *Undefeated*, I decided to take *Sexaholix* to Broadway. I don't want to say I'm the hardest-working man in show business. But Mr. Brown was looking over his shoulder.

I whipped *Sexaholix* out of nowhere. I started writing it in Australia during all my *Moulin Rouge!* downtime and it just flowed. I'd always wanted to do a relationship piece. I was dying to do a war-of-the-sexes show and talk about dealing with the wimmins. And it was an opportunity to explore all my screwing up in that department. Now that I was with Teeny, my soul mate, I could look back on it all more objectively.

And I got death in there, too. Yeah, sex and death, the two Big Subjects. I'm up there with Tolstoy. And Woody Allen.

Looking back, I can see how my shows have kept getting more and more personal. *Mambo Mouth* is just a collection of characters. *Spic-O-Rama* is my dysfunctional family in camouflage. *Freak* is much more direct and open about my fucked-up childhood and my father's abusiveness and all that. And *Sexaholix* is as flat-out true as I could be about my sex life and relationships. It was like I had to keep writing and writing to get closer and closer to revealing myself. Peeling the layers of the onion.

I don't know why it worked out that way. Most writers seem to do the opposite. Their early work is the most directly drawn from their own lives, and then as they run out of things to write about themselves they start writing more about other people. I don't know why I did it backward. Typical of me, I guess. I did it my own fucked-up way, and it worked out.

So *Sexaholix* is me, John Leguizamo, in the present day, no bullshitting around. I used Serge's real name this time. Pissed him off again. I'll be buying his love back for the rest of my life. And I played Teeny's parents really broad, exaggerating their whiteness for comic effect. So *Sexaholix* not only pissed off my own family again, but Teeny's too. It's a good thing I'm making so much money. Christmas is a bitch.

I was a little antsy about taking *Sexaholix* to Broadway. Doing raunchy material there can be dicey. *Puppetry of the Penis* was happening at the same time, but that was off-Broadway. You have to be careful on Broadway. You get a lot of tourists, family groups, senior citizens. Sometimes for the matinee there'll be more wheelchairs and walkers parked in the lobby than at St. Vincent's Hospital. You don't want half the pacemaker section going code-blue on you cuz you said a cuss word, like those people who had heart attacks watching *The Bible According to Mel Gibson. Full Metal Jesus.* Whatever it was called. I didn't even tell the producers the show was called *Sexaholix* until it was too late for them to back out.

Another thing that was a little dicey about doing it on Broadway was that Teeny and her family and all her friends came. I was used to insulting my own family on stage and paying the price later, but Teeny's family and friends are so different from mine—they're like Jew WASPs, the whitest Jews I ever met—and I didn't know how they'd react. It made me kind of nervous up there, wondering if any of them were in the audience, gritting their teeth, sharpening their knives.

To make things worse, Teeny's dad was hard of hearing, so he made her bring him back like three or four times so he could catch the whole thing. Through the whole show he's going, "What'd he say?"

"He said 'pussy,' Dad," Teeny would whisper.

"What'd he say?"

"He said 'pinga,' Dad."

"What the hell does that mean?"

"I'll explain later, Dad."

Afterward, she asked him what he thought of it.

"I'd like it better if he didn't mumble," her dad said. "And why can't he speak English? Why's he speaking Mexican all the time?"

With the exception of my family and maybe Teeny's, *Sexaholix* was a huge success. Sold out sold out sold out. I did it for six full months. Six months, seven shows a week. That still kills me. Seven shows a week is inhuman. It was doing so well the producers wanted to extend the run, but I couldn't. You get so tired. If I could have done five shows a week, I could've lasted a year. But the seven shows a week murderlized me. On top of that, I tore my hamstring early in the run, so I had to go to a lot of physical therapy. It was tough. (Tiny violin playing in the background.)

It's not that I got bored with the show. Like the others, it kept changing. I'm never satisfied with my work anyway, so I keep messing with it. I kept editing *Sexaholix* until I had it down to a lean, mean laughter-and-tears machine. Oh man, if I could go back through

Pissing everybody off again in *Sexaholix*.

all the movies I've been in and edit those fuckers the same way . . . they'd all be shorter and tighter. All of them. But you can't. It's finished. In my plays, I can edit and edit and rewrite and rewrite, so it stays fresh for me.

It's more the physical punishment. I get really tired. My body gets so worn down. I ain't a young pup anymore. And the lifestyle I have to lead when I'm doing a long run gets really tedious. I live like a fucking monk. I mean a nonfucking monk. I can't talk or smoke, to save my voice. I can't drink. I can't have coffee. I have to keep in shape, stretch a lot. Because my body starts to hurt from the adrenaline that pumps through it every night on stage, that fight-or-flight combo of sheer exhilaration you get from performing in front of an audience, and abject terror you get from performing in front of an audience. It's a rush when you're up there, but afterward it leaves you totally drained and sore. And then you have to do it all over again the next night, and the next, and the next. Your muscles start to ache from doing the same movements every night. It's like full-body carpal tunnel syndrome after a while. I learned a bunch of kung-fu stretches that helped—until I hurt myself pushing them too far.

Yeah, theater may look like a job for pussies, but try it sometime. It takes a real man, bud.

Sexaholix went through mood swings, just like the other plays. It depends on how I'm feeling, what kind of day I've had. Like if I'm in a cranky mood the angry parts of the show really stand out. Other nights the more touching parts will be emphasized, or the funnier parts. And the audience still has an impact on me. Not as much as my early days, now that I'm a seasoned Broadway performer. I know what to expect. It used to kill me when a matinee audience would sit there quietly through the whole show, then jump up and give me a standing ovation at the end. I'd hate them. I'd be like, "Where were you at the rest of the show?" Those quiet audiences used to make me angry and hostile, and then I'd give more, really put out to get some kind of response from them. You can literally hurt yourself that way. And then you've wasted your voice for the evening show.

Now I know how to deal with all that. Fuck 'em if they don't laugh at my jokes.

Sexaholix was the first of my plays I toured around the country. I'd always felt like my humor was too New York. No one would understand it in Minneapolis or wherever. But I'd tested the waters a little—with *Spic-O-Rama* in Chicago, and small runs of *Freak* there and in San Francisco—and they'd gone really well. And people all over the country liked the HBO specials. So I figured it was time.

I toured *Sexaholix* to twenty-four cities. It was like the Rolling Stones or something. I felt like such a rock star. Phoenix, Seattle, San Francisco, Houston, Atlanta, Dallas. All over the map. It was wild. And people dug it. They were screaming and rowdy and talking back—just like in New York. Tampa, Austin, Portland—I couldn't believe the audiences. God they were fun. Sometimes I'd get boos and hisses from the Latinas in the crowd at the part where I break up with Evelyn and take up with Teeny, the white girl. But that was okay. You do material like mine, you learn early on how to deal with hecklers, how to make it all part of the show.

A few cities were a bit strange. The Minneapolis audience was oddly quiet—except for one drunk white lady who wanted to come up on stage and tell dirty jokes. People booed and we had to sit her down.

I got nominated for another Tony Award. I was up against two other solo shows—Elaine Stritch and Bea Arthur. That's right—me against the Golden Girls. I thought I was a shoo-in. I was the only one nominated who could climb the steps to the stage.

But I lost out again.

Losing is okay. It's good for you. Like eating your vegetables. It makes you strong.

I wasn't bitter. I just happened to be wearing a sign saying I DEMAND A RECOUNT when *People* took my picture.

So I still haven't won a Tony. The HBO version of *Sexaholix* got nominated for another Emmy, but we didn't get it. Maybe the committee was remembering the speech I gave when I won it for *Freak*.

"I don't deserve this. I didn't deserve herpes either."

I don't know. Sometimes I really am my own worst enemy. Sometimes I really am just a Puck-up.

One night in the midst of all the *Undefeated* and *Sexaholix* busyness I was tucking Boogie and little Bubba into bed, and Boogie said, "Daddy, can a girl be a bastard?"

"What? Who said that to you?"

"Grandma."

"Which Grandma?"

"Both."

Grrr. That's what I got for letting those old ladies around my kids. Plotting against me behind my back. I was used to that from my mom, but Teeny's mom too? Oh, the treachery. The effrontery. The balls on them old broads.

"Now, Boogie," I said, "you know I love your mother too much to marry her. Go to sleep."

As I closed the door, I heard her say to her brother, "We'll just tell everybody we're adopted."

The little Judas brat. Turning on me.

But she didn't need to worry. Teeny and I were going to be together always. Always in love, always loyal.

Why?

Cuz we weren't married.

Sure, marriage had come up. We'd been together eight years at that point. We had two kids. Our moms had been dropping hints for years. Broad hints. Hints like anvils falling out of the sky.

We'd talked about it. Discussed what we both brought to the table.

She was Jewish. I wasn't.

She came from money. I did too—now.

She went to the best schools. I knew where they were.

See? We were perfectly matched. Soul mates on permanent booty call.

And Teeny knew I wasn't a bad father. I give my kids everything— private school, trust funds, a Jamaican nanny. "Children, get me my smokes. And roll me a fatty from your father's stash." I even gave them a way into the white world. They were rich little Jewaricans. Half Latin and half Jewish. So when they grew up they'd be able to dance *and* balance their own checkbooks. Credits, debits, *wepa!* Credits, debits, *wepa!*

We just never thought we needed to make it official and get married. We knew where we stood. We didn't need a license. We weren't going fishing.

I know you're thinking it was just me. I'd failed once at marriage, so I was gun-shy. I'd grown up watching what happens when a marriage falls apart horribly, and I didn't want to do that to Teeny and our kids. I still hadn't grown up and couldn't handle the responsibility.

Fuck you. Teeny felt the same way I did. Marriage just wasn't a big deal to her. She knew we loved each other and our kids. She had faith in me, and in herself, and in us. She didn't care what our mothers thought, or all her married friends. She thought it was kind of funny when her friends stumbled over what to call us.

"This is John. He's Teeny's . . . um . . . manfriend? Bedmate? Live-in sperm donor? Designated fuckpal? Just what is the correct term these days?"

And then came *Sexaholix*. And I'm on Broadway, and touring all over the country, and on HBO, telling millions of total strangers how Teeny and I were never gonna get married. Nope, no sir, no way. Didn't want to, didn't need to. Nuh-uh. Negatory. Not gonna happen.

And that's when everyone started to meddle big-time.

Teeny took her best friend to see the show, and afterward she was, like, "Well? What did you think?"

"Oh, he was great," her friend said. "Very . . . earthy. But funny. Really funny. . . . But honey, don't you think it's a little insulting the way he keeps saying he's never going to marry you? Doesn't that make you feel a little . . . cheap?"

And then my mom got on me about it.

"Listen, John, I don't like the way you say you're never gonna marry Teeny. Can't you cut that part out?"

"Mom, I can't cut that out. It's a big part of the show."

"But think of the children, John. *Ay, pobrecitos!* Do you want everyone in the world to know my grandchildren are bastards?"

"They're not bastards, Ma. They're just . . . unwedlocked."

She sucked her teeth and shrugged.

"Listen to you, Mister Fancy with his big words. Someone should wedlock you up until you get some sense."

So Teeny and I talked about it. It wasn't like we were antimarriage, exactly. We'd just never thought it was necessary. But now . . . I don't want to say we were pressured into it. But part of our reason to go for it was just to shut everyone up.

We waited until the summer of 2003, after I'd finished my big Broadway run of *Sexaholix*, and *Undefeated* had premiered, and I had a couple of weeks before heading off to shoot my next film. And we got married.

We didn't do it with a lot of hoopla. A small affair, just family and closest friends, maybe forty people tops. No press release, no giant reception. We did it casual, on the down-low. Cuz that's how we both wanted it.

We held the wedding on the lawn of some friends' house upstate. It was a beautiful summer day, blue sky and sunny. The lawn was big as a golf course and swept down a gentle green hill to the Hudson River, where white sailboats skipped across the glistening water. Birds twittered in the enormous trees that dotted the estate, and ducks wandered up from the river's edge to check us out. Total white-people country. I felt like I was back in the Fresh Air Fund.

The caterers set up a tent with big clouds of flowers on long, white-clothed tables. Before the wedding I followed them around, rearranging the seating-assignment cards. They were trying to mix my family and Teeny's, and I was trying to keep them apart. Also, my dad was coming with his third wife, and I wanted them seated as far away from my mom as possible. Across the river would have been good.

We'd hired a video crew, and they wandered around the grounds shooting the proceedings. Funny what you see on a wedding video, what went on behind your back. Like every time they pointed the camera at Teeny's dad or mine, each of them is standing off to the side somewhere, alone, staring at everybody else, hitting the champagne hard and often.

At one point the lady holding the videocam points it at Teeny's father.

"So, it's the big day," you hear her say to him. "Are you happy?"

He squints at the camera for a long beat, then shrugs.

"Canada's not far. Everybody's nice there. I'll still have time . . ."

"Yeah, sure," he mumbles. Still playing the OG.

Teeny and I were both nervous as kids. I must have sneaked a pack of smokes pacing around the lawn, and the guy doing Teeny's hair said she was so jumpy he had to Krazy Glue her to the chair to keep her still.

Finally it was time for the ceremony. Rows of wooden chairs were set up on the grass, with a center aisle to keep the bride's and groom's families apart. I'm not sure what to call the guy who did the officiating. We couldn't have either a Jewish or a Catholic wedding, because I'm not and Teeny's not, so he wasn't a rabbi or a priest. This guy was someone Teeny had found through the caterers. He was like an accountant or a bank teller in his day job, but he'd gotten some sort of mail-order preacher's license that allowed him to marry people in the state of New York, except only on alternate weekends or something.

My Moms was very suspicious of the whole thing.

"You're not going to have a priest?"

"No, Ma. He's like a justice of the peace."

"Is that legal?"

"Of course it's legal. I think."

"In the whole state of New York you couldn't find one priest?"

"They're all in jail, Ma."

We did stand under a kind of hupa, for a light touch of Jewishness. There was a tiny hint of Catholicism in it, too. But mostly it was a mail-order sort of affair.

For all the acting I've done, in front of millions of people, I've never felt more nervous than standing up in front of those forty people and playing the part of the groom in my own wedding. You should see me in the video. I look petrified. Deer in the headlights. About to crap my nice wedding suit.

Then Teeny came down the aisle, looking beautiful in a simple white dress with a big bouquet of white flowers in her hand. Instead of the usual wedding march, we'd chosen our own song for this moment: Etta James singing "At last, my love has come along . . ." That got a laugh out of everybody.

Boogie was our flower girl. She looked adorable toddling down the center aisle, throwing handfuls of petals in everybody's faces. Little Bubba was supposed to be the ring bearer, but he ran wild on us. Teeny's sister had to chase him down and wrestle him for the rings.

We stood there and stood there while the mail-order preacher rattled on. I got the feeling he didn't get asked to do a lot of weddings and he was milking this one for all it was worth. I wasn't listening. I was daydreaming that I still had a chance to make a run for it. Down the hill, jump in the river, swim out to one of those sailboats. They'd carry me to the other side. I could still make my escape. Hitchhike to Canada. Canada was close. Everyone's so polite in Canada. They'd welcome me with open arms.

I never really heard what the preacher was saying until I watched the video. He actually got off some good lines. Like when he said Boogie and Bubba were "children rare and fortunate to be at their parents' wedding." People giggled.

There was a scary moment in the ceremony when the preacher asked our two dads to come up and light a pair of large candles, symbolizing the two families. Then Teeny and I were supposed to take those two candles and use them to light one bigger one, signifying the families were now joined. Both of the old men were drunk by this point, and neither of them looked too steady on his feet. I didn't think either of them should be trusted with matches. I could see the report on *Entertainment Tonight*:

"Tragedy struck the wedding of actor-playwright John Leguizamo this afternoon, when a freak fire destroyed the posh New York estate where the ceremony was held . . ."

When it was my dad's turn to light his candle, little Bubba suddenly popped up out of nowhere, shouted "Happy birfday!," and blew it out. Yeah, the rotten apple doesn't fall far from the tree.

Then the preacher said to the crowd, "I ask now that you all voice your consent to this union."

I looked out at them. Teeny's family kind of muttered and shifted around in their chairs. My dad sat there stone-faced. My mom was crying too hard to say anything.

"Can we do that once more with a little enthusiasm?" the preacher frowned.

"Hurray," they all cheered half-heartedly.

The preacher rambled on and on, while Teeny and I stood there like the figures on a wedding cake. Then, just to drag things out even more, he asked various friends and family members to come up to the front and say a few words. This was the part of the ceremony I'd dreaded the most. Who knew what some of these loonies might say?

Teeny's father tottered up first, champagne glass in hand.

"This is a great day in Mexican-American relations," he grinned. He turned to me. "Who loves ya, *hombre*? *Viva Zapata!* Treat my little girl like a queen or I'll roast your cojoanies on a spit."

Teeny's mom bum-rushed him back to his seat.

My dad stumbled up there next. He got most of the way through his speech without embarrassing me. Until the part where he raised his glass and said, "And so, John and Tiny, I am very happy for you both."

"*Dad,*" I stage-whispered.

"Because I know, Tiny, that John loves you very much."

"*Teeny, Dad.*"

"And I know Tiny is a good mother to John's children."

"*Teeny!*"

"And so, John and Tiny, I wish you both the very best."

He stumbled off, looking very pleased with himself.

My cousin Mirtha, who's been like a sister to me and Serge since we were kids, got up and told a story about a time the three of us went to visit Grandma Dulce. We were sleeping over, but we couldn't get to sleep because my grandma had sleep apnia and was snoring so loudly in the other room. So I led the two of them creeping into the kitchen, where we found my grandma's saltine crackers. Grandma Dulce loved saltine crackers. They were salty and brittle, like her. I took a bunch of them and crumbled them up. Then we snuck through the dark into Grandma Dulce's bedroom, where she was snoring like a bear. I went up to the bed, where she was lying on her back with her mouth open, and poured the cracker crumbs in. She started hacking and coughing, but she didn't wake up—she just rolled onto her side and stopped snoring. And we kids could finally get to sleep.

I'm still not sure what the point was of telling that story at my wedding. Either my cousin was trying to show how clever I was, or what a cruel, devious little monster I'd been. It got a good laugh, though. In show biz, nothing else matters.

When it was Serge's turn to speak, he decided to sing us a song instead. Mister Opera Singer.

"This is my favorite song from *Pal Joey*," he announced. It was called "I Could Write a Book." Kind of Freudian of him, I thought. Still competing with his older brother, even at his wedding. But I let him have his moment in the sun. Nobody but family was looking.

It was my Moms who totally mortified me. When it was her turn she cried for like five minutes before she could even speak. Everybody on Teeny's side of the aisle was rolling their eyes and drumming their fingers. And then, sobbing, my mom began to tell the story of how my father abandoned us. At my wedding she's going into this. With him sitting there. My heart sank into the lawn.

"I was so scared, because their father left us with nothing. *Nada*. Goose eggs," she's sobbing.

Oh man. Teeny's family are wrinkling their brows and wondering what the hell she's going on about. My dad's face is getting darker and harder-looking by the second. Teeny's staring at me like *Do something*.

"Ma," I whisper out of the corner of my mouth. "Not now, Ma. *Please*."

"Ay, we were like homeless peoples!" my mom is wailing, in full *telenovela* overacting mode. "Thrown out on the street like garbages! I didn't know how I will feed my children!"

"*Ma*," I'm hissing.

But she's on a roll. She knows exactly what she's doing. And so does my dad. It's been a quarter-century since they broke up, and still neither of them can pass up a chance to bad-mouth the other in public. And ruin another wedding for me while they're at it.

By the time all the speeches were over I was a nervous wreck. When it came time for Teeny to slide the ring on my finger, I held out my right hand instead of the left.

Talk about a Freudian slip. I blame my family.

When the preacher finally pronounced us man and wife, I think I'd sweated off five pounds.

Then it was time to eat and dance. It was funny to watch Teeny's family trying to dance to Latin music, and my family trying to dance to rock. Finally both sides gave up. Her family only danced when it was a white-people song, and mine when it was a brown-people song.

And then Boogie went over to the DJ, grabbed his mic, and started belting out "Old MacDonald." I felt so proud. Commandeering the microphone, just like her dad . . .

Teeny says that marriage and fatherhood have calmed me down. Or worn me out. I'm still working very hard, and in my mind I'm just as driven as ever by my demons to succeed and produce. I just don't quite have the stamina I had when I was in my twenties and thirties. Teeny says I'm still a maniac obsessive freak by normal standards, but compared to my younger self I'm almost a slacker.

With two kids, getting any writing done is impossible. When I'm working I want to be with them, then when I'm with them for a while I want to be at work. Compared to raising kids, acting is so easy it's like a vacation for me.

Nowadays I'm pooped by nine p.m. I crawl into bed, then the kids crawl in after me. Boogie climbs in at two a.m. because she's cold. She starts elbowing me and clenching her teeth, which sounds like a coffee grinder played through a boombox. Then her cat comes looking for her, cuz they're like interspecies twins. Her cat has asthma. He coughs, wheezes, and hacks louder than Grandma

Dulce used to. He crouches at the foot of the bed and gacks up these terrifying hairballs bigger than my head. They look like they're going to sprout legs and attack. At four a.m. Bubba crawls in with us cuz he had a nightmare. He sleeps perpendicular to my head, and the minute he falls asleep he starts punching and kicking me and telling me to get off him. Maybe he's dreaming that my head is one of those hairballs come to life.

At five a.m. the alarm rings. I catch some sleep driving on the way to work. Then I'll work all day, then maybe pick the kids up at school, hang around with them, play with them. By the time we get them fed and wrestle them into bed again, Teeny and I are exhausted. You should see our sex life.

Actually, if you do see it, could you tell it to come home? I miss it.

Raising kids is such a trip. Especially if you're still just a kid yourself, like me. Sex isn't the only adjustment you make. Like I used to be real paranoid about my furniture. I grew up to be a typical Latin that way. When people came over I'd never offer them anything to drink, cuz I was so scared they'd spill on the carpet. It was an expensive carpet. Handwoven in Tibet. By virgins. I was so proud of it, which made me crazy paranoid about it. We'd have friends over, and after an hour or so they'd be like, "Um, do you have anything to drink?"

"No," I'd say.

"I'm kinda dry," they'd say, and smack their lips.

"Stick your head under the faucet," I'd tell them. "It's Brita."

Teeny would elbow me and give me The Look, then go get everyone drinks. I'd sit there staring at them every time they took a sip. Sweat beading on my forehead, fingers digging into my thighs. I was like a character in a Hitchcock film. Oh, it was torture.

Eventually we worked it out and only served club soda.

Now I'm much more relaxed about it. Or I've given up, anyway.

Two kids running around the house, dropping their sippy cups on the carpet, spitting up on the sofa, tormenting the cat until it runs up the drapes. You get used to the idea that your home is going to be a wreck for the next eighteen to twenty-one years. I used to be so paranoid about my high-end stereo and my hi-def Japanese TV with the flat screen big as a drive-in. Now I come home, Boogie is pouring her juice into the DVD player, Bubba is Magic-Markering stick figures all across that flat screen, and I don't freak. Really. After Teeny has revived me with the smelling salts, I very, very calmly and quietly explain to the little fuckers that if they ever do something like that again to Daddy's equipment, Daddy's going to sell them to child sex-slave traders in Thailand.

Actually, I should sell one of them, to pay for the other one's education. Flip a coin.

"Daddy, where's Bubba?"

"Bubba went to live with another family, honey. Eat your animal crackers."

Jesus, school is expensive. Of course we have to send them to private schools. This is New York City. Public school here is like SWAT training. We couldn't do that to them. In my day you just dumped your kids into PS Whatever, and if they survived long enough to graduate you bought them a Happy Meal and gave them a pat on the back and sent them out to find a job. Now you have to enroll them in the very best pre-pre-pre school to get them on the inside track for college. Kids in the womb are studying prelaw. When I make a movie now, I just have them sign my paycheck over to the principal. Last year we spent $16,000 on art supplies for Boogie. Art supplies? When I was in school we had one crayon per classroom.

Ah, but what the hell. I don't mind. You can't take it with you. Who would I leave it to? Homey?

So yeah, I'm trying to adjust. Balance the workaholic stage-screen-

and-TV career with middle-aged fatherhood. I keep telling myself, "Everything in moderation, dude," but doing *anything* in moderation goes against all my conditioning. There's a psychological term—I'm sure I don't have it right but it makes sense to me—"outmoded self-defense mechanisms." The behaviors that helped me when I was getting in trouble at home and on the street, that helped me survive early in my career and have driven me all these years, don't necessarily help now that I'm older and want to start enjoying life a little more. I'm a little old to be playing Puck all the time.

I read in some outdoor-adventure manly-man type magazine an interview with this young guy who was famous for snowboarding down the Himalayas or bungee-jumping out of helicopters or something. And he said he didn't want to be like his mentor, who had reached the age of forty and wasn't physically able to do the stunts anymore but had not prepared himself for another life. He was just miserable and depressed because he had no other interests or hobbies, no idea what to do with the rest of his life. The old *AH-OO-GAH* went off in my head, and I've been trying—I say *trying*—to make my own adjustments to life after forty. To keep my interests alive, or else get some new interests real quick.

But I still dig what I do so much. I love acting, I love writing, I love producing. Plus I'm still making mad cheddar, which pays for our four pieces of real estate, and the fancy schools, and the nannies, and the trainers . . .

So, because I can't quit working and I want my family with me, I drag them around a lot between the East Coast, West Coast, and wherever I happen to be doing a long movie shoot. We're like carnie folk. I uproot them every now and then, take the kids out of school, away from their friends and everything they dig, and haul them off to Canada, Ireland, L.A., Florida, Ecuador.

Yes, I know I'm kind of repeating the patterns of my own childhood, when my parents moved us every year of my life since I was born. The rotten apple really doesn't fall far from the tree. The Leguizamo Legacy continues.

But how and when do you break the cycle? I should probably go back to therapy, but when the hell would I find time to talk to a shrink? And they're so expensive. Ever notice the words "the rapist" are in "therapist"?

Then again, maybe I'd enjoy it. I love talking to anyone who'll listen to me, even if I have to pay them.

I'm of two minds about it. Maybe I should use one of them.

ACKNOWLEDGMENTS

I wanna thank my wife, Justine, for letting me think I'm the boss sometimes . . . and my kids for sharing their daddy-time, my Moms for all her math, full-bro for never letting me forget, cuz Mirtha and Nancy, Tias, half-bros and stepsis for all the support, all my high school buddies, stepmoms, new buddies, and all my suits Lambo, Jace, Goli, and Ina. I gotta thank all the crews for putting in hours and effort way beyond any spoiled actor . . . I mean we're not digging ditches or doing brain surgery. Thank you for helping me get over myself.

PHOTOGRAPHY CREDITS

215   'MOULIN ROUGE' © 2001 Twentieth Century Fox. All rights
       reserved.

216   © Mary Ellen Mark.

222   'MOULIN ROUGE' © 2001 Twentieth Century Fox. All rights
       reserved.

232   'SPUN' © Newmarket. All rights reserved.

236   Courtesy of Universal Studios Licensing LLLP.

246   'UNDEFEATED' photograph courtesy of HBO. HBO is a registered
       service mark of Home Box Office, Inc.

248   Courtesy of Custom Film Effects.